TODDLER
TAMING

Jerry Pitman - swimming

TODDLER TAMING

A SURVIVAL GUIDE FOR PARENTS

by Dr. CHRISTOPHER GREEN

Foreword by Sidney Q. Cohlan, M.D.
Illustrations by Roger Roberts

Fawcett Columbine • New York

A Fawcett Columbine Book
Published by Ballantine Books

Copyright © 1984 by Dr. Christopher Green and Dr. Hilary Green
Illustrations copyright © 1984 by Doubleday Australia Pty Limited
Foreword copyright © 1985 by Random House, Inc.

Library of Congress Catalog Card Number: 84-91682

ISBN 0-449-90155-6

Cover design by Georgia Morrissey
Photo by Suzanne Szasz
Text Design by Holly Johnson at the Angelica Design Group, Ltd.
Manufactured in the United States of America

First American Edition: July 1985

10 9 8

To the caring and compassionate staff who make the Royal Alexandra Hospital for Children one of the great children's hospitals.

CONTENTS

Foreword   ix

Author's Note   xi

Introduction   xiii

1 Different stages for different ages   1

2 Behavior: what's normal? what's average? what's tolerable?   7

3 The difficult child: whom do we blame?   17

4 Don't let them grind you down   22

5 Making life easier for yourself and preserving your sanity   27

6 Discipline that works—most of the time!   47

7 Tantrums and other tricks   58

8 Nasty habits in nice children   72

9 Sleep problems—at last, the cure   87

10 Toilet training   110

11 Myths about diet   121

12 Feeding without fights   137

13 Fears, comforters and security   144

14 Fidgets, fiddlers and hyperactives   159

15 Playgroups, pre-schools and attempts to produce the infant Einstein   173

16 The good, working mother   182

17 The toddler and the single-parent family   186

18 Getting the best out of grandma   190

19 The handicapped child: behavior and discipline   194

20 Common toddler illnesses   200

Notes   218

Further reading   219

References   219

Index   220

FOREWORD

For American mothers struggling through the ups and downs of life with a toddler (long ago characterized as the "terrible two's") this book will be as welcome a rescuer as a St. Bernard with a keg of "spirits" around its neck. Beleaguered American parents will discover that they are not alone: Dr. Green's self-centered, negative, tantrum-prone toddlers from "down under" in Australia are mirror images of our own native creatures.

To the parental question "What are we doing wrong?" Dr. Green offers compassionate insight and realistic advice devoid of jargon and dogma. He is keenly aware of the feelings of frustration, inadequacy, ambivalence, and guilt generated by the confusing mosaic of conflicting advice in print and on the air. In defense of parents, and with a penetrating, down-to-earth sense of humor, he proposes reasonable, workable strategies to cope with the day-to-day insurrections.

The primary emphasis throughout *Toddler Taming* is based on established evidence—from longitudinal studies—that children are born with genetically different behavior and personality potentials. Some 40% are relatively "easy" children. As Dr. Green puts it, "It would seem that children in this 40% would do well whether the mother is competent or hopeless and the father is a saint or Jack the Ripper." Another 10% are "little monsters from the word go . . . it is hard to change their pattern with any technique less powerful than an anesthetic!" The rest are in-between. It is for this group that the book's sage and pragmatic advice will be most rewarding. It should help harassed parents over most of the inevitable hurdles without guilt and with the hopeful promise that toddlers are not forever.

Parents are also different. Rigid instructions on how to cope with specific behavior problems will not fit the needs or capabilities of every family. Dr. Green's honest approach is best summarized in his own words: "There is no absolute 'right way' of bringing up children, although some ways may be less wrong than others. The way that feels right and works for you has to be the best."

My own delight with this book is biased. I've been saying the same things for over forty years.

SIDNEY Q. COHLAN, M.D.
Professor of Pediatrics and Associate
    Director, Pediatrics
University Hospital
New York University Medical Center

AUTHOR'S NOTE

Thanks to:

My wife, Dr. Hilary Green, for researching, editing, encouraging, and being a very special person.

James and Tim, without whose help this book would have been completed much earlier but would have contained less practical wisdom.

Dr. Paul Hutchins, colleague and fellow toddler tamer, provider of encouragement and common sense advice.

John Coveney, hospital dietitian, my mentor on mealtime without tantrums.

Roger Roberts for his splendid illustrations.

Michael Morton-Evans, whose typewriter turned my dyslexic ramblings into a form of English.

INTRODUCTION

Most parents fare well with their cuddly, compliant babies. They may worry about tiredness, feeding, weight gain and minor illnesses, but generally they are in control and feel positive. When a toddler bursts onto the scene, many parents receive a nasty shock. They wonder why their placid, angelic baby has suddenly become negative, stubborn, and at times even demonic.

I used to be an expert on child care. I knew all the right methods, I lectured, I wrote learned treatises. I could tell anyone how they were doing it wrong. Then a strange thing happened—two toddlers hurtled into my own life. I found them extremely active, exhausting, and hard to control, and I began to learn more about toddler behavior than I had learnt in all my ten years of specialist training. I then understood what many parents go through.

Toddler behavior fluctuates from minute to minute and day to day; the resultant erratic mixture is good, not so good, or frankly appalling. Parents experience many moments of immense joy and satisfaction interspersed with exasperation and even depression or utter despair. Most parents have little idea what constitutes normal toddler behavior and even less idea how to manage these difficulties when they arise. Many, quite incorrectly, believe they are the only ones who can't control their kids and think they are hopeless, second-rate parents. Life is quite tough enough now without immobilizing ourselves with such misplaced feelings of guilt.

The so-called helping professions have often done little to help. Whole forests have been cut down to publish academic theories on child care; many of these expert authors imply that some form of permanent psychological scar will result if your children are not brought up the "Right Way." The more I work with toddlers the more sure I am that there is no one "Right Way." In general I believe if parents are encouraged to do what feels right and works for them, they won't go far wrong. As for the learned theories, they complete an about-face each decade and as the learned experts confuse themselves, real children and real parents remain singularly unimpressed but *happy.*

This book is *not* a theory packed, latter-day bible of child care. All I wish is to give some practical common-sense advice, boost parents' self-confidence, and make them feel happier and more in control. Happy, confident parents can do wonders for their children.

The consistent use of the pronouns "he" and "his" when referring to a toddler may offend or irritate some readers. I make no apology: I have used these words for practical reasons and in no way is it an indictment of boy toddlers! Little girls are equally responsible for the characteristics I describe.

Whether your "bundle of joy" is a full-time or part-time angel, or a little devil, this book will have something for you. My ideas are unlikely to win the Nobel Prize for Medicine, though if this book can help parents stop fighting with their children, a peace prize might be in order.

Dr. Christopher Green
Sydney, 1984

TODDLER
TAMING

DIFFERENT STAGES
FOR DIFFERENT AGES

BEHAVIOR DEVELOPMENT

Little do the doting parents of that joyous bundle of newborn perfection realize the bumpy course that may lie ahead. In the first
five years, the baby's behavior, demands, and needs will change
dramatically. These changes often catch the parents off guard,
sending them into a tailspin.

In simple terms there are three major stages of development
between birth and eight years of age. How to recognize and cope
with them is what this first chapter is all about.

The first stage is from birth up to the age of one year. Stage two
is toddlerhood, to four years old, and at stage three another magic

transformation occurs—to the early school-age child. Some children pass through these stages peacefully, the changes passing almost unnoticed, while others batter through painfully—with their nearest and dearest suffering from fallout. Certainly, as children grow in size and cleverness, their behavior alters. Sadly, this is not always for the better.

The baby: Birth to one year

The baby from birth to one year is a cuddly little article who spends most of the year getting to know mom and dad while they get to know him. This is the important process of bonding. The aim in the first year is to develop a secure and trusting child who has a secure and trusting relationship with his parents. When he is hungry he should be fed; when he is frightened he should be comforted; and when he cries he should be cuddled. You cannot spoil a baby in the first year of life.

A major change occurs in the middle of this period which affects the parents' handling of the baby. In the first six months, the baby can usually be looked after by any consistent caretaker, thus allowing him to be passed around a gallery of doting relatives or left with a baby sitter while mother is at work. At about six months of age, however, the baby becomes very close to, and demanding of, one person. This attachment is usually to the child's main caretaker, the mother. At this stage dad shouldn't despair; his turn comes a little later!

After this time it becomes more difficult for the caretaker to separate from the child, which presents various problems, especially if baby sitters are necessary or the baby needs hospitalization. After the first birthday the difficulty of separation starts to decline. By the age of four and a half, most children are able to go off to school independently with little worry.

The word "bonding" needs some qualification to be understood properly. Mythology would have us believe that when parents first hold their treasured new arrival, as their eyes meet for the first time, violins play and peace and joy will reign forever. What a beautiful idea! Unfortunately for many parents it is about as realistic as the story of Cinderella. A significant number of mothers feel little for their babies for weeks, or even months, after the birth. For a few, maternal feelings may take a very long time to develop. Like many poorly understood emotional happenings in our lives, the more we worry about feeling "the way we are expected to feel," the more difficult it is for those natural feelings to appear.

The other problem with the bonding theory is that, although the mother may have all the love and bonding emotions you could ever wish to hope for, a significant number of babies are extremely difficult to bond to. In fact, these probably make up over 10 percent of all babies. And what little horrors they are! They arch their backs, spit out their bottles, violently resist being cuddled, and are obviously quite unaware that normal babies are supposed to be angelic and full of love. Others make the situation even worse by screaming with colic most of the night or day.

It is not surprising that, as the parents pace the floor in the wee small hours, drive a car around the block several times at four a.m. (much to the annoyance of the neighbors) or resort to medication, they wonder what happened to the simple joys of parenthood. As for bonding—well, that may become a luxury reserved for doves, and Barbara Cartland!

The terrible toddler: one to four years

At one year of age the baby prepares for the second behavioral change. This is the onset of toddlerhood, and it is now that parents are put to the full test and start to feel their age. Although toddlerhood starts at one year, it is really 18 months before it gets going in earnest. It hits a peak around two, with a gradual easing off by two and a half and vast improvements by the time the fourth birthday is reached. Between the age of one year and 18 months, there appears to be a sort of no-man's land with some babies behaving so well that they need no discipline, while others have hatched into fully fledged toddlers who show all the attendant difficulties. Many more boys than girls seem to have a stormy passage through toddlerhood.

LEARNING CONTROLS

In the first year, the aim is to encourage bonding and establish a mutual feeling of trust and security with the baby. With the toddler, the main aim is learning controls and how to separate a little, so he will move some of the way towards becoming a little adult. By controls I mean:
1) control of bodily functions (toilet training);
2) control of impulses; for example, learning that demands cannot be met immediately;
3) control of behavior; for example, frustration control and tantrum control.

At the beginning of toddlerhood, the child has no voluntary restraint over his bowels and bladder, but by the time he is half way through this stage, these should be well in check and they should remain so.

A two-year-old is highly impulsive and impatient, believing that

he only has to snap his fingers to get what he wants. If his request is not met immediately everyone will get a piece of his mind. By the age of four, most toddlers have ceased to be impulsive, but the transition is achieved only with quite a bit of pain for the parents. Quite a number of adults appear never to have progressed past this toddler stage of impulse control. Picture, if you will, the husband snapping his fingers as he sits with his feet up, waiting for his wife to fetch him a can of beer, and the minor tantrum when it does not rapidly appear.

While the toddler is learning to control impulses, as well as his bodily functions, he is also beginning to learn to share, to mix, to separate from his mother, and to control the frustration of failure or of not getting his own way. He is even, believe it or not, getting a smattering of common sense and something that vaguely resembles a conscience.

WHAT MAKES TODDLERHOOD SO DIFFICULT?

Parents with toddler-age children expreience almost three times the risk of psychological disturbances of parents with babies or school-age children. There is ample scientific evidence to back up this claim, but why do the problems peak in children of this age? The answer is simply that toddlers have some amazing characteristics which make their management difficult. Their extraordinary behavior can often rock the stability of the soundest parents. Some of the difficulties are discussed below.

NEGATIVITY

Children learn to say "no" long before they learn to say "yes," and at the age of three this simple little word flows out with the clearest articulation—due mainly to two years of non-stop practice. It has been said that the word "no" is used by toddlers whose parents over-use the word from the child's earliest age. This would be a nice, simple explanation, but we find that even with the most positive, best parents, the child will use the word with great regularity.

SENSELESSNESS

Toddlers live only for the present, neither thinking deeply about events that took place more than five minutes ago nor worrying much about the future which, for them, is a mere ten minutes away. Battles are fought with no thought for the repercussions and reason generally falls on deaf ears. There is little understanding or acceptance of our often odd, but much prized, adult values. In short, this is an age devoid of reasoned thinking, when the word "conscience" does not occur in the vocabulary.

STUBBORNNESS

As the toddler is developing self-control he soon discovers that he can also exercise quite a bit of control over others. All that needs to be done is dig in the heels, flex the muscles, and watch

the amazing effect this has on everyone around. Stubbornness without sense is bound to lead to conflict, and when negativity and a total lack of interest in anyone else's rights are added, you have a sure fire combination for parent demolition. Certainly this behavioral quartet has for a long time been recognized as a potent threat to parents' health. Perhaps, in years to come, children leaving maternity hospitals should have stamped on their backsides the warning "toddlers are a health hazard!"

Not only is stubbornness without sense a danger to parents' health, it is also a hazard in the course of life preservation. A determined two-year-old may well decide to have a tantrum in the middle of a busy highway, the only concern being the theatrical impact of the performance. The impending disaster as cars and trucks thunder down on the assembled gathering does not enter the child's mind. That's the future, and we don't worry about that at this age.

SELF-CENTEREDNESS

Most toddlers have tunnel vision, which focuses only upon their own needs and happiness. It never occurs to them that other people may have rights too. When a child is playing and wants a particular toy, it is unlikely that he will ask politely for it, as the "smash and grab" method is a much more effective way of getting what he wants. The idea of taking turns and sharing is quite foreign and, although toddlers enjoy being with other children, they tend to play beside them rather than directly with them. This self-centered behavior is normal for most toddlers—although it has been known to extend into adulthood! Some of the world's notable dictators have shown skills that even the most inventive toddler would envy.

BEHAVIOR: WHAT'S NORMAL?
WHAT'S AVERAGE?
WHAT'S TOLERABLE?

There are great variations in the stages of toddler development; no two children or households are the same, and many factors influence behavior. What is deemed to be a problem depends very much on the "eye of the beholder." One family harboring a little terrorist may view the situation with utter despair while another might regard the same antics as some clever form of circus act, which they enjoy. All this makes it difficult to collect useful data concerning behavior, and the figures that are available cannot be applied equally to every child of a certain age.

2

FACTORS THAT INFLUENCE BEHAVIOR

The hereditary temperamental make-up of both child and parents
has the greatest influence on the types of behavior we see. A cool,
calm, organized parent with a cool, calm, organized child will not
know what a behavior problem is. The same cannot be said of the
anxious, disorganized parent, who has a "short fuse" and is trying
to cope with a child with a similar personality. Parents and children come in all mixtures, and all will experience different mixtures of behavior.

The mother surrounded by helpful family support will experience behavior problems of a different type and frequency from
those experienced by the isolated parent who valiantly struggles on
alone without any help. Different marriages will also experience
different kinds of behaviors. Some marriages are strong, with a
united, positive team managing the child. Others are weak with
little shared care or support, and in some cases even major attempts from one partner to sabotage all of the other's best efforts.

Life in the eighties is far from easy. The worries of work,
money, and competition, and all the other stresses of modern society, influence parental happiness to differing degrees. This in turn
affects the child's happiness and behavior.

The vast range of "normal" toddler behavior is discussed in this
chapter. Many of their "little ways" may seem unacceptable and
negative, but because they are so common, they are probably best
viewed as normal. Some figures from American, English and Aus-
tralian studies are included to give an idea of the occurrence of
these kinds of behavior.

THE WIDE SPECTRUM OF NORMAL

All toddlers

- crave attention and hate to be ignored. Some are quite satisfied
  with their parents' best efforts; others would grumble unless
  twenty-five hours a day, eight days a week were devoted solely
  to their care.
- separate poorly from their caretakers. The toddler prefers to
  play near his mother and does not let her out of his sight for
  long. Being placed with an unfamiliar baby sitter causes initial
  problems; being locked in a room or becoming separated when
  out shopping constitutes a major trauma.
- tend to be busy little people. Some are extremely active and
  hardly ever sit still; others are just "active."

- have little road sense; their impulsive and unpredictable be-havior is a hazard even in the apparently sensible child.
- have little respect for other people's property. Their "fiddly fingers" are drawn as if by magnetism to everything they pass. Ornaments are broken and cupboards are rearranged. Those ten active little digits have an amazing power to spread a sticky, jam-like substance over every surface they meet— rather like a small bee distributing pollen.
- tend to be stubborn and willful; some are quite militant, but others will bend to reason.
- tend to be blind to the mountain of mess they generate. The tidy toddler, who is neat and even picks up his own toys, is the exception rather than the rule.

Many toddlers

- will sit and concentrate, drawing, doing puzzles or pre-reading tasks. A minority will settle for a long time, but most become restless in about five minutes and look for an escape. Quite a large proportion of active little boys will not sit and settle in their toddler years even for short periods.

- are cuddly, affectionate, "giving" children. But a minority resent handling, are distant, and seem to give a poor return of love to their parents.
- are determined and independent. Some become so belligerent that they refuse to be fed or dressed, even though they are far too young to do either task unaided. Other toddlers are passive, dependent, and quite happy to be pampered and directed.
- are compulsive climbers. At an early age they will organize an expedition to the summit of the couch, and, once this has been scaled, will set out to conquer kitchen cupboards, tables, and anything that "happens to be there." Other toddlers are more sensible and have a healthy fear of the "painful stop at the end of the drop."
- eat well, although many do not consume the quantities or quality of food that their parents might desire. Some children take food extremely seriously, while others find it merely an interesting plaything. Some go off their food almost completely around their first birthday, and a proper eating pattern may not return for anything up to a year. Some will tolerate a narrow, unimaginative diet; others will eat everything in sight. Some eat main meals; others were born to be "snackers."
- continue with a daytime sleep until the age of three years. Others, however, discard this at about 18 months and nothing the parents can do will bring it back. Most toddlers go to sleep before eight o'clock each night, but others stay on the rampage until close to midnight. Some are lazy in the morning, finding it hard to get out of bed; others wake at an ungodly hour and disturb the whole household. With children who are on the rampage from before dawn to midnight, it is often hard to change their pattern with any technique less powerful than the administration of a general anesthetic!
- have fears. Dogs, loud noises, new situations, and strange objects and people cause distress in over half of this age group.
- display a multitude of irritating habits.

How common are behavior difficulties?

About one in four toddlers exhibit behavior that causes significant concern to their parents. Probably only about one in ten parents of toddlers do not experience some minor behavioral irritation or quirk.

In the late 1950s a California group surveyed the behavior of 800 toddlers. Twenty-eight per cent of mothers claimed they had some serious concern with behavior; 91 per cent said they had

lesser concerns over some aspect of care.[1] In 1973, 705 London three-year-olds were followed up and their parents interviewed.[2] About seven per cent of toddlers had moderate to severe behavior problems; an additional 15 per cent had less major, but genuine ones (a total of 22 per cent). In this English study, the less severe problems occurred equally in boys and girls, while the moderate problems seemed to occur almost twice as often in boys, and the severe ones were three times more common in boys. Many parents with terrorist boy toddlers would agree with these figures.

A study begun in New York in 1956 followed up 133 children from birth to six years.[3] During this time the researchers were most interested in temperament and behavior. The New York Longitudinal Study, as it was called, showed that 40 per cent of the group fitted into the "easy child" category, being a joy to look after as babies and children. Parents, teachers and pediatricians all found this group easy. It would seem that children in this 40 per cent, whether the mother was competent or hopeless, the father a saint or Jack the Ripper, would do well.

More than half of the 133 children, however, were not so easy to handle. Ten per cent of the study group were little monsters from the word go. They were difficult as babies, difficult as toddlers, and their difficulties accompanied them into school. Parents, pediatricians and teachers all suffered under the strain. These were particularly negative children, extemely loud in both voice and crying, and easily frustrated; they had irregular sleep and feeding habits and showed great difficulty adjusting to any change. They slipped into tantrums with the greatest of ease. This is the group of children that age their parents and baby sitters, and as they pass through school they precipitate nervous breakdowns in delicate teachers. Though saint-like parents have more chance of managing such children, they are extremely difficult for anyone.

A further 15 per cent of the total were described as "slow warm up." These had many of the same difficult characteristics as the last group, but less severely. The difference was that, when handled with care, understanding, persistence, and patience, they had a sporting chance of doing well. In this group parenting was a major challenge; exceptional parents managed but normal parents struggled.

With the angels, impossibles, and semi-monsters accounted for, 35 per cent of the total remained in a group that was neither very easy nor very difficult. The ease with which they could be handled depended on the parents and particular blend of easy or difficult temperamental characteristics that the child had inherited.

Another New York study, the Chamberlin study, followed up 200 children from the age of two until school age.[4] It demonstrated the main behavioral worries for parents at different ages and set out to stir up specialist pediatricians to give more help. The behavior patterns commonly seen at ages two and four were listed. The author then ranked them in the order that causes greatest concern at those two ages. At age two, the toddler's stubborn and willful characteristics top the list, causing the parents the most worry. Second place was shared equally between tantrums and "getting into everything." Continuing the Toddler Behavior Olympics, at age four the gold medal was still won for stubborn, willful behavior, although now verbal abuse and "back talk" were also included as problems. The silver medal went to whining and nagging, and the bronze was awarded to lack of sharing and fighting.

In the Chamberlin study, a number of parents were interviewed and asked to describe their children's behavior at three different ages. Some of the findings are listed in Table 1.

Table 1. Mothers' Behavioral Description of Their Children at Ages 2, 3 and 4 (percentage of age group)

Behavior	Age 2 %	Age 3 %	Age 4 %
Eats too little	50	26	37
Doesn't eat the right kinds of food	64	43	54
Resists going to bed	70	46	56
Awakens during the night	52	52	56
Has nightmares	17	18	36
Resists sitting on toilet	43	2	2

Behavior	Age 2 %	Age 3 %	Age 4 %
Has bowel movement in pants	71	17	1
Wets self during day	75	14	7
Wets bed at night	82	49	26
Curious about sex differences	28	45	75
Rubs or plays with sex organs	56	49	51
Modest about dressing	1	7	26
Fights or quarrels	72	75	92
Jealous	54	47	42
Hurts younger sibling	44	51	64
Hits others or takes things	68	52	46
Stubborn	95	92	85
Talks back (acts fresh)	42	73	72
Disobedient	82	76	78
Tells fibs	2	26	37
Constantly seeks attention	94	48	42
Clings to mother	79	34	26
Whines and nags	83	65	85
Cries easily	79	53	58
Temper outbursts	83	72	70
Active, hardly ever still	100	48	40

At the Royal Alexandra Hospital for Children in Sydney, Australia, I run a two-night program called "Coping with Toddlers Course" for parents, which is designed to provide a humorous practical romp through the common worries that beset parents.

Between 200 and 500 parents turn up each night and I ask for a show of hands from the audience as I ask the various questions about their children. This is a highly selected audience and a non-scientific method of collecting data, but some of the figures that result are interesting:

- 15 per cent of those that attend claim that they can never take their child to the supermarket because of tantrums and the trail of devastation left in his wake;
- 98 per cent spank their children despite what experts tell them;
- eight per cent are confident that when they get home after the course ends at 10 p.m., they will be greeted by a toddler wide awake and in full flight.

At a recent meeting of specialists in our hospital, I asked twenty-eight pediatricians to answer questions about their own children. These covered a wide area, with behavior featuring quite strongly, and some of the general questions yielded interesting, even amazing, answers, For example, four of the experts did not know the date of their children's birth; three were uncertain as to whether their child was fully immunized; and nineteen stated that their storage of drugs at home was far outside the guidelines set down by the hospital's Child Safety Centre. In the behavioral area, twelve had endured at least one colicky baby, and although experts in this city often dispute the benefit of drugs in helping colic, nine out of the twelve used medication, six swearing by its efficacy. Three pediatricians had had children with breath-holding attacks, four had struggled with toilet training, and eight had had to cope with feeding difficulties. Eleven of these experts had experienced at least one child with sleep problems, and thirteen considered that their discipline was often far from effective.

All this goes to prove just one thing. Toddler behavior worries the majority of all parents, whether they be psychologists, plumbers, process workers, or pediatricians. If we care about our kids, we all find ourselves in the same boat. No matter what we do, it seems that about one in ten of our children is going to cause us considerable difficulty, and a quarter of them, at least some concern. When I look at Chamberlin's figures I always wonder "who are the children with normal behavior?" Are they the docile, compliant, non-whining, non-stubborn minority or the real-life terrorists who haunt our homes?

It is upsetting that few parents have any idea what constitutes normal toddler behavior. They spend much of their lives feeling guilty, inadequate, self-recriminating, and believing they are the only ones who cannot control their kids. Life is tough enough without immobilizing ourselves with such ill-found guilt.

Many parents fear that this anti-social behavior in their two-year-old is the first sign of juvenile delinquency in later life. This sort of behavior is quite normal at this age. With the passage of time sharing and social justice will miraculously appear in their repertoire, and the terrorist side of their personality will fade forever.

CHANGE, TENSION, AND UPSETS

Toddlers are extremely sensitive to their environment. Hens will stop laying if frightened or if their domestic happiness is upset, and toddlers' behavior will alter for similar reasons. At age two, the toddler may have just become fully toilet trained and while the parents are still congratulating themselves, and the washing-machine is getting a well-earned rest, this control may evaporate overnight following as simple a change as grandma coming to stay for the weekend. Another toddler may have been sleeping soundly through the night since birth but, on recovering from the first bad cold, may develop an anti-social wakening habit.

Behavioral gains are made and lost with great rapidity as the environment changes. If such minor triggers can have such impact, it is easy to see what damage hospitalization or parental fighting can cause. At this sensitive stage, any disturbance in the environment causes problems. Particularly harmful is the fighting that takes place in the warm-up period prior to a divorce; it can be immensely destructive and have a long-term detrimental effect upon the child.

FLUCTUATION

Parents become extremely confused as they see toddlers' behavior changing from day to day and week to week. When the child has a good day, it is put down to normal behavior. But when the child has a bad day, this is put down to some outside influence. Teething is the great stand-by: emerging teeth have for centuries been blamed for toddler problems; lack of sleep and dietary aberrations make good reserve scapegoats. It never seems to occur to parents that, just as adults can have good and bad days, so too can toddlers. Trainers allow racehorses this indulgence. We certainly don't blame sore teeth for our off days.

Nonetheless, parents often find it hard to accept these variations in a toddler's behavior. As they witness their child's behavior change rapidly from easy to difficult and back again, parents may convince themselves that the toddler has some form of epilepsy or a Jekyll and Hyde personality. Don't worry. It's all quite normal.

The early-school-age child: four to eight years

Somewhere between the ages of three and a half and four and a half years, the child gradually slips out of toddlerhood to become an early-school-age child. This third behavior stage is once again quite different from all that has gone before. The child now thinks of the repercussions of his actions, exhibits quite a bit of sense, and develops a strange fascination for rules. It is at this stage, it is thought, that many a bureaucrat is born! Many five-year-olds at school will sit at their desk, not only obeying the class rules themselves, but taking the role of class policeman, reporting the slightest transgression of their classmates to teacher. At this stage, parents can cash in on this obsession with rules of their own, now at last being able to lay down "laws for the house" that have a fair chance of being obeyed. At this stage of development, the child can be treated more like a little adult with more trust, democracy and reason.

Although there are always worries and problems with children, life should never again be quite as difficult for the exhausted parents of the burnt-out toddler.

3

THE DIFFICULT CHILD
WHOM DO WE BLAME?

HISTORY

In the nineteenth century, writers were in no doubt that the cause of all deviant behavior was bad breeding. Some put forward the notion that "the born criminal and lesser sinners were beyond help due to their abnormal make-up."

As the twentieth century dawned, this notion gradually changed, and environment was thought to be the major influence on children's behavior. By the 1950s this notion had become highly refined: all behavioral blame was laid squarely on the shoulders of inadequate mothers. It seemed irrelevant whether the marriage was stable and the parents exceptional. Mother still collected the blame, regardless of the untold unhappiness, guilt and suffering it caused.

The folly of the fifties

As a doctor who has lived through the aftermath of this era of psychological abuse of mothers, I am amazed that such an attitude could ever have existed. I would have thought that any professional who views life with his eyes even partly open could not help but see the immense variation, based on simple heredity, in all aspects of human nature. Any parent with more than one child must observe their completely different personalities. This difference cannot be accounted for solely by the different standard of care each child receives. I do not believe that most families give out different care to different children, although some children are difficult to love owing to heredity and may generate more anger and irritation in their otherwise tolerant parents.

An example of genetic influence can be seen by anyone visiting the nursery for the newborn in any hospital. There you will find children who have never been in the care of their mother and yet have totally different personalities. In one crib there might be a beautiful, quiet, loving baby exuding affection, cuddling in tightly, and feeding with ease. In the very next crib could be a child in identical health who is irritable, arches his back, cries most of the time, dislikes being held, and is forever spitting out his food. One child would be a joy for any parent; the other would be a trial even to the most well intentioned family.

The cause of difficult behavior: the view in the eighties

Behavior and temperament are now known to have great variation and a strong hereditary component. This hereditary influence gives us the basic material to work with, but the final product depends very much on environmental factors, such as parenting. It is now accepted that children's behavior is a product of both heredity and environment. In Chapter 2 it was postulated that 40 per cent of children were destined to be easy, probably being well behaved in even the most undesirable environment. Ten per cent were probably going to be exceptionally difficult in anyone's hands and would try the patience of a saint. Another 15 per cent had difficulties that should be almost completely overcome with high class parenting or would become worse if badly handled. This left 35 per cent whose behavior would be dependent on their temperamental pattern and the parents they chose to be born to.

It may seem a silly observation, but sometimes a family gets a child that does not suit them. I know that in my working day there are people who irritate me profoundly, but luckily I am able to escape to the quiet of my own home at the end of the day, far away from their annoying influence. When a child who does not suit a family arrives, the parents are unable to exercise this privilege of escape and have to force themselves to make the baby welcome. When a peace-loving, polite, quiet, obsessively tidy family is hit by a human tornado, their equilibrium is, not surprisingly, shattered. To survive this onslaught, major adjustments have to be made. It is just as upsetting when a sporting, active father spawns a docile, passive boy more interested in picking flowers and quiet pursuits than playing football.

If a difficult child is born to a family, they are stuck with that child. They can't just send him back like some disagreeable parrot from a pet shop. What can be done, however, is to adjust your handling of the child to help him through his difficulties and get the best results with the fewest headaches.

Other hereditary influences

Other children exhibit strong genetic traits, with patterns of behavior similar to those of their parents. Parents often mistakenly believe that children watch their lives and selectively extract the best points, being oblivious to their many weaknesses. In reality the reverse seems to be true, with children actively seeking out their parents' weaknesses and firmly establishing similar habits.

I see many children who are difficult to live with, and I believe they are not very unlike their parents. There are, for example, totally disorganized children who turn out to be very similar to their totally disorganized parents. Some children are sent to me because they are unenthusiastic and have little drive to do anything in life. These children often come from equally boring parents.

I also see many over-active, impulsive fathers who always have to be on the go. They frequently produce active sons who are often as over-active, impulsive and intolerant as they are, which leads to a major personality clash. I was recently brought three-year-old twins whose father complained that they could never sit still and were forever rocking and head banging. In my office I watched them rock from foot to foot, always slightly out of time, like defective windshield wipers on a car. It soon became clear that father was an over-active, driving athlete who had never sat still from birth. The more he complained about his children's over-activity, the more I noticed him rocking, swaying, kicking his feet, moving his hands—exhibiting a problem far more severe than his normal children.

The whole question of heredity and environment becomes confusing when the parents have behavioral difficulties that cause marital disharmony and a far from satisfactory environment. When the child exhibits similar difficulties, one is never certain just how much of this is caused by genes and how much by the poor environment.

Is behavior worse in the eighties?

Forty years ago, children's behavior problems appeared to be much less common. Many writers have blamed the current increase on the artificial colorings and other poisons we give our children. I do not believe this is the main cause; there is, I think, a much simpler explanation. Forty years ago, if one went to a doctor seeking help for one's child, it would be in the knowledge that all blame for the problem would be laid firmly on the mother, and some long-term psychotherapy for the parents might be suggested. This, in itself, must have been a major deterrent from seeking help, preventing most troubled parents admitting to anyone but their closest family that they could not handle their offspring. Behavior problems may seem to be more common these days because of the break up of the extended family and the highly competitive world our children live in. I believe that it's not so much an increase in the problems themselves as an increase in the awareness of them, now that parents are prepared to talk more openly about them. Now that they realize that criticism will not be levelled at them, parents are coming for help early, and this is a healthy change for the better.

Conclusion

Some children are born easy and some children are born just plain difficult. There is little we can do to change the basic material we have been given to work with, but much we can do to improve the way we handle children's behavior to make the best of what we have.

4

DON'T LET THEM GRIND YOU DOWN

For mothers, life today is certainly not as easy as it was in our parents' day, but why should this be so? After all, those terrible epidemic diseases of childhood, which terrified our parents, have been virtually abolished and our homes are full of labor saving devices. Though children in this decade are no worse behaved than in the past, child rearing is more difficult, for two main reasons. First, most families suffer because they have lost the support of the extended family; in other words, they lost granny as a live-in helper. Second, competition and unrealistically high expectations of ourselves and our children cause considerable unhappiness and some loss of good, old-fashioned discipline.

BEWARE THE
MEDIA-GENERATED MYTHS

Present-day life seems to be one constant round of "keeping up with the Joneses." We seem to spend our lives constantly checking that we are performing as well as everyone else. This continual competition weakens us. Looking back through medical literature, it is fascinating to see how ideas reappear. Alfred Adler, a psychiatrist working in Vienna in the late nineteenth century, at the same time as Sigmund Freud, was interested in competition, writing about the "drive for power" and its effect on behavior, happiness and self-esteem.

We constantly strive for the perfection we see in magazines and on television. The "perfect marriage," "the perfect husband," "the perfect white wash," and, of course, "the perfect child-rearing method." Needless to say, nothing is perfect, and most of what we are striving for is a myth generated by the media. All those people who appear regularly in the popular television "soap operas" are just actors and the events depicted are utter fiction. Our heroes, who seem so controlled on the screen, are just as likely to feel tired and unhappy as the rest of us, going home to the harsh realities of life and escaping by—yes, you guessed it—turning on the television! And what a lot television has to answer for! As someone once said, it has succeeded in turning children from an irresistible force into an immovable object. And, once we have become as immovable as the rest of them, we are force fed a diet of idealistic materialism.

Recently one of Australia's glossy women's magazines celebrated its tenth year of publication. A cynical reviewer commented: "The typical girl featured needs a career, a husband, children, a home, jewels, clothes, excitement and travel." Faced with this picture it is little wonder that so many women feel they've been cheated. They begin to think that the role of being a good mother is unexciting and lackluster and not at all what real life is about.

BEWARE OF LEARNED AUTHORS

The assault on the parent's psyche begins in the maternity hospital, when, on discharge, the baby is put in your arms along with your "owner's manual." This little book tells you when to change the formula and indicates the frequency with which you must come back to see your doctor. It also describes the workings of your new baby, giving such useful information as "around the age of six weeks, the night feeding will miraculously stop, leaving unbroken sleep thereafter." To add insult to injury, the book is peppered with glossy pictures of smiling children. On the cover is an attractive, well-groomed mother, immaculately dressed with a toothpaste advertisement smile, no dark rings under her eyes, and not an ounce overweight. This bears little resemblance to the new mothers I work with.

Browsing through the shelves of my local bookshop recently, I was fascinated to note how most subjects related to child-rearing seemed designed to undermine the average mother. Titles abound on such subjects as *Teach your child to read by the age of 4*, *Happy Families*, and *The Joys of Breast-feeding*. These titles make no allowance for those parents who don't want to breast feed forever, whose child won't sit still long enough to learn to read, and for those families in which there is little happiness.

Books that set unattainably high goals and generate feelings of parental inadequacy should be reclassified as fiction and relegated to the appropriate library section. Life is tough enough without some smart philosopher producing learned writings to make us feel as though we are second-class citizens.

BEWARE HELPFUL ADVICE

One commodity that has never been in short supply is free "helpful advice." The neighbors, the playgroup mothers, the girl at the supermarket checkout, utter strangers, and interfering well-wishers will all throw in their opinions at the drop of a hat. Some of this advice may be sound, but much will be misguided, inaccurate, or merely provided to advertise the superiority of the giver. Don't listen to those who condemn your children in a self-righteous manner, blaming all the children's imperfections on your handling, while behind them stands that angelic model child. Angelic children certainly are more likely to have "super parents," but the largest part of the behavior and personality is in genes and the luck of the draw, rather than exemplary parenting.

BEWARE THE COMPETITION OF PRE-SCHOOL AND PLAYGROUP

These days we tend to release our children into society much earlier than was fashionable thirty years ago. At the age of one, when a child goes off to playgroup, we focus our attention on every detail of his development and compare him with the other children there. Others exhibit their children to show off their abilities, like a circus ringmaster displaying his performing dogs. Those who are not walking are immediately deemed slow; those who bite, push, and don't mix are branded potential "juvenile delinquents" before even reaching the ripe old age of two.

Around the age of three, the little ones graduate to a nursery school. Here some perform as ideal children, behaving exquisitely and separating easily from their parents. Others do not demonstrate this model behavior, crying copiously or withdrawing unhappily into a corner to sulk. Once the initial separation hurdle is overcome, other problems arise.

I have had children referred to my clinic accompanied by notes such as "Please investigate this three and a half year old child. He is failing at cutting out with scissors." What a drama! And it can get worse. Many children of such tender years are even expelled from pre-school—an amazing start to one's life. In my day I just cannot imagine anyone having thrown a child out of pre-school— though I must admit I did have one little friend who was expelled, but only after he achieved the dubious distinction of sinking his teeth up to the gums in the arm of a nun! At the time of writing, the world's most expelled toddler is in my care. At the age of three and a half, he can boast three expulsions and refusal to entry to a further *seven* establishments. This must be some sort of record.

BEWARE THE "HELPING PROFESSIONALS"

The "helping professionals" have a great ability to crush parents' self-confidence and make them feel inadequate. It is easy for us to imply superiority, giving the impression that we know how to bring up our children perfectly and that behavior problems only occur in our patients' offspring. But, believe me, pediatricians and other professionals are only human and worry just as much as any other parent about their children and how to handle them. Some, unfortunately, are still steeped in the archaic ideas of the fifties and find it impossible to give practical advice on behavioral matters without psychoanalyzing the parents. It's all a bit like the weather forecaster who can tell you with great accuracy what the weather did yesterday and all last week but is completely useless when it comes to helping with today, tomorrow, and the future.

Choose your professional well. We are called the "helping" professions, which implies that we should be good at helping, but unfortunately this is not always the case. Watch out for the school of thought that insinuates that unless you bring up your children "the right way," some form of permanent psychological damage will ensue, leaving the child scarred for life—that's another popular canoe paddled down the stream of child care.

Despite our inability to decide what exactly is the correct way to bring up children—and fashions in theories of raising children have changed almost as frequently over the past fifty years as fashions in clothing have—the children survive, which just shows how resilient they are to all the conflicting and confusing advice we have given to parents over the generations.

There is no absolutely right way of bringing up children, although some ways may be less wrong than others. The way that feels right and works for you has to be the best.

In conclusion, life today is tough, largely owing to the competition and the unreasonable goals we set for ourselves. Both society and our children make it extremely hard for us to relax and do what we inwardly feel is right for us and our children. Most parents are doing an amazingly good job. They don't need criticism; they need encouragement and support.

5

MAKING LIFE EASIER FOR YOURSELF AND PRESERVING YOUR SANITY

The ideas outlined in this chapter should make life easier for the parents and happier for toddlers. All these suggestions are common sense, but though they may be easy to follow in theory, they may not be quite so easy in practice. Give them a try anyway!

STRUCTURE AND ROUTINE

Little children tend to be much more secure and happy when they live in an organized, structured environment. As well as knowing when they are going to be fed, when it is bedtime, and when it is time to go to nursery school, they also need to know the behavioral limits that their parents will tolerate. Most children thrive on routine; late nights, late meals, unexpected visitors, or dad going away for the night will immediately throw them out of kilter. Wherever possible, parents should try to organize the day well in advance so they can warn their children what lies ahead for them. Disorganized parents can produce disorganized children, and the combined effect is a sure recipe for chaos.

CONSISTENT DISCIPLINE: ONLY ONE SET OF RULES IN THIS HOUSE

Toddlers can become incredibly wound up and confused if they receive conflicting messages from each parent. We are not always aware that we are transmitting differing, confusing messages, and it is an unusual family in which both parents agree completely about discipline. Nonetheless, great efforts must be made to pull together, and it is vitally important that one partner does not interfere and counteract the other's attempts at discipline.

In each home there can only be one set of laws. If today the police let you drive on the left hand side of the road, tomorrow the middle, and then the next day you are given a summons for not driving on the right, you would have good reason to be confused, insecure and angry. The same goes for the toddler living in an environment of inconsistent, rapidly changing laws. They also become confused, angry, and unmanageable.

In some marriages one parent is so pig-headed and has so little respect for the other party that every statement is countermanded. This is a common situation when a couple is preparing for separation and divorce. The child is quick to spot the disagreement between the parents and will play off one against the other until the situation becomes intolerable. When there is such major disagreement between the parents, there is little benefit in giving any behavioral help, as nothing is likely to work until the warring parties have separated and stability returns.

Divorce and separation in themselves, however, are not the great evils to the child we are sometimes led to believe. If the break is made cleanly, without open or subtly hidden hostility, the child will usually escape relatively unscathed. It is the anger, inconsistency and those degrading tricks that parents use before separation, as well as the ensuing custody battles, that do all the harm. What makes me want to weep is angry parents who use the child as a weapon with which to beat their partner. This is a common form of child abuse that seems to be quite accepted in our "advanced" society.

DON'T BLAME GRANDMA

Parents with uncontrollable children are often quick to blame someone else for their problems. So often I hear parents say "How can I discipline him when the next day he goes to his grandmother and she spoils him?" This is a complete red herring and a figment of the parents' imagination. You cannot go through life blaming baby sitters, teachers, and others for your child's imperfections. The buck, as the saying goes, stops here, with you. Anyway toddlers show an amazing ability to cope with different disciplines in different situations. Of course they realize they can behave differently and will be disciplined accordingly when at pre-school or grandma's, but they know there is a different set of rules in their parents' home, and they accept that.

AIM FOR CALM AND PEACE—
DON'T STIR THEM UP

Although most parents know what situations bring out the worst in their youngsters, they continue to stumble into them with amazing regularity. We know, for example, that tension, anger, noise, windy days, restriction, crowds, and excess activity are all potent

detonators. If you are looking for a life free of explosion, then they
are best avoided.

Tension and overkill

Although we realize that tension upsets children, most of the upsets in our lives are impossible to control. One of the silliest
remarks a doctor can make to his patient is "relax, stop being so
tense." If it were that easy to relax, you wouldn't have been in the
doctor's office in the first place. Families live with many tensions
as they worry about jobs, money, relationships, housing, and the
hundred and one other things that go into making up the average
troublesome life. I have no miracle cure to stop these worries, but
I am equally aware just how infectious tension can be, and how it
stirs up children.

One form of futile and unnecessary tension follows "overkill"
punishment. If, for example, the child commits some major crime
early in the morning, punishment should be meted out immediately, followed by forgiveness and peace. Some parents are amazingly slow to forgive their children, continuing to use a form of
negative psychological warfare throughout the day, which ensures
high tensions and resultant bad behavior, as well as guaranteeing
maximum parental unhappiness. Overkill punishment and holding
grudges is far more successful in generating parental hypertension
and ulcers than in producing stable, loving children.

Tension and inevitable happenings

Tension can also be minimized to some extent if you try to view
life with a degree of philosophical acceptance. Some things happen
in life that are just inevitable. They will occur whether we burn
ourselves out with worry and tension, or lie back and adopt the
philosophical approach. An example would be, say, the occasion on
which your three-year-old child is sick and wakes up at least five
times during the night. This is an inevitable occurrence caused by
the sickness, and it is totally outside your control. You can either
accept this and take what sleep you can salvage gracefully or resent
the situation deeply and become so angry that when at last your
head hits the pillow you find you are too keyed up to sleep.

It is fairly difficult to view life from the calm plane of a philosophy appropriate perhaps to a meditating Indian guru. On the other
hand, beating your head against a brick wall is futile, unless you
happen to subscribe to the school of thought that admits it is painful, but so lovely when you stop! To be accepting and sensible in

matters of child rearing does not mean that you have to sit around cross-legged, chanting mantras and chewing vegetarian delicacies. We might all become amateur gurus if we stopped "blowing our tops" and started using our brains.

Noise

Loud music is known to make teenagers want to dance and great armies are moved to march off and fight at a mere fanfare of trumpets. Likewise toddlers will become greatly stirred up in a noisy situation. It is hard to discipline the young in a home where the adults are arguing, children are fighting, and the television set is going full blast. Calm and peace are highly infectious and toddlers think and behave best when the volumes are low and they are surrounded by the minimum of distraction.

Activity

All children are stirred up by activity. Toddlers love rough play and get very excited and wound up when horsing around with a parent. If you spend time stirring up your child, you must also set aside time to help him unwind. The child who comes straight to the dinner table from some major horseplay will probably display appalling manners and behavior.

But wound-up children shattering mealtime peace is not half as bad as the effect they produce at bedtime. When over-excited and over-exercized late in the evening, the toddler becomes impossible to settle down to sleep. Recently I saw a four-year-old boy's minor sleep problem turned into a major one by activity. His intelligent father took the boy out for an evening jog, believing this would tire him out and help him fall asleep. The poor child returned home out of breath, with a bounding pulse, and psyched up like a marathon runner with another 10 kilometers to go. Hours would pass before he could settle to sleep, and all the while his well-intentioned parents were quite unaware of what they were doing.

Activity and horsing around are to be encouraged, but there is a time and a place for everything, and just before bedtime is not the right time.

It takes two to fight

An obvious piece of common sense that is often forgotten is that, no matter how much one party wants to fight, it is not possible unless someone else accepts the challenge. If you've got your dander up and are spoiling for a fight, the result will depend completely on how the object of your fury reacts when you meet. If they also explode and get out of control, a marvelous fight is guaranteed. If, on the other hand, they refuse to be drawn into battle, and remain cool, calm and collected, there can never be a fight.

You only have to go to the complaints counter in a major department store to find out what calm, controlled people are like. As the customer's voice ascends in octaves of fury the only reaction coming from the other side of the desk is invariably "oh, how interesting" or "Yes, quite. I'll draw it to the manager's attention." Parents, too, have this power to encourage or prevent fights, depending on how they react. Fighting with toddlers is a futile and soul-destroying occupation, so exercise your veto in order to stabilize your blood pressure, maintain your sanity, and generate some domestic peace.

BEWARE THE TRIGGERS

Minor triggers can create big explosions, and it is obviously infinitely preferable to avoid the trigger than have to mop up after the "big bang." If you stand back and try dispassionately to analyze your child's repertoire of cunning tricks, you will find that it is in fact pretty small. You are probably being stirred up by the same trigger day in, day out. By triggers I mean those situations that always seem to lead to trouble, like dragging their feet until they are almost late for school, or refusing to bathe or brush their teeth. Among toddlers, most fights start when the child is diverted from doing something he does not want to stop, such as playing when he should be in bed or when the chimes of the ice-cream truck are heard but you are not prepared to supply the necessary funds.

Look carefully for the triggers and see if you can discover exactly what it is that sets off your child's bad behavior. With a bit of cunning, they can be got round.

BEWARE TODDLER MANIPULATION

Toddlers are masters of several techniques usually reserved for the secret police. One of the favorite methods of destroying a prisoner's sanity and will to resist is brain-washing. The technique is simple. One day the guard walks in, puts his arm round the prisoner's shoulder and says "I am your friend, Comrade." The next day the guard enters, takes the same pose and then hits the prisoner over the head with an iron bar. As this fluctuating behavior continues, the prisoner becomes confused and insecure, which leads to even-

tual disintegration of the mind. Even better psychological disturbance can be attained if the technique of sleep deprivation is
added. After days of disturbed sleep, the average prisoner becomes
so emotionally exhausted that he finds he cannot think straight and
will eventually confess to anything.

So it is with toddlers. They confuse their parents, changing
their behavior from hour to hour and day to day. Sometimes parents find it impossible to believe that this is normal toddler behavior, and immediately take the child to the doctor for
examination of a "split personality." Many parents with young
children also suffer from sleep deprivation. Their night-time peace
is ruined to such an extent that by day they become irritable, irra-
tional, and with all the sparkle of the living dead.

Another small trick carefully designed to jar a parent's nerves is
the skillful interruption in mid-sentence of everything that mom or
dad says, destroying clear thought processes in all but the most
resistant of toddler-hardened minds. Non-stop, irrelevant questions can heighten until the parental brain is completely numb.
Toddlers demand constant attention and there is absolutely nothing more tiring or emotionally draining than focusing one's full
attention on one thing all day—except perhaps trying to juggle
three live hand grenades with the thumb of your left hand in a
splint.

Little children also have an incredible ability to make their
mothers feel inferior. Many will act the complete angel when outside the home, reserving their demonic side for the exclusive ap-
preciation of their parents. There's no point in telling anyone—
they're just not going to believe you! Other children are difficult in
their mother's care but behave perfectly for their father. This can
cause quite a few parental bust-ups.

PREFERABLY POSITIVE

Ideally, children should live in an environment full of love, attention and encouragement. Most of us aim for this, but somehow it
seems much easier to slip into that negative, punitive rut that gets
us nowhere.

Ample Grade A attention should be given (see Chapter 7), but
this is impossible when our children are annoying us, when we
feel unwell, or when the housework or the cooking have to be
done. At these times, it is all too easy to adopt that negative battle
stance where life becomes a series of "no," "don't," "stop it," and
slap. After living through a day like this, parents feel physically
exhausted and numb behind the eyeballs. At bedtime, when they

think back over the day, they weep when they think, "What good thing have I said all day? Is this what the joy of parenting is all about?" The next morning parents greet the dawn with a negative sigh, "What awful thing is he going to do first?"

We are only human and it is difficult to adopt a saintly, positive attitude through all adversity. A helpful technique is one we use with the parents of handicapped children. We actively seek out good points in what, at first, appears an utter desert of bad news and general negativity. We look carefully for talents, skills and good points, and once they have been recognized we build on them in the hope of lifting some of that black cloud of despair and gloom that surrounds the family.

With toddlers, if all appears negative and full of unending bad behavior, head out on a voyage of exploration to discover some good behavior. In some children, their performance is so bad that a vivid imagination is needed to spot anything that remotely resembles good behavior. With them, we reward the "nearly good," using this as the thin edge of the wedge to build up more positive relations and, we hope, better behavior.

Trying to be positive is a highly admirable but often quite impractical goal. Sometimes it is easier to concentrate on avoiding being negative, which in the long run has much the same effect.

One way to avoid slipping into the negative spiral is to actively set out to cut down the number of times the word "no" is used. This is best achieved using two techniques: first, by having more sensible expectations of the child, and second, by trying to remove temptation by making the house childproof.

SENSIBLE EXPECTATIONS

"Normal" toddler behavior in all its gory detail has already been described, so you should by now be under no misapprehensions as to what it's all about. You may already have lowered your sights somewhat and begun to approach toddler management with slightly more sensible expectations. Some of the more common areas of conflict are described below.

Mess and breakage

Toddlers by nature are noisy, dirty and messy. If allowed to pour their own drinks, a good proportion of it will inevitably land on the floor. In wet weather, mud and dirt walk into the house with your toddler, and toddlers are rotten judges of the dirt-resisting properties of your best carpet. They have absolutely no sense of the adult monetary system and our strange values, failing to realize the difference between breaking a milk bottle and a priceless Waterford crystal vase. Animals they fondly cuddle yelp for release and ornaments they handle in genuine interest seemingly disintegrate in their fingers.

Toddlers aren't malicious; they are merely impulsive, non-thinking and invariably accident-prone. If you leave anything of value in their reach you have only yourself to blame if it is broken.

Broken toys

If you give a toddler an expensive toy there is a sporting chance that it will be broken before the sun has set. Toys do get damaged, and it is stupid to blame the toddler; it is probably you who should be reprimanded for spending too much money in the first place or buying poorly made articles. Little children do not need expensive, easily broken toys. They have such an imagination that an old cardboard box or the tube from the middle of a toilet roll can give hours more creative fun than any expensive plastic creation.

Father's return

By evening, the toddler is bored with his mother and as he hears father's key turn in the lock he happily comes to life with renewed energy. Dad is viewed as an exciting new entertainment-giver, and the toddler has little respect for dad's tiredness after a long working day and his wish to sit down, put his feet up, and talk to his wife or read the evening paper. It's far from easy, but fathers must try to see life from their child's point of view and allocate a period of attention at the time of their return each night. The child will expect it and is unlikely to accept rejection without a fight.

Social honesty

Children of this age have not yet developed the quality of "social dishonesty" which is expected of any of us who wish to succeed in the grown-up world. Toddlers are not backward in pointing out different skin colors and people's handicaps, as well as informing people of their disastrous hairstyles or ugly features. When out visiting, if the cooking tastes rotten, the child will not beat around the bush, using the vague dishonesties of an adult; he will say it in plain English for all to hear.

Whether we should change the toddler's dishonesty or the adult's dishonesty is an interesting philosophical point that we will not argue here. Suffice it to say that, in the long run, it is hard to live in the crazy world of adults without behaving like one.

MAKING YOUR HOUSE CHILDPROOF

The more realistic you are about your child, the less you will have to say "no" to him. To make a real impact on the flow of negative utterances, your house should be fortified like a Roman fort and made as childproof as possible.

Fiddly fingers and the collapse of the dream home

Newly married couples move into their dream house, taking pride in displaying their prized possessions. When the baby is born, a few changes are needed. When the toddler bursts onto the scene, a major rethink is called for. As he starts fingering the ornaments and taking the house apart, some stubborn parents adopt the attitude that "we were here first and we will live in this house on our terms."

Sure, you can leave all those tempting trinkets lying around, and the child will eventually be taught not to touch them, but it is rarely worth the months of trouble and argument. Most parents believe it is easier to keep temptation out of the toddler's way for one or two years, and in this way have the minimum of fights and the maximum of joy.

High shelves, locks, open and prohibited areas

As soon as the child approaches toddler age, you should survey your house and lay plans to childproof it. You cannot be expected to fortify the whole place like some suburban Fort Knox, but a few modifications are well worth the effort. Breakables and items you want to keep out of toddler's reach should be kept on a high shelf or in a childproof cupboard. If you have good furniture in a good room, it is often wise to keep this out of bounds for most of the time, to prevent the spills and breakages that are sure to cause fights. While some restriction of access is a good idea, the child must have ample room to exercise and must be allocated some "play areas," such as the saucepan cupboard or the laundry sink.

Don't complain when your toddler flushes your best teaspoon down the toilet; devise a toddler-proof fastener for the cutlery drawer. Don't complain when he draws all over the walls using the pen you keep beside the telephone; keep the pen on a higher level.

Immobilize the refrigerator (if necessary)

Some parents come to me with what they believe to be a really profound question. "Dr. Green, how do I stop him taking chocolate out of the fridge?" The obvious is to keep all such temptation out of the house, but if you are not prepared to go quite that far, immobilize the refrigerator.

The favored technique for refrigerator immobilization is to use a short piece of elastic cord, the type used to clip articles on the roof rack of the car. The hooks can be clipped round the back of the fridge, and although the doors may open a short distance, they slam closed before the toddler's arm can extract the goods. This method usually allows parents easy access, while providing the child with a form of exercise not unlike a chest expander.

Make-up, creams and indelible markers

Many toddlers have amazing artistic talents, particularly when it comes to finger painting on the floor or the mirror. Make-up, creams, and indelible markers should be kept well out of reach. Any pen with ink that is not easily and instantly washable must be kept under the tightest security.

Dangers, dogs, and sharp toys

Houses with windows that come down to floor level pose a danger to the child, who will suffer severe cuts if he falls through the glass, and even greater injury if he rides his tricycle through an unprotected first floor window to the ground below. Block such dangers with furniture or fit temporary bars across the window pane.

Safety plugs should be fitted over electrical outlets as young children have the sort of fascination with electricity that a snake has with a mongoose. It is not a bad idea to have a commercial circuit-breaker fitted to your junction box outside, and then at least you can rest safe in the knowledge that even if he does poke a hairpin into the electric toaster he will survive to poke another day.

Toys with sharp edges that are likely to cut or damage either him or something else are best removed altogether. It is imperative that all medicines are stored safely in a securely locked cupboard high up out of harm's way. It's a common mistake for people who are very conscientious about storing medicines to leave even more dangerous products within easy reach in the kitchen or laundry.

Bleach, rat poison, weed killer, drain cleaner and any caustic compound are the main offenders, and they must be locked well away.

Pets and toddlers generally mix well, but there is no place in the same house for a savage dog who bites when teased, however important his role as a guard dog may seem. Such animals should be sent back to the jungle where they belong.

Fortify the compound

Coping with an active toddler can be extremely difficult if there is no access to a small piece of secure garden. You need fences and gates to prevent the child escaping into the road before you can relax. If surrounded by busy traffic and inadequate fencing, in the interests of the child's safety all doors leading from the house must be immobilized. The best methods are a high-level fastener, security chain or a deadlock.

The playpen

The playpen is a marvelous invention for keeping active children with fiddly fingers out of mischief. Although sound in theory, this rarely works in practice, because extremely active children resent being restricted and will reject the notion of staying in a playpen. Some parents tell me that what they really want is a large playpen in which they can place a comfortable chair, then sit and read a book while the child runs wildly around the house, unable to get within arm's length of the parent.

Absconders and harnesses

Though no toddler has any road sense, most do not like to be separated from their parents when out of the home, and they will tend to stay close by. Some toddlers, however, will take off like a horse out of the starting gate at the first sign of open space. Some of these children enjoy being chased after; others have no fear of separation from their parents, get lost with monotonous regularity, and place themselves in great danger. This period of attempting to abscond is generally quite short-lived, and although I greatly dislike the use of harnesses, in some instances they must be preferable to exhausted parents worrying themselves and the local policemen into nervous breakdowns every time they venture out with their child.

Apathetic, helpless parents

Never a week goes by without some brilliant parent telling me of a new childproofing technique she has invented. Other parents seem to have no imagination, initiative or motivation to improve the difficulties that consume them. They are apathetic and helpless, as they sit there and tell me "it's impossible to lock the door," or "impossible to immobilize the gate," or "impossible to stop him drawing on walls."

As I sit comfortably at home and watch astronauts blasted off from earth to fly round the world many times before landing back where they started, it seems unbelievable that in this same super-scientific world an intelligent 25-year-old cannot devise some method to prevent a two-year-old child from opening a door. We do not need the high technology of computers, space suits and rocket fuel: a piece of elastic or a length of string can all produce dramatic results.

Fighting with children is such a waste of time and emotional energy, that if you are not one of the lucky 40 per cent who have an easy and angelic child, please be sensible and childproof your home.

AVOID NO-WIN SITUATIONS

Beating your head against a brick wall has already been listed as one of the least productive occupations in life. For those who seek a peaceful existence, it is wise to reserve time and energy for worthwhile causes and avoid at all costs those that cannot be won. In a small number of situations the toddler will always have the upper hand, and when fights develop the parents can never win. The main areas to look out for here are feeding, sleep, toileting, and discipline outside the home.

Feeding

It is relatively easy to sit a child at the table and place food in front of him. Some clever parents can even get food into the reluctant child's mouth by using great feats of cunning, but no one has yet discovered the location of the switch that makes the toddlers chew and then swallow the food. I am sure there is a Nobel Prize waiting for the person who discovers how to make toddlers eat, but until that happens it is best to accept failure in the food fight.

No toddler has ever starved to death through stubbornness, and forcing food down a child's throat only causes feeding problems and gives the stubborn toddler a means of really upsetting his parents when he wants to.

Sleep

In exactly the same way as you can lead the proverbial horse to water but cannot make him drink, parents can put a child to bed but they cannot make an unwilling child go to sleep. If the parent demands that a stubborn toddler go to sleep immediately, the little rascal will generate unbelievable powers of wakefulness, just to show who's boss. It is pointless forcing children to sleep. You must simply be content with keeping them in their room and adjusting the volume of noise to a tolerable level.

Toilet training

You can take your child to the toilet, and if the right approach is used, he can be made to sit there for a certain length of time. But no parent can force a stubborn child to use the toilet against his will. Put yourself in the place of a two-year-old who has been extracted from his favorite game to sit reluctantly on a cold, hard toilet seat. He is exasperated enough by the inconvenience to the time schedule of his busy day, and when his mother insists that he use the toilet, this is the last straw. As she says, "You will use the toilet at once," you can see his eyes twinkling with devilment and a smile come onto his face as he says to himself: "That's what she thinks!" After the child has sat for the approved, but unproductive, five minutes, mother eventually abandons it as a no-win situation. Often this is not the end of the saga, and a short time later the little fellow appears with a coy smile and a sagging diaper and the air is full of unpleasant odors.

Fighting over toilet training slows training and ages parents. Getting worked up over it leaves the child with a trump card that can be used mercilessly to batter parents when the spirit moves.

Discipline outside the home

In my practice, about a sixth of all young children consistently upset their parents when they are taken outside the home. The greatest embarrassment is when the child seeks out a prominent public place to perform the latest and most theatrical tantrum. For best effect, a crowded street or supermarket are favored venues.

Designers of modern supermarkets have much to answer for, as they have created an environment sure to bring out the worst in any toddler. Outside the complex, you encounter those coin-operated highway robbers which, for a small sum, mechanically bounce your child up and down. Parents should be warned against ever putting a coin in one of these machines, as once this has been done, it becomes impossible to walk past them without tantrums when no ride is allowed.

Once inside the supermarket, the noise and bustle stir up the child. The next decision is whether the youngster should ride in the shopping cart or run beside you, fingering the groceries and knocking over the displays.

Each child has an individual time limit for shopping, and once it has expired every effort should be made to get out as soon as possible. Getting out of supermarkets is never easy at the best of times, because checkouts tend to be slow and crowded. To make things worse, the management takes great care to leave its displays of sweets alongside the slow-moving line, and—surprise, surprise— the most tempting items are always placed on the low shelves well within reach of little fingers. They know what they're doing, these people!

Imagine the effect on a three-year-old who grabs a chocolate bar and is immediately told by his mother to put it back. He stops to think for a minute, checks out the audience, and then throws himself on the floor in a most proficient tantrum display. At this point there are only three options left open to the mother:

1) she repents, accedes to blackmail and gives him the chocolate bar;
2) she ignores the outburst and walks on; or
3) she gives him a sharp smack.

None of these remedies is likely to work. If he is given the chocolate bar, he will demand one every time he goes to the supermarket. If his splendid mother ignores him and walks away, half the assembled shoppers will mumble, "Women like that shouldn't be allowed to have children." If she spanks her child, the other half will look aghast and self-righteous, and stare at her accusingly as if she were a child-beater.

Supermarkets pose a number of other problems. Many of those angelic, quiet children who appear to be sitting quietly in the shoping cart have nasty habits the minute their mother's back is turned. They make their own selection from the nearest shelf or transfer at random mother's carefully chosen goods into a passing cart. This causes considerable confusion and embarrassment at the checkout. Some children run wildly up and down the aisles; others feel impelled to touch everything in sight. A good game is taking one of the cans out of the base of a pyramid and watching the whole lot crash to the ground. Then there are the absconders, who disappear the minute you get inside, invariably end up in the manager's office, and are next heard of when a voice comes over the public address system announcing: "Will the mother of a noisy two-year-old with a faded yellow T-shirt and dirty face come and collect him immediately, before he is involved in a nasty accident."

There is no correct treatment for children who have tantrums in public places. Whichever method you use poses problems, a great deal of embarrassment, and is generally not very effective anyway. All efforts should be made to concentrate on tidying up the tantrums that occur in the child's own home. Once this control has been achieved, it always spreads outside to the supermarket, busy street, and on visits to other people.

Misbehaving when visiting or in the car

Children tend to be better behaved when out visiting friends than when in their own home, but a small minority make it very difficult for their parents when they go out. At times like these one soon discovers who one's real friends are, and visits should probably be restricted to these select few for the time being.

Other children can be extremely difficult when out in the car, often screaming and fighting in the back seat, which is dangerously distracting for the driver. A tantrum that occurs in a speeding car in the middle of rush hour is completely untreatable, and the child is invariably aware that there is nothing his parents can do. I recently witnessed a minor road accident following which a distraught mother got out of her car, most apologetic, and said that such had been the volume of noise in her car that she had been past the point of being able to drive safely and simply had not noticed the car she hit. Children who fight and scream in cars must be responsible for a significant number of accidents each year. This is a no-win situation, and often the best you can do is to improve the home behavior, knowing that once this improves outside behavior will follow suit.

PRESERVE PARENTAL SANITY

It is not only children who have rights. Parents have rights too. Maintenance of the parents' stability and marriage is as important to the children as it is to the parents themselves. Here are some ways of strengthening the parents' psychological well-being and looking after the marriage.

Don't let the child put a wedge between parents

Couples spend the first years of marriage adjusting to the idea of sharing life together. No sooner has this state of equilibrium been achieved, than a child arrives on the scene to permanently rearrange the family. Some husbands who have been pampered like children get a shock when they find there is now a real child on the scene who is stealing all the attention. Besides losing much of the limelight, they also have to contend with erratic mealtimes, lack of social life, their wives' tiredness, and a high level of environmental noise.

Nerves and marriages benefit greatly when the parents can spend some time alone together. It is not at all satisfactory that the child be allowed to romp around all day, stay up until all hours of the night constantly interrupting every adult conversation, and then cap it off by demanding to sleep in the middle of the marital bed.

Parents must be encouraged to use relatives and babysitters so that they can go out by themselves. If they can manage a whole weekend by themselves occasionally, it works wonders. It's a sad fact of life that once children have grown up and left home, some parents have forgotten how to talk to each other and live alone together. It is our business to ensure that there is "life after the birth of children" and "life before death" for parents.

A young child can easily play off one parent against the other. Most children are much better behaved for their father than they are for their mother, for a very obvious reason. The mother who spends all day with her toddler becomes so well known that the child has worked out all her weaknesses and is able to manipulate them to the full. Father leaves for work early and often arrives home late in the evening as an exciting stranger. The child has not seen enough of him to be able to work out his weak spots. Were the family to go in for role reversal with dad becoming the child-minder and mom the wage earner, a reversal in abilities to discipline would follow. Any father who believes himself to be a superior parent and criticizes his wife's mode of discipline is arrogant, misguided, and needs a firm kick in the pants.

Explode the myth of the twenty-four-hour-a-day mother

The myth is that all women were designed to be twenty-four-hour-a-day mothers. Certainly this role suits some admirably, but others are happier and better mothers if in full-time work outside the home, while most of the rest benefit greatly from having some time to themselves. Fathers are able to escape to the relative peace of their work, usually unaware of the degree of physical and emotional stress involved in trying to be a good twenty-four-hour-a-day mother. Mothers must have the right to escape, and to have some peace and time to themselves. There is usually a grandma, a neighbor or some form of temporary child care facility where the child can be taken while mom has an hour or two off.

With a child of any age who is irritable, particularly badly behaved, or severely handicapped, it is especially important that a certain amount of external day care is considered. This should also be arranged for any children whose mother has reached the stage of being past coping; day care is essential so that she can recharge her batteries.

Some mothers are much happier and better parents if they return to part-time or full-time employment. If this is the case, I would encourage them to go back to work. Everyone will benefit in the long run.

Whip dad into action

By my calculation, fathers are responsible for 50 per cent of the material that makes up any child. As equal shareholders, they should be encouraged to take an equal part in child care. On returning home from work each evening, for example, a father can enter the scene like the rescuing US cavalry and take the child off to be entertained. This is invariably the time of day—that impossible hour leading up to the evening meal—when the child is tired, hungry, bored, and wants mother's attention. Mother is also tired, hungry, and irritable, and she cannot give that attention and cook a meal at the same time. Every mother will know well the time of day I mean. This is one occasion when father can come to the rescue and do his bit. Fathers can also take care of a child one night a week, to allow mom out to classes, sport, or just to keep in touch with the real world.

A misguided expert once declared that two children were easier to look after than one. The theory was that they entertained each other, and kept themselves out of mischief. I suspect that two children are four times harder to look after than one. Though they may well enjoy each other's company and can entertain each other, their joint talents at getting into mischief are immeasurable and by the law of compound interest four hands can do greatly more damage than two.

Many stressed moms get great relief if father will take one child off whenever possible, usually on a Saturday morning. This splits up the terrorist cell and makes life easier for both parents. Fathers are particularly suited to taking youngsters to run off energy in the park, or taking them outside to help in the garden or around the house. They have much to offer in making life at home easier and must be used to the full.

When the going gets tough—get out!

Despite all the behavioral advice in the world, there comes a point when some children's behavior becomes unbearable. This usually

happens on those wet, windy days when the single bedroom apartment seems oppressively small. When the whining starts, it seems
to reverberate around the walls and ceilings, going right through
your head and jangling your nerves. At this point, discipline becomes difficult and I believe it's best to cut one's losses and run.
Take the children and head for the wide open spaces. Noisy children never seem so loud when their efforts are muffled by the
great outdoors, and the movement of the baby carriage is usually
very soothing to the active toddler. It's worth getting wet just for
the peace of mind!

One very upset mother I recently cared for told me: "When I
am losing control, I get outdoors straight away. There things never
seem quite so bad, and even if I was driven too far, I know that I
would never hit him in public." Now there is a piece of wise,
honest advice.

Out of control and birth control

When I see parents who cannot cope with their children, I ask
them what their plans are for further additions to the family. Most
parents who have a difficult child swear that it will definitely be
their last. Whether it is, of course, is another matter entirely. I
am often asked if the first or second child is the most difficult. The
answer is that the last child is probably the most difficult.

Occasionally parents whose children are completely out of control tell me that they may have more, but that "It's all in God's
hands." Far be it for me to interfere in other people's affairs, let
alone their religious beliefs, but if parents cannot cope with their
present brood, I can assure you that an extra child is only going to
make matters worse. Perhaps these parents should seriously consider some reliable form of avoidance rather than leaving all the
responsibility in God's hands.

6

DISCIPLINE THAT WORKS—
MOST OF THE TIME!

Parents with newborn babies manage to cope pretty well in the first year, but as soon as that negative, stubborn, self-centered terrorist toddler appears, many wonder what has hit them. As their own discipline methods falter, they are bombarded with a mass of free advice and helpful opinion from assorted relatives and armchair philosophers, who managed successfully to screw up their own children and are now determined to do the same to yours. Some experts dispute the need for any sort of discipline, in the belief that model parents so influence children by their shining example that discipline is largely unnecessary. If you happen to be one of the fortunate few who has been rewarded with an easy child, this may indeed be true. For the rest of us, however, discipline is most certainly necessary. But we must choose our methods carefully.

It may seem strange, but young children tend to feel much more secure when they live in an environment that has structure and clearly defined limits. Not only does good discipline make children happier, but it gives a much needed foundation to help them cope with the limits and restrictions of school and life in general. Children who have experienced little discipline before school find it hard to change overnight and fit into the limits of a kindergarten class. Some children are strong enough to take this in their stride, but many react badly, and become withdrawn, sullen, and unhappy. The result may be that the child will then refuse to go to school at all.

I am in no doubt as to the benefits of discipline, but I worry about some of the stupidity that is displayed by parents in this area. In this chapter various types of discipline are discussed, some of which are effective most of the time; some will work occasionally; many methods are best forgotten altogether.

THE REIGN OF TERROR

The reign of terror is an old-fashioned remedy based on the belief that any child can be battered into shape if the parents are firm enough. This method was fashionable in Victorian times, and many a drawing-room echoed to such sayings as "little children should be seen and not heard."

Some parents still believe that a house run on strict authoritarian lines can produce the perfectly behaved child. These dictatorial families believe they have created a child who is well-behaved and perfect; in short, a being closely resembling the reincarnation of his God-like parents. On the surface the child may appear well-behaved, but underneath this thin veneer of compliance lies resentment and potential for rebellion. Model children produced through intimidation continue to present this model picture just so long as the threat is present. Once the threat is lifted they rebel; for example going wild when their parents go away for the weekend, getting boozed up or having "super orgies." They leave home at the first possible opportunity, making a rude departing gesture as if to say "Thanks for nothing, dad." Like government by intimidation, discipline of children by intimidation is only good as long as the intimidation continues. It never leaves respect, long-term stability, or happiness.

SPANKING

When lecturing to parents I delight in asking how many of them are child spankers. From an audience of about a hundred, a few hands tentatively poke up; heads turn uneasily as parents fear that they may be the only child beaters in the auditorium. The next question is: "How many of you do not smack your children?" Out of a hundred parents, rarely will more than two hands appear.

Whether it is a good way or a bad way to treat children, the fact of life is that these days most parents spank their children some time or other. Although a great many experts have philosophized on the evils of this punishment, most parents I see continue to be of the opinion that a well-aimed smack is quite justified in certain well-chosen instances. If you are one of the 98 per cent of parents who are going to use spanking as a form of punishment, could I plead that it be restricted only to the following two situations:

1) after some dangerous, life-threatening act, or
2) to defuse the rapidly escalating, no-win confrontation.

Following some dangerous, life-threatening act, an immediate hard smack will strongly reinforce the message that whatever has just taken place must never again be repeated. Cats may have nine lives, but as those of us who work in big hospitals know, this does not extend to children. Children only escape once or twice when climbing out of second-floor balconies, dismantling electrical appliances, playing with fire, or running across busy roads. A painful smack may produce minor emotional trauma, but it is a small price to pay if it significantly increases the chance of keeping a child alive and healthy.

Other parents find that a quick, sharp smack may be most valuable in defusing a deteriorating situation that is about to get hopelessly out of control. In toddlers, most major behavioral wars start with some insignificant trigger that sets in motion an ever-increasing cycle of trouble. It is preferable to nip this swiftly in the bud rather than wait until it has escalated to mammoth proportions and upset the entire family. A well-timed smack may well defuse the situation, diverting the child from escalation to the more easily controlled "dry tear" crying of the Hollywood actor.

Spanking misused

Having mentioned two situations in which spanking might be considered, it must be emphasized that spanking does more harm than good in every other instance. There is no doubt that, used as the main form of discipline, spanking is negative and emotionally degrading, as well as being an extremely ineffective form of control. Any form of discipline that is over-used loses its potency, and spanking is no exception.

Usually when spanking occurs, the child is hit by a mother who has lost her temper. She is naturally upset at her loss of control and feels guilty and sorry for what she has done. This by itself would not really matter, if it were not for the intelligence and highly refined manipulative skills of the toddler. In this case, our soft-hearted mother is already feeling guilty and the toddler is well aware of the fact. As the crying starts, the child is aware that she is feeling even more upset and, recognizing the mother's distress, he cries even harder. The vicious cycle continues until mom can stand it no more and picks up the child for a big cuddle. This may indeed be a most charitable way for a good mother to behave, but in this instance it is quite wrong. Mother has in fact rewarded the wrong behavior and given the message "doing something naughty gets a cuddle." The right way to deal with it is for her to walk away from it completely. In this instance spanking is a hopeless form of discipline which has backfired and resulted in the child being rewarded for the very behavior mom was trying to extinguish.

Another occasion in which the smack leads to more trouble than it is worth is when, after the child has been smacked, he does not cry but immediately returns the smack. The parent then returns the blow and the toddler reciprocates. This is a no-win situation, and a minor war develops that is much easier to get into than it is to get out of. As the battle heats up, the parent gets more angry, and although the toddler is receiving a few minor flesh wounds, it becomes the best game for weeks.

Toddlers are negative, stubborn, and have little sense. If their parents also exhibit these qualities, any fight will go on "to the death," with each party showing an unthinking determination to cast the last blow. Most toddlers are not only more intelligent, but also more theatrically talented than their parents ever realize. When spanked, they look the parent straight in the eye, either communicating the message in words or Oscar-winning dumb insolence. "It didn't hurt . . . see if I care." Of course the smack hurt, but the child is well aware that denial will infuriate and punish the smacker. Such are the acting talents of some toddlers that I have had children referred to me accompanied by a note from the family doctor, "Please investigate the nerves in this child's legs. He appears to feel no pain!"

Whether spanking is good or evil, it continues to be used by almost all parents. If it has to be used, then it should be administered carefully, selectively, and certainly not used as the main form of discipline. Parents must be careful that, although they may appear to win the first battle with a smack, the resulting war is not lost because of the skilled follow-up mounted by the intelligent and theatrically talented toddler.

DEBATING, ARGUING—IS THERE A PLACE FOR DEMOCRACY?

I am constantly amazed by how much parental energy is consumed in arguing, debating, and being democratic with little children. Holding learned, philosophical debates with toddlers has hit almost epidemic proportions in my practice, and it is about as effective as discussing differential calculus with a Masai warrior. Parents seem to have read somewhere that every little detail of what is going on in life must be explained to their child. This is a commendable and charitable action, but it often leads to troubles that pass unrecognized by the highly intelligent, but functionally blind, parents. Toddlers crave attention, and one of the main ploys of guaranteeing a constant flow of this commodity is asking endless questions. If you examine these questions you will find that the repertoire is small, little interest is shown in the answers, and the same question is repeated hundreds of times, or for as long as the parents will rise to the bait.

We know that children like to ask questions and, if not overdone, this is a rather sweet characteristic of their age. If they are interested in the answers, then of course they must be given all supporting details explained with honesty and simplicity. The problem is that debating and questioning may have no relation to the quest for knowledge and may be only used as an attention-seeking ploy. When debating with children of any age parents must ask themselves, "Is the child genuinely interested in the answer to the question?" Or they must consider whether the answer matters or whether the way they are being stirred up is the real reason for the exercise.

Take for example the case of an acrobatic toddler who is jumping off your dining table onto the floor. It is natural to tell him to stop. He immediately asks "Why?" Well, one could easily embark on a discussion concerning the lack of strength of modern furniture or possibly mention Mrs. Smith, who lives in the apartment downstairs, outlining the characteristics of the nervous disorder that accounts for her intolerance for loud overhead noise and her allergy to large sections of plaster landing on her head from the ceiling above. All this will avail you naught. I believe that the question "why?" should be answered, but if it is purely manipulation, parents should immediately pull rank and say, "Because I don't want you to." You might as well be warned now that, although countless philosophers have debated at length the finer points of love for mankind, good and evil, this is a futile exercise with a toddler, who is far too obsessively self-centered to care for humanitarian principles.

With arguing and debating children give explanation and knowledge, but don't give attention for the wrong reason.

SHOUTING

We all know that shouting at children is a poor form of discipline, yet most of us continue to do it. Young children are so sensitive to the noise, activity, and tensions around them, that shouting tends to stir them up most effectively. The more the parent shouts, the more boisterous the child's behavior becomes, and so the vicious cycle develops. In the interests of a quiet life, shouting should be kept to the absolute minimum. It rarely achieves anything worthwhile and serves only to shatter your nerves.

THREATS

Thinking back to my student days in my home town of Belfast, I clearly remember bus travel to and from the hospital, and two things stick in my mind. I will never forget the winter rush hour with its overcrowded buses, their interiors smoky and thick with brown globules of condensation dripping from the roof. The occupants only took their pipes or cigarettes from their mouths to embark on a spasm of coughing that would have done credit to a tuberculosis ward. Equally vivid is the memory of the mothers with their uncontrollable offspring who crowded onto those early morning buses. The trip from city center was punctuated by "Stop it," "Do that again and I'll smack you," "I'm warning you for the last time," or "I'll get the man to put you off." Threats, empty threats—the most common and futile form of discipline.

Threats, if not over-used, work on some children, but only if, after fair warning, the threat is carried out as promised. Of course on those early morning Irish buses the children knew their exhausted mothers were all talk and no action. They had heard the threats so often before it was all water off a duck's back, a daily ritual that stirred up the mother and did nothing for the child.

DELAYED PUNISHMENT

Young children do not have a very far-reaching view of life, thinking back no further than the preceeding ten minutes and looking no further forward than the next ten. An hour hence, tomorrow, or next week is all quite beyond their understanding. Discipline for the toddler must, therefore, be immediate. Withholding some treat tomorrow or waiting until dad comes home are both unfair and ineffective. If the toddler has to wait until father comes home, he has long forgotten his misdeed and the delayed punishment will come as a thunderbolt from the blue. This does more to frighten and confuse the child than improve his behavior or act as a long-term deterrent.

With toddlers, punish immediately and make that the end of the episode. Parents who hold a grudge, continue to fume, and engage in psychological warfare for the rest of the day do great harm to their own health, upset their child, and guarantee a day full of tension.

DIVERSION TACTICS AND REMOVAL OF PRIVILEGES

Sensible mothers who find they are in danger of running headlong into a confrontation or tantrum situation become quite skilled at quickly diverting the child's attention before the obnoxious behavior has a chance to get properly underway. There is a psychological moment that comes just before all control is lost, and the clever parent will skillfully use this in the cause of peace. The method is discussed in greater detail when we look at toddler tantrums.

Removal of privileges is quite an effective technique in the school-age child, particularly after the age of seven years. The child who won't do homework, stays out late, or commits some major transgression can have his bicycle impounded or television viewing restricted. In toddlers this is pointless and should not be attempted.

NEGOTIATED SETTLEMENT

The technique of negotiated settlements is common in sorting out industrial disputes, where union members may agree to build an extra car a day in exchange for say, a longer coffee break and ten weeks vacation a year. Bargaining and debating with toddlers is generally a waste of time, but the early-school-age child is often interested in coming to such a settlement.

With some children over the age of four, I will get the parents to draw up a list of the kinds of behavior that they would dearly like to see eradicated and then balance this with a list of things that the child himself would very much enjoy having changed. Though we rarely revolutionize a child's behavior completely with this method, there is always some improvement. Recently I saw a girl of three years 11 months whose parents were greatly upset that she still sucked a pacifier day and night. She was a bright little girl, and as she was clearly aware of the consumer society in which we live, we negotiated a simple contract in her presence. On her fourth birthday she was taken to a large toyshop where she chose her favorite doll. What happened thereafter had been fully negotiated and went most smoothly. When the girl reached the cash register the shop assistant handed her the doll and in exchange, the little girl handed over her pacifier, which was then deposited into the permanent care of a convenient trash can. Negotiated settlement had passed off without a hitch.

BEHAVIOR MODIFICATION BY ENCOURAGEMENT AND REWARDS

Whenever the phrase "behavior modification" is mentioned, parents usually expect to learn some sinister technique of the type used by secret police to mold unwilling members of society to their way of thinking. Others have heard that behavior modification has been used to train dogs, pigeons, and circus animals and take exception to any suggestion that it might be used on their darling child. There is nothing startlingly new about behavior modification; it has been around for centuries and is probably the most effective method for disciplining children. It is a technique that is part of our everyday life and is used just as often on our friends, colleagues, bank managers, and other assorted members of humanity as it is on our children.

Behavior modification is a simple technique by which one uses rewards to build up the behavior one wishes to encourage, while ignoring the undesired, bad behavior. By rewarding the good you hope that it will be repeated, and by trying to ignore the bad you hope that it will go away. Admittedly this is a highly simplistic view of the technique—and I can hear disbelievers grumbling that it is silly and that you can't ignore bad behavior. Let me assure you that it does work.

We know that toddlers are frequently negative and obstinate. When a stubborn, determined parent confronts a stubborn, determined toddler it is extremely unlikely that either party can win.

Upset parents get wound up and disturbed by fights, so they suffer much more than the toddler, who has a short memory and will have forgotten the confrontation long before the dust has even settled. The reward-based behavior modification approach suits toddlers extremely well because it leads to far fewer fights and results in parents being much less tense. Let me give some examples.

Example #1

A four-year-old boy I saw once, while lying across his mother's knee to be examined, involuntarily straightened one of his legs and kicked me. Seeking a bit of fun, I jumped back holding my knee and pretending to make a great fuss. Ten seconds later, he kicked my other knee and I reacted similarly. By the end of the interview the little terror was jumping on my toes and kicking my shins with all the gusto of a spectator at a football game. Admittedly this is a rather odd way for a doctor to behave, but it clearly demonstrates what happens when one rewards a behavior, in this case making a fuss when kicked. A more sensible and conservative doctor would never have noticed the initial kick, taking it for what it was, an accident, and by ignoring it the subsequent behavior would not have built up.

Example #2

A three-year-old hyperactive boy destroys my office each month as he rearranges all my belongings and jumps on all my furniture. This boy spends his days running wildly around his home, going from naughtiness to naughtiness. As he speeds about his exhausted mother shouts at him in vain "Don't," "Stop," "I'll smack you," and although these irate and useless shouts do not constitute high-grade attention, nevertheless they are a form of reward and in a strange way encourage the bad behavior that they are supposed to stop. On the rare occasion that the child quieted down enough to perform some useful activity, his exhausted mother would give a sigh of relief, give thanks for the peace, and go into another room to get on with her housework.

This poor woman had become so ground down that she did not realize that she was using behavior modification techniques to build up the wrong kind of behavior. She was shouting at the over-active, destructive acts and giving them her attention, while the good behavior, which came when the child settled, she ignored and left the room.

Example #3

A four-and-a-half-year-old boy has difficulty with bowel training and is still soiling his pants. I work with him and get him really enthusiastic for a cure. A special chart is kept on the family's refrigerator door and every time he sits on the toilet great praise is given and a gold star is fixed on the chart. He is not forced to use the toilet, but when he does and the result is positive, then four extra stars are given along with liberal praise. When he is clean all day with no soiling, extra stars are attached and a small present given. This is an example of behavior modification where sitting, using the toilet, and being clean are rewarded, thereby building up and reinforcing them and gradually curing the soiling symptom. On the occasions that the child refuses to use the toilet or soils his pants, this is not dramatized but rather ignored as undesirable behavior.

Rewards, not bribes

Behavioral experts quite rightly disapprove of bribing children, although rewarding our children is to be encouraged. There is a subtle difference between reward and bribery. A bribe is a form of blackmail, in which the child is told that he can have something after he has performed a certain task. The behavior modification reward is given when there is no talk of what will happen until after the good behavior has appeared, and then the reward comes as an immediate and pleasing reinforcement. There are what the experts call "soft" and "hard" rewards. "Soft" rewards refer to praise, fun and encouragement; "hard" rewards are items such as sweets, stickers, or plastic soldiers. Most toddlers are very happy with soft rewards, particularly attention; older children are often more aware of the world monetary system and may expect hard rewards.

In summary, behavior modification is not some dubious new technique, but a well-tried method of molding behavior. When this technique is used properly, much can be achieved without recourse to raised voices, tantrums, force, threats, or parental insanity.

SELECTIVE DEAFNESS TECHNIQUE

It is possible to build up a toddler's undesirable behavior by inadvertently giving him attention for the wrong reasons. When attention is being sought for the wrong reasons, and the parent realizes it, a highly effective technique is selective deafness. Here the parent pretends to hear only the responses they wish from their child and cuts out all those that are generated for the sole aim of parental annoyance. Selective deafness is a technique that I first observed when watching how many husbands react when their wives are talking to them. It may be a most irritating way to treat one's wife, but it is an excellent way to manage the toddler who is trying to stir up his parents with a well-performed repertoire of verbal insults.

Take, for example, the three-year-old boy with conscientious, attentive parents who is thwarted in some misbehavior. He turns to his mother and declares "I hate you." We all know that he doesn't really hate his mother, but is merely trying to punish her. This outburst is best handled by the selective deafness technique. Indeed, most whimpering, whining, crying, bad language, debating, and refusal to obey is best handled by this method.

TIME OUT

Time Out is a most effective form of discipline for all children. When parent and child are having a major confrontation, it is vital that the parent keeps cool and remains in control. The best time for using the technique of Time Out is at the point when control is about to be lost. It allows the warring parties to be separated, giving both time to cool off. The technique consists of putting the child alone in another room for a time until the situation is sufficiently defused. It is not a method of punishment, rather a means of keeping everyone cool and avoiding battles. The technique is discussed more fully in Chapter 7.

CONCLUSION

There are many possible ways to discipline a toddler and many different opinions on the need, or lack of need, for such discipline. Attempts to relate "strict" or "permissive" child-rearing methods to the development of behavior problems has proved fruitless, despite volumes of material on the subject. The general principles outlined in this chapter apply to all toddlers, although we should not lose sight of the totally different personalities, and thus different disciplinary needs, of the individual child.

Have confidence in your own abilities at parenting, remembering that whatever works and feels right for you is what you should be doing, despite what the so-called experts may say.

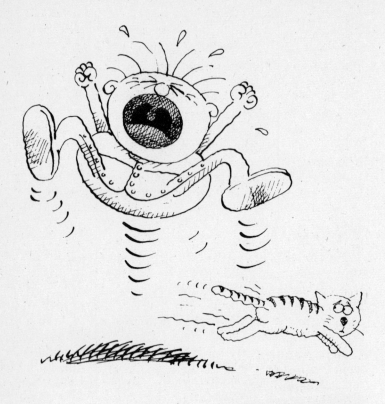

7

TANTRUMS
AND OTHER TRICKS

Tantrums and other attention-seeking tricks make up the largest part of the behavioral harassments suffered by the average parent. Literature abounds with learned theories as to why tantrums and the like occur, and this can make fascinating reading for the academic parent. It has been my experience, however, that these ideas are of little help to all those real parents with real children, who at this moment are crying out for good, practical help to keep them on the rails and maintain their sanity. In this chapter, I outline my own philosophy on how to interpret toddler behavior, then give some practical, proven, methods of controlling such behavior.

INTERPRETING BEHAVIOR

At one stage in my career, I undertook some formal training in child psychiatry, during which I was taught how to interpret behavior in psychodynamic terms. We talked of bonding, sibling rivalry, castration anxiety, Oedipal conflict, and other high-blown notions. When I say we talked, I mean this was by far our greatest skill; we were able to tell any mother how she had caused the problems in her child. Unfortunately, we were much weaker in giving the practical help, emotional support, and management advice that was really needed. Fascinating though these theories are, I have since learnt to interpret toddler behavior in much simpler terms. My method, although somewhat lacking in science, is amazingly easy.

When a little child puts on some particularly anti-social act, you stand back and say to yourself, "If I was doing what that little creep is doing, what percentage would there be in it for me?" In toddlers, the answer is nearly always the same, "to gain attention." Although the precipitating event on many occasions may be frustration, insecurity, competition, or whatever, the anti-social act is designed for one purpose only, and that is to attract attention.

Toddlers crave attention and hate to be ignored. When some parents are told that their child is misbehaving to gain more attention, they look in disbelief, saying "How could he want more attention? He gets our full attention—always." Some children who receive attention twenty-four hours a day still feel dissatisfied, wishing it to be increased to at least twenty-five! This demanding behavior, although it puzzles and frustrates parents, is not restricted to the toddler. Many parents who have everything also feel dissatisfied, resentful, and seek even more.

Attention is extremely important to the daily functioning of the toddler, so we should look carefully at the different sorts of attention we give to ensure that it is not being given for the wrong reason.

GRADES OF ATTENTION

Attention comes in many varieties. The best is high quality attention (Grade A) consisting of playing, reading, cuddles, and fun. At the other end of the scale, the worst grade (Grade Z) is no attention at all; the parent just ignores the child. When teaching parents, I like to point out that the attention toddlers crave comes in twenty-six different grades. Grade A is high class attention, Grade Z completely ignoring, and there are twenty-four progressively poorer qualities in between these two. There is no scientific basis to my twenty-six-grade theory; it is merely my way of looking at attention. Let us now speculate what types of behavior might fit into some of the alphabetical slots.

Grade A attention

As parents, we all set out to give as much Grade A attention as possible. This is a most worthy goal, but although we aim high, we are only human. Most of us slip into the intermediate grades, which has the effect of rewarding undesired behavior and thus selectively building up many irritating and unwanted habits.

Grade B attention

I reckon that the Grade B slot is awarded to that skillful art of incessant question asking. The toddler who is not getting his mother's full attention may ask non-stop questions. There is no real interest in the answers, but a great deal of attention is generated by the interrogation process. Grade B attention is not as good as the play and fun of Grade A, but it is preferable to the ignoring of Grade Z.

Grade C attention

Probably debating and arguing feature at this point on the scale. The little child who argues with his parents often has no interest in the rights and wrongs of the argument; his mind is focused solely on getting attention. Debating with one's parents is in the same class, giving the child a great buzz and doing little for the parents' health.

Grade D attention

This slot is most probably filled by the wall kicker and door slammer, the type of child who will employ strenuous efforts to stir up his mother. The door goes slam! slam! slam! "Stop it!" shouts the mother. Slam! goes the door again. "I'm warning you!" shouts the mother. Slam! goes the door again. All this generates quite a bit of attention, and although nowhere near the quality of Grade A, it is enough to justify the effort to the toddler who might be feeling rather bored.

Grade G attention

Having skipped a few grades this space is probably best reserved for one of the nastier toddler techniques—verbal abuse. This poisonous art is aimed at the hard-working, sensitive mother and consists of comments like "I hate you" and "You love Johnny more than me, don't you?" They are guaranteed to get through to the soft heart of the toughest mom and give the child a fair return for his efforts.

Grade H attention

Yelling, bad language and saying "no" all the time probably fill this slot. These activities are sure-fire methods of stirring up the most peaceful household and aging even the most dutiful of parents. The attention produced is of poor quality, but the great volume is an adequate compensation.

Grade J attention

Turning off the television in the middle of a program or pushing older brother's homework books onto the floor wins this one. A fair bit of attention can be successfully gained from this anti-social set of exercises.

Grade K attention

The theatrical escapades that follow a spanking warrant a Grade K attention in the toddler's eyes. If the child can "keep his cool" after the initial sting of the smack, he may use the situation to mount a powerful psychological counter-attack. The child looks the parent straight in the eye and declares that he felt nothing, or cries with such expertise that he manipulates his parents into giving him a cuddle. A good attention-getter this, even though it is a mite painful at the outset.

Other grades

A selection of progressively more irritating attention-seeking exploits fill these other grades, including tantrums, whining, refusing to eat or use the toilet, breath holding, vomiting on demand, throwing toys, and playing off one parent against the other. All these will gain a degree of attention and are, therefore, useful weapons in the toddler's armory of cunning.

Summary

Parents should remember that attention comes in many grades and be careful that it is given only for the right reasons. Reacting for the wrong reasons has the knack of reducing the good behavior and building up the child's most undesirable qualities.

TANTRUMS

Tantrums are one of the main anti-social hallmarks of the toddler. They start after the first birthday, but generally by the age of four, peace has returned, as most children learn that tantrums don't pay. A few children seem to escape the natural cure, however, to become those adults we all know who lapse into childish tantrums when they do not get their own way.

Children are born different; some are quiet and controlled, with a great frustration tolerance; others come with a remarkably short fuse.

The tantrum as an art form is occasioned by a number of different stimuli. Not all tantrums are caused simply by a parent's thwarting a willful child in mid-activity. Some come from the inner frustrations of the toddler himself, who is impatient with his own lack of ability.

Stage-managing the most artistic tantrum

The highest quality toddler tantrums are produced with all the skill of a Broadway stage production: every detail is designed to elicit the very best audience reaction. Once the tantrum has started, its length and intensity depend on the sort of feedback the actor receives at the theater.

On center stage is the willful toddler who has been prevented from doing something that seems immensely important to him. He quickly sizes up the situation and makes instant preparations for a spectacular tantrum. First, he takes a quick look over his shoulder to check that the proposed area for crash landing is clear of hard, potentially hurtful objects. Next he sizes up the audience, checking that they are well positioned and watching, and possibly that the lighting is adjusted to the best effect. Then, quick as a flash, he's off. CRASH! He hits the floor, body writhing, and the performance has commenced.

Treatment of tantrums

Treating tantrums is extremely simple in theory, yet amazingly difficult in practice. Two techniques are commonly suggested:
1) the firm, cuddle method, and
2) the pretending to ignore method.

THE FIRM, CUDDLE METHOD

Many of the academic writers on childhood behavior subscribe to the theory that most tantrums are the result of a blown fuse in a frustrated child who is full of tension, violent feelings, and internal rage. They believe that, although this behavior may be upsetting to the parents, it is much worse for the unfortunate child who is seeking to find his inner controls. My ignoring technique would be considered counter-productive, and they would say that the child really needed support and encouragement. The recommendation would be to hold the child firmly against the parent's body until the rage subsided. This would give the child the feeling of warmth and external control as he fought to calm his internal rage.

This textbook technique certainly works quite well with some toddlers, and I occasionally use it with some of those amazingly irritable and impossible babies I meet in their first year of life. But personally I dislike the method and, although I realize that in theory it may be a most noble way to treat a toddler tantrum, I believe it is more designed for "super textbook parents" rather than the real-world parents I normally meet. When moms are devastated, tired, run down and past thinking about scientific child care, I believe few are capable of, or even safe, being asked to hold a wriggling, angry child. I believe that it is very one-eyed to look only at the child's needs. Parents have rights, too, and they also need to remain calm and emotionally in control. I am firmly convinced that the best way of preventing the futile fights of tantrums is to separate the warring parties until each has had a chance to calm down. What is more, I believe that if more parents adopted this approach there would be fewer instances of child abuse.

THE PRETEND TO IGNORE METHOD

Method #2 works in this way. First, the tantrums must be ignored completely. This is easier said than done, particularly in a small apartment on a wet day. Parents are ordinary people, and no smart professional has any right to expect performance of superhuman feats. Parents do have one trump card, however, in that the child, though clever, is unable to tell if they are really ignoring him or just bluffing. Parents may get inwardly as angry as they like, but outwardly they must act calm, cool and collected. The parent has to match acting skills with the toddler, and the cool, sensible parent will win every time.

So the stage is set. The determined toddler has done his pre-take-off checks and is just about to fling himself on the floor in a tantrum. The parent, having decided to use the "pretending to ignore" method, should now adopt one or all three maneuvers: diversion, if possible, pretending to ignore, and Time Out on losing control.

DIVERSION

Diversion is a slightly dishonest but highly effective technique used by many clever parents to abort the tantrum before it gets underway. It has already been mentioned that it is preferable to tackle behavioral outbursts at the stage of detonation rather than trying to mop up the devastation after major explosions. In this instance the parent must act at that precise psychological moment when the child is just gathering his energies to fling himself on the floor. Some real or imaginary item of enormous interest has to be discovered to catch the child's attention. For example, just as the child is about to drop to the floor, the mother runs to the window and exclaims "Oh, look, there's a funny dog in our garden," or "There's daddy home early." With interesting diversions such as these, the child thinks for a second and will usually run over to the window, whereupon the mildly dishonest, but peace-loving, mother notes that the dog has disappeared or it was another car very similar to daddy's that just drove past. Many experts might abhor the use of such deceitful methods, but in the interests of peace this technique is often effective.

PRETENDING TO IGNORE

Pretending to ignore comes into play if diversion tactics have failed and the toddler is already writhing on the floor. At this stage it is vital to pretend to ignore the child. The secret here is not to stand watching the profoundly irritating performance, but to busy yourself in some useful activity that will make the ignoring much easier. Some very tough parents I know are able to lift up the newspaper and read it, while staying in the same room as the child. Most parents find it much easier just to walk calmly out and become absorbed in some energetic activity elsewhere. A good retreat is the kitchen where you can wash the dishes squeaky clean or carve away at some poor innocent vegetable.

Once you leave the auditorium, you will hear the tone of the tantrum alter, usually to a higher intensity, as the star of the show sees his audience melting away. The faint-hearted toddler will, at this stage, give up the unfair struggle and peace will return. Unfortunately, most toddlers are militantly determined and will pursue their parents wherever they go, dropping on the floor at their feet for repeat performances. Once again parents must pretend to ignore this, but the persistent child will eventually start kicking your heels and annoying you until you are forced to react.

At this point, Time Out is called for. There is a good chance that the parent is now coming very close to losing patience and an all-out battle is about to ensue. If parental sanity is now threatened, it is time to use this invaluable technique.

Time Out

When a child reaches a pitch of crying and aggravation that can no longer be ignored, this is the moment to decide whether to plunge into a full-scale battle or use Time Out. There shouldn't be a moment's hesitation: Time Out it should be.

THE METHOD

The technique is simple. The parent simply picks up the child, in a cool, matter-of-fact way, without anger or fuss, and puts him firmly in another room.

The main purpose of Time Out is not to punish the child, but to separate the warring parties and give enough time for them both to cool off. Big bangs start with little triggers, and it is much easier to use this method to defuse the situation in its infancy than to wait too long and have to mop up after an ugly scene.

WHICH ROOM?

The question now is which room do you use for the best effect? Bedroom? Living room? I favor using the child's own bedroom, though the "experts" are always quick to tell me this is a mistake. They believe that if the bedroom is used, the child will associate this with punishment and develop a fear for this part of the house, which will result later in sleep problems. This is a most predictable academic response, which, though sound in theory, is not true in practice. If putting the toddler in his bedroom will put him off sleeping, then presumably putting him in the dining room will put him off eating, putting him in the living room will put him off sitting, putting him in the kitchen will put him off helping with the cooking and so on. It's simply not true. I choose the bedroom because it is usually sufficiently far away and soundproofed from the rest of the living area of the house to give the two parties good separation as they cool off.

SHARED BEDROOM

Difficulty arises if the toddler shares a bedroom with an obsessively tidy and possessive brother or sister. Parents find it hard to relax for fear of what might be happening when that angry, attention-seeking child with fiddly fingers starts to reorganize his brother's or sister's treasures. In this event, it is necessary to use another "neutral," room in the house.

NEVER LOCK THE DOOR

Time Out in the bedroom must never be mistaken for that deplorable carry-over from the last century of locking children in their room. This only serves to terrify the children and has little to offer in the way of any beneficial behavioral effect.

MAKE SURE HE CAN REACH THE HANDLE

The child must be put in his room and the door closed, but ensure that he can reach the handle from the inside. If this is not possible, then a chair should be made available for extra elevation. For stiff, difficult-to-open doors I suggest a sock tied between the two handles, inside and out, which allows the door to close across but leaves no risk of it becoming jammed shut with the child trapped inside. The child must be able to come out when he has cooled off.

NAUGHTY CORNER

Putting a child to stand in a corner of a room may work well in a classroom situation where there may be a designated "naughty corner," but in my experience parents who have tried this technique at home find that it does not work. The child sneaks out of the designated corner as soon as the parent's back is turned, is then told to go back, tries to escape again, and the time that follows is punctuated with rude noises, gestures, and other harassments. This is a useless form of discipline as it causes parents continued aggravation while, at the same time, providing the child with an enjoyable game.

When Time Out does not work

When I suggest Time Out to parents, they often tell me that they have already tried this method and find that it does not work with their child. On being questioned further, I find a number of similar problems are mentioned.

IMMEDIATE REAPPEARANCE

The first is that the child comes out immediately. Where, I ask, is the parent at the time of said child's reappearance? Usually I discover that the answer to that is "standing outside the door." Of course, the child is only too well aware that there's a welcoming party waiting and thus gets the greatest satisfaction from a triumphal re-entry. In my experience it is extremely rare that a child will leave the bedroom before some cooling off has taken place. This can only be achieved if the parent has beaten a hasty retreat to the far end of the house, having put the child in the room. I am amazed by the number of parents who complain that the child is out of the room before they have got six feet from the door. It seems unbelievable that a two-year-old can run across a bedroom, manipulate a door open, and escape faster than a fit adult can sprint from the scene. If this is the case, however, then all I can suggest is that the parent enroll immediately in a fitness class in order to learn to move faster than the toddler!

STILL NOT IN CONTROL

If the child releases himself before he is fully in control, it is important that he is put straight back and certainly not greeted by a parent who is standing outside, waiting for a fight. Some parents believe that a gentle smack should be administered before returning the child to his room, not so as to cause pain, but merely to leave the child in no doubt that he is not welcome until better behaved.

KICKING AND FORCING THE DOOR

Another complaint is that the toddler kicks all the paint off the door. I believe that paintwork is easier to repair than a parent's shattered nerves. Most parents who complain that Time Out fails because of the door being kicked or noise in the bedroom are themselves at fault. Many stand listening outside the door and the toddler realizes that he has an attentive audience and obliges by putting on an enormous performance. This defeats the whole purpose of Time Out, since the child gets a great deal of unwarranted attention and the parents get worked up and upset.

Occasionally parents tell me that Time Out doesn't work because their toddler tries to "force the door handle." When asked what the parents are doing at the time, they usually reply that they are "holding the other side." Parents get themselves into silly situations without realizing it: they should escape to the furthest end of the house during Time Out.

WRECKING THE ROOM

When parents tell me they cannot put their child in his room because he is liable to wreck it, most are in fact only speculating that this will happen; few have put it to the test. In the last three years, I can think of only two children who have genuinely messed up their bedroom during Time Out, and not only was this habit quickly eradicated, but Time Out was also found to be miraculously successful.

One of these children was an extremely willful four-year-old girl, who was intelligent, outgoing, and generally bored with being at home with her mother. She had many tantrums when she could not get her own way, and when put in her bedroom, she would wreak havoc. When I heard that Time Out had been tried unsuccessfully, I started by getting the parents to perform a careful survey of her room. This was cleared of all breakable objects, as well as pens, paints and other messy substances. The first time after this that she was placed in her room she did not cry, because she knew that a little rearranging of her belongings would teach her mother a lesson. Ten minutes later she came out of the room, in perfect control and looking extremely pleased with herself. Her mother glanced in the door and saw the bed wrecked and clothes all over the place. Mother merely remarked, "Oh dear, that looks a bit of a mess." The little girl was taken completely aback, realizing that she had been unable to precipitate the usual rage reaction in her mother. As she sensed a "change in the air," she was extremely careful to avoid any tantrums for the rest of the day. When bedtime arrived, she was sent to get into her pajamas but soon returned, as she could not find them in the mess. "I think they may be under that pile of clothes," said mom helpfully. The child then asked how she was going to be able to sleep in her unmade bed. No problem, said mom, she would just lift the blankets off the floor and plonk them over her. The same procedure was followed next morning when the girl looked for her clean clothes. Again the untidy pile of clothes was pointed out, and the message came across loud and clear: wrecking one's room got no major reaction from mother but caused considerable inconvenience to the wrecker.

I talked to the mother by phone first thing the next morning, and we decided that mother and daughter should set about tidying the room together in an enthusiastic and positive way. All the clothes were gone through and those that were too small were put aside and sent to the "poor children." As the toys were tidied, mother and daughter made a list of possible presents she would like for Christmas, which was fast approaching.

I was surprised by the control and strength of this mother and delighted that the habit, which in the past had prevented the effective use of Time Out, was quickly extinguished. In the wake of the showdown, mother and daughter were able to salvage the situation, build a much closer relationship, and turn a disaster zone into a fun place to live. The room was never damaged again and the tantrums were greatly reduced. Once again, I emphasize that wrecking rooms during Time Out is, in my experience, a rare occurrence.

UNREALISTIC EXPECTATIONS

Parents frequently expect Time Out to produce miraculous results, which it was never designed to produce. Many expect the child to come out heavy with humility and repentance, and to stand before them and make a public apology for being naughty. Others refuse to let the matter rest, constantly reminding the child how naughty he has been and thereby maintaining a high level of tension, which is guaranteed to destroy everyone's happiness for the rest of the day. The purpose of Time Out is to allow both parties to cool off and thus prevent major fights. The child does not have to apologize. The only expectation is that he re-enter in a more reasonable frame of mind.

Other parents claim that Time Out doesn't work because the child repeats the undesired behavior, showing that the method is ineffective. If a child comes out of his room still in the middle of a tantrum, or if he walks straight out and immediately repeats the same action, then he must be put straight back in his room. This, in my experience, is very rare. But parents more frequently complain that similar behavior is repeated at some other time during the day.

Time Out is only aimed at defusing a rapidly escalating situation at a particular time, and once this has passed and peace is regained, the method has shown itself to be effective. It is foolish to presume that five minutes of Time Out will prevent all nasty behavior for the rest of the day. No method I know, other than possibly a straightjacket or perhaps a prolonged period under general anesthesia, could give such a guarantee!

Some parents feel they have been cheated when the child goes into his room in mid-tantrum and remains there to play happily with his toys. I must repeat that Time Out is not a punishment; it is a technique aimed at separating two people who are hell-bent on having a major battle. Whether the child plays with his toys, stands on his head, or sings *Waltzing Matilda* in his room is irrelevant, just so long as he cools off and parents are allowed a little time to relax.

CONCLUSION

Time Out is a very effective technique when used properly. I use it with toddlers, the handicapped, and even some disturbed older children. It is a powerful method of maintaining peace in the home, and if used in the way mentioned, it reduces a lot of emotional tension without frightening or upsetting the child. As the tension settles and the child understands clearly the limits placed upon him, this leads to a closer and happier life for all.

Using baby to achieve attention

The child who has studied long and hard perfecting his parent-stirring techniques will be far from pleased when he sees that they no longer get the desired results. Most children at this stage throw in the sponge and decide to surrender. A few children with un-crushable determination, however, refuse to give in gracefully, and they will develop more powerful methods to get their own way. In my experience, the heavy artillery often involves the newly arrived baby, who suddenly finds himself in the middle of someone else's battleground.

Most families seem to be planned so that a new baby arrives just when the toddler is about 18 months old. This ensures that, throughout the first year of the new baby's life, his brother or sister will be at the most militant stage. The toddler is also far from happy at the appearance of this new arrival, who has taken much of his mother's attention away. It seems fair to him that the baby should suffer in the course of the toddler gaining a little extra attention.

The baby is a most potent weapon in the toddler armory, as mothers of newborn babies tend to be sensitive, clinging and over-protective. They find it hard to accept that a grubby, careless tod-dler with little sense should be allowed to manhandle their bundle of perfection. The clever toddler is quick to realize that to gain maximum attention all that is needed is to approach the baby and give it a sharp poke. The mother will react in a moderately spec-tacular way, the response being bettered when the toddler brings up the big guns, such as jumping on baby or tipping his carriage. The *pièce de résistance*, however, is reserved for special occasions: the toddler pokes a finger to within three inches of the baby's eye, which is usually quite close enough to guarantee a major tantrum from mother.

If parents have been strong enough to get rid of other kinds of anti-social attention-seeking behavior, there is no reason for them to surrender to these strong-arm toddler tactics. It is important that the mother does not over-protect the baby, or this unequal division of care and attention will lead to undesirable rivalry and jealousy. My teaching is that babies are by and large pretty unbreakable. Within certain limits the toddler should be allowed to play with the new baby, climb in his crib and poke him, just so long as he doesn't hurt him. While all this is going on, the parents must try to keep out of the situation. It is best if they stand near the door and watch out the corner of their eyes to ensure that the baby comes to no harm. As for putting fingers near the baby's eyes, I don't believe this is a malicious act. The eye is a truly amazing and beautiful part of a baby and I think most of the poking is only the exploring of an inquisitive little child.

In summary, it is important not to jump into a rage every time the toddler approaches the baby. This parental reaction leaves the toddler holding a potential "big gun" that can be used at any time to cause upsets. It is even more dangerous if the toddler is scolded for going near the baby, while at the same time the baby gets a cuddle. This surely sows the seeds of major sibling rivalry.

8

NASTY HABITS IN NICE CHILDREN

When I talk to parents of any kind and in any city, the same problems always seem to feature at question time. This chapter deals with these commonly asked questions.

WHINING

Whining is one of the most parent-destroying activities that any child can indulge in. Naturally we expect children who are tired, sick or teething to whine, but there still remains a great band of healthy, well-rested children who continue to devastate their parents with this vile habit. In my experience, boys generally take the prize for over-activity and really bad behavior, but when it comes to whining, the fairer sex takes out the gold medal every time.

There is great variation in a child's ability to whine. Some will wind up to full volume at the drop of a hat; others work their way towards it in fits and starts, prolonging the agony as skillfully as any torturer from the Spanish Inquisition.

Some whiners seem to lack that basic ingredient called "sense." They know when to start but seem unable to know when the right time is to stop. At present I look after a seven-year-old, mildly retarded girl, who must surely rate a place in the next *Guinness Book of Records.* As well as her enormous ability to whine like no other seven-year-old, she has the unique habit, when disciplined, of running out of the front door into the street, grabbing the arm of the first unsuspecting passer-by, and shouting, "Save me, save me. They're going to beat me!" Even without the whining, you can see the sort of torment the parents are going through. Well, her world record-breaking whining binge commenced about midday when she could not get her own way over something fairly trivial. Commencing at high volume, and despite all attempts at distraction by her parents, the whining continued until bedtime. Mercifully she fell asleep, only to wake up at two a.m. asking for a drink, whereupon she started whining over the same matter. On waking up the next morning, she immediately began to whine. It was a total of three and a half days before the adjudicators clocked her off. Not only is she a quite remarkable little girl, but the parents are astonishing in their ability to withstand such a battering to their mental stability.

The treatment for whiners is the same as the one for tantrums. It is basically:

1) divert the child's attention;
2) ignore him as much as you can;
3) Time Out in his bedroom; and
4) get out into the wide open spaces

Skillful mothers can divert lesser whiners back to the straight and narrow by noticing something around the house or setting off on some interesting activity. Mom can suddenly notice a cat in the garden, remember the laundry needs to be hung out, or make a fuss over feeding the goldfish. All these are of some benefit in the not very determined whiner.

If diversion does not work, the child must be ignored. Mortal man has only a limited ability to actually ignore whining, so pretending to ignore it is probably the best we can hope for, but it gives an equally strong message to the offending party. When the parents can no longer ignore the irritation, then the situation is coming close to a blow-up when somebody is going to lose control, everyone will become very unhappy, and little will be achieved. This is the moment to employ the Time Out technique discussed in the previous chapter.

As a last resort, when diversion, ignoring and Time Out have all failed, mother must sweep up the offending party and head for the great outdoors. Most children suspend hostilities as soon as they escape from the restrictions of the home battleground, and with the minority who continue, the whining and whimpering never seem so bad when competing with bird song and noisy motor vehicles.

BITING

The residents who man the hospital's busy Casualty Department once asked me if I would come and lecture to them, and I presumed they wanted to hear me expound on some high-powered medical topic. To my surprise, I found that what they wanted to hear, more than anything else, was how to manage children who bite! It seemed that in our city biting had reached almost epidemic proportions, which was upsetting not only our casualty officers, but also parents, playgroup leaders, and any child or adult within biting distance.

In my experience, biting is purely a playgroup habit found mostly in the one to two-and-a-half years age group. Experts who have written on this topic state that it is a symptom of a tense, anxious child and, although it is interesting to know the theory, in practical terms I find it a great deal easier to stop a child biting than to stop a child feeling tense.

The treatment for a biting child is as follows:
1) If bitten when carrying the child, put him down at once and walk away;
2) If your child bites another in your own home, use the Time Out technique, or a smack;
3) If your child bites others at playgroup, give the toys and all the fuss to the injured party.

Many babies in the first year of life suddenly sink their teeth into whoever is carrying them, unaware of the pain they may cause. Although this is not a malicious act, it is important that the baby be made to realize that it is not an acceptable form of behavior. Rather than shouting, becoming angry or slapping the baby, it is preferable to put him down on the floor immediately. It does not take the average baby long to work out that, if he wants the pleasure of a good cuddle, he shouldn't indulge in cannibalism.

Slightly older toddlers often sink their teeth into some soft part of the neighbor's child. Apart from being extremely painful for the assaulted party, this sort of behavior can often lead to feuds far more vicious than ever witnessed by the Campbells and the Mac-Donalds. As soon as the bite takes place, the guilty party should be put in his room for a bout of Time Out. Some parents might prefer a short, sharp smack to Time Out. Personally. I wouldn't agree, but if it works for you, then you should consider it.

Child biters in playgroups are very common, and although some of these biters are certainly tense, anxious children and we should be as kind and sympathetic as possible, some semblance of discipline must be maintained. At playgroup, I usually suggest that the child who bites is moved to a far-off corner and ignored, while the injured party gets all the attention and the use of some favored toy. The biter will generally get the message fairly quickly and desist from his anti-social behavior.

Over the centuries parents have moved away from most of the painful, biblical punishments so beloved by the Victorian disciplinarians. One, however, still seems to remain fashionable among mothers, and that is "an eye for an eye and a bite for a bite!" Enlightened though this may have been in those far-off days, I believe it is best discarded in this modern age. More often than not, all it leads to is a painful and prolonged physical encounter with both parties suffering.

FIGHTING

Little cats, little lambs, little lions and little humans all enjoy fighting. In the animal world, it has the effect of building up muscles, improving coordination, and toning up the self-preservation instinct. In children in the eighties, I doubt if it has any such noble purpose. Certainly it is a habit that causes great anguish to parents and leads to considerable confusion over how to handle the warring parties.

The skilled art of fighting with one's brothers and sisters is really only in its infancy during toddlerhood, and it doesn't get properly underway until the school years. Constant bickering among children seems to be a never-ending source of fun to them, but it causes frayed nerves and an aching brain among parents. Of course, if you could keep the two warring parties to Marquis of Queensberry rules, life would be much easier, but this is rarely the case.

Fights usually occur when a child is tired and bored, and there seems to be nothing better to do at the time. Most toddler fights seem to be associated with "baiting" and taunting. Some children

have an extraordinary ability to stir up everyone around them, and
I am sure that many of them could start a fight in an empty room.
As the little plotter walks past his sister quietly doing her homework for instance, a book mysteriously falls to the floor. In mid-
program the television suddenly changes channel or the child
stands on his head blocking the screen. His beautiful sister is in-
formed that she is ugly. His brother's cars are hijacked in the middle of a game. Passing children are poked, tripped, or otherwise
irritated. These are all baiting ploys used in the pre-fight warmup.

Some children are immensely gentle and rarely complain. It is
their misfortune that they become the targets of taunters.

Other children have an extremely short fuse, and they will react
quickly and unthinkingly when irritated. These unfortunate children are often branded as aggressive, but this is rarely the case.
They do not set out deliberately to hurt anyone; they just react
poorly to stress.

Some children, like many adults, never stop complaining. Parents are forever getting an earful over allegations of injustice or
favoritism. At mealtimes someone always gets a bigger portion; at
bedtime someone else always gets a longer story; and generally life
seems to be totally without justice for the complaining child. One
mother I know got so fed up with mealtime fights that she started
weighing out all desserts individually on the kitchen scales at the
dining table to ensure that her school-age children all got perfectly
equal helpings.

I would have chosen the selective deafness technique in preference to this melodramatic act. With fighting, taunting, complaining children it is best for the parents to keep out of it as much as
possible. When books are dropped on the floor or the television
channel is changed, the child may be asked to right the wrong. He
is then either diverted to some useful activity or separated and put
in another room. When children throw things or actually come to
blows, you are forced to intervene, taking the role of a household
United Nations Peace Keeping Force. Once you are involuntarily
involved, it is best to first separate the warring parties, divert their
attention, and try very hard not to take sides. As a rule the real
rights and wrongs of the episode are never as clear cut as they may
seem. The child who does the hitting is very often the one who
was being taunted in the first place.

You cannot stop children fighting, but you can divert them, separate them, put them outside the house, and prevent them from
hurting themselves or damaging your property. When possible, it is
best to keep out of the situation and not to take sides, thus allowing the children to lay down their own ground rules and establish
their own level and codes of conduct.

Jealousy can also lead to fights. Humans are basically competitive, jealous animals and their offspring are much the same. When the newborn baby arrives, most normal children will feel some jealousy as the attention, which was once all theirs, has to be shared. Beautiful, bright, easy-to-love children may cause jealousy in their brothers or sisters who are not equally endowed with these desirable qualities. Although as parents we try hard to be fair and give equally to all our children, nothing in life is completely equal or fair, as the average child is quick to discover.

Tension and insecurity also cause fights, although this occurs mostly in the school-age child who behaves badly, hits other children, or becomes the class clown as a reaction. He is frequently branded aggressive, when his real problem is more likely to be some unrecognized specific learning, concentration, or socialization problem. Such children, because they cannot compete equally at school, become tense and stressed and thus begin to behave badly and fight.

BREATH-HOLDING ATTACKS

These are among the most alarming of all toddler behavior traits. Some children have been reported as having up to ten attacks a day, others one a month. Luckily the vast majority of toddlers never indulge in this nasty habit.

Breath-holding comes in two forms, the more common cyanotic (blue) type and the rarer pallid (faint) type. With the cyanotic attack, the child voluntarily holds his breath to the point of passing out; it is a kind of super tantrum used to stir up anyone preventing the child from getting his own way. Although less common, the pallid form is associated with a painful experience. For example, the child sustains a minor hurt and passes out rapidly in a form of fainting fit.

The cyanotic (blue) attack

These attacks most commonly occur from 18 months to four years, although they may occasionally be seen before the first birthday in the really negative child. This is not a new behavior pattern brought about by the hectic life-style of the eighties. Hippocrates described something very similar happening among the terrible toddlers of ancient Greece.

What normally happens is that the child is thwarted in the midst of some action that is vitally important to him, and reviewing his repertoire of reactions, he decides that breath holding will be a more effective reprisal than one of his lesser tantrums. He then cries about three long cries, the last going all the way until his lungs are completely empty of air. The audience waits in anticipation for the next breath, but the ensuing silence is deafening. No breath is heard. Over the next fifteen seconds the child voluntarily holds his breath, which inevitably leads to him going blue in the face and passing out. Once unconscious, the child loses voluntary control of his breathing; the body immediately switches over to "automatic pilot" and breathing restarts, with full consciousness returning about fifteen seconds later. Occasionally the episode may end in a minor short convulsion, leaving the parents even more upset.

Breath-holding attacks terrify parents, and although the treatment is extremely easy for a doctor to give, it is amazingly difficult for the parent to administer. However, if breath holding is to be stopped it must be viewed in the same light as the tantrum or any other form of attention-seeking behavior. It must simply be ignored. Totally ignored. Making a fuss about it will only ensure that it is repeated.

First, the parents must assure themselves that the attack is not caused by any other medical problem and will not damage the child in any way. Once they are convinced of this, the techniques of diversion and ignoring must be used. If diversionary tactics fail, and the child stops breathing, he must not be allowed to hurt himself. Usually he will be on the floor, but if still upright, it is best to set him down gently, well clear of any dangerous or sharp objects. He must then be left completely alone, and although watched carefully while unconscious, once consciousness begins to return, the parents must move away and ignore him.

Some experts suggest splashing cold water on the child's face as he starts to hold his breath. This may be effective, but it will only work if done in the first 15 seconds of voluntary breath holding. After that it is pointless and probably dangerous once unconsciousness has occurred.

I have no illusions that this is an easy treatment, and I know that firmness and ignoring the child, although hard, are the only effective methods of curing this behavior. After the child reaches the age of four, breath holding becomes extremely rare.

The pallid (faint) attack

This is not the true breath-holding attack, as it is more like a simple fainting spell than a form of attention-seeking tantrum. Children who have pallid attacks seem to be particularly sensitive to pain or fear, either of which may trigger off an attack. (They are generally thought to become the sort of adults who faint at the thought of a hypodermic needle or the sight of blood).

A two-year-old may be walking under a table when he hits his head hard on the edge. In the pallid attack, he would not cry out or hold his breath, but will simply go limp and fall to the ground. His heart rate drops dramatically, and he looks very pale. This is the child's equivalent of an adult faint, and they usually recover very quickly.

As for treatment, if the child is lying flat, nothing else needs be done and nature will remedy the situation. If the attacks are genuinely the result of some involuntary reflex in a sensitive child, then the child should be cuddled and fussed over upon recovery. Although this seems quite logical, most authors on the subject in the past seem to have doubts about whether or not there may be some minor attention-seeking component in this action, and it is suggested that the parents maintain a low profile and do not fuss too much over the child.

Let me reassure parents with children who suffer from breath-holding attacks, however, that it is not a serious condition. In the event, it is the parents more than the children who require sympathy.

THE ABSCONDER

Any toddler worth his salt, who has read up on his child psychology, will realize that he is meant to be clingy and loath to be separated from his parents. A small percentage, however, seem ignorant of this fact, and they are forever running off and getting lost. Absconders are a real trial to their parents, who are forced to take part in high speed pursuits down the main street, hide and seek in the supermarket, and the interminable wait for the voice to come over the loudspeaker informing them that the infant absconder has been coralled and is awaiting pick-up.

Luckily most absconders develop sufficient sense to stop the habit within a six month period, but some may take years to grow out of it. I have little success in treating children who run off. I am able only to suggest that the parents remain fit and vigilant at all times, or resort to the less desirable back-up of a toddler harness. One of the last children I had to fit with a harness had the curious habit of jumping on passing buses; fortunately he was always extracted before the bus started off!

IMPULSIVENESS

Thinking before they act, looking before they leap, or displaying any sort of sense at all cannot, by any stretch of the imagination, be classed as the toddler's strong suit, but some seem to be even more disastrously weak in this area. The impulsive child is a classic leaper before looking: he runs onto the road before waiting to see if anything is coming, and gets into fights without stopping to think first of the outcome. If all this is also accompanied by a lack of sense, the child can never be allowed out of sight. Constant supervision and no chance for the parents to relax leads to a great feeling of tiredness.

The lack of sense by itself makes problems worse, as these children are extremely slow to learn from experience, producing the same difficult behavior day after day despite quite exemplary management. The parents despair at their apparent lack of effectiveness and wonder what they are doing wrong. It's a bit like beating your head against a brick wall.

There's not much you can do. The toddler will grow out of it in due course, and all you can do is wait patiently for that happy day.

BAD LANGUAGE

Bad language is not a major problem in toddlers. Most of the obscene language they know is learnt at school, along with all the other appurtenances of a normal education, and is regurgitated parrot-fashion at home. When a toddler swears or uses bad language, he is usually only copying someone he has heard at home or at pre-school. Toddlers are great mimics and they have mighty retentive memories—just remember that the next time you hammer your thumb instead of the nail or express your opinion of someone else's bad driving!

Toddlers also have an extraordinary interest in "lavatory" talk. Bottoms and bodily functions seem to make fascinating topics of conversation, probably because in the toddler's world of limited experience, these are subjects that they can talk about with real authority. The bodily function fascination usually disappears of its own accord before the age of six and before that it can be gently doused, generally by diverting the child's attention to something else.

When new, undesirable words come from the toddler, the chances are that he will not know what they mean but is aware of the interesting effect they have on his parents. In handling this problem some degree of selective deafness is suggested and a quiet caution like "we don't really want to hear that." If the parents throw a tantrum every time the child uses a certain word, it again gives him a potent weapon to stir up the household any time life begins to look a bit boring.

Undesired language shouldn't be allowed to upset the parents, but it should be gently molded out of the vocabulary. A major confrontation will lead to nothing but trouble and will probably only serve to implant the behavior even more firmly.

If a household is run on democratic lines, it is only fair that if parents are allowed to use excessive bad language, then the toddler has the same right. If you don't want your toddler to use bad language, then you must stop using it yourself. It's really as simple as that.

STEALING

This is mentioned purely because no such crime exists in children under five years old.

Adults are obsessed with who owns what, and they spend thousands of dollars guarding, insuring, and locking away all their treasures. Toddlers are fortunate in not having reached this stage of life; they are totally uninterested in all the hang-ups of possession, titles, and deeds of ownership. Although they may collect up items and money, this is not with any malicious intent. All that is required, therefore, is a gentle reminder, when objects are taken, that they should really be left alone. Nothing more should be said. When out visiting a slightly firmer line is required, more for the benefit of the person whose house you are visiting than as a genuine reprimand to the toddler.

INTERRUPTING ADULTS

One of the greatest sources of irritation with small children is their inability to refrain from interrupting when adults are talking. In some houses it is almost impossible for parents to talk to each other when there is an awake toddler around. Parents often find it hard even to communicate by cuddles and kisses without the star of the show trying to force his way in between them.

The child has three problems. He thinks his wise sayings are of earth-shattering importance and that everyone must immediately shut up and listen. He does not like others stealing his much enjoyed position center-stage, and he knows that if he does not say his piece immediately it will be forgotten and lost forever.

Some children become absolutely impossible when visitors call and want to talk at some length to their parents. The child interferes so much that tempers are lost or the visit becomes a complete waste of time for all concerned. Visitors who are real friends should realize that the toddler needs a lot of attention, and if they are not sharp enough to see this, their absence is probably not a great loss anyway.

Some children refuse to let their parents talk on the phone. They successfully prevent this by either making so much noise that conversation is rendered impossible, or they create such havoc in the house that the call has to be abandoned.

Several years ago I looked after a young handicapped boy whose favorite trick was to wait until the phone rang and then set off at high speed round the house, turning on every possible electrical appliance he could before the call was terminated. When his mother got off the phone the house was buzzing with the noise of vacuum cleaners, food mixers, hair dryers, while fires and lights blazed like a crystal palace on a Saturday night, and the electricity meter raced round and round like a Grand Prix car.

Now the bad news . . . I have no answers to help those whose children behave in this way, except to assure you that it is perfectly normal behavior. I suppose that visitors who try to monopolize parents are pretty boring to a toddler, who tries to discourage them. Long telephone calls are fairly anti-social at the best of times and are best reserved for the evening. The constant interruption of conversations will resolve itself by the end of toddlerhood, by which time the child will have a better short-term memory, be less impulsive, and will have learnt to wait his turn.

VOMITING ON DEMAND

When I come into my office on a Monday morning to be confronted by the pile of work I should have done the week before and I'm feeling a trifle delicate anyway—as one tends to at the start of a new working week—there is nothing I dread more than having to see a child who vomits on demand. This problem can be treated, but one has to be very tough.

Some children, owing to a weak valve at the top of the stomach, can regurgitate their food frequently and effortlessly. Other children have completely normal anatomies but find that profuse crying or coughing can lead to vomiting. The last, and luckily the rarest, group are those who vomit on demand for the sole purpose of punishing their parents and getting what they want.

Children from the first group, with the weak valve, need a proper X-ray diagnosis, medical treatment and reviews. Those from the second group, who find that coughing or crying leads to vomiting, need some special management. They must never be left to cry hysterically as this often leads to disaster. If they are put in their room after some major transgression, they must not be allowed to cry for long periods: the controlled crying method outlined in Chapter 9 should be used. Spasms of coughing in children usually do most damage at night-time, as coughing is always worse at that time and the horizontal posture denies the stomach the beneficial effects of gravity. If a sensitive child has contracted a respiratory infection and consequent spasms may lead to vomiting, it is best to take some precautions before bedtime. The last meal should be well before bedtime and if a nightcap drink is required, I strongly urge lemonade in preference to milk. It is not that it is any more likely to stay in the stomach, but if it does reappear it is much easier to clean up than second-hand milk in the middle of the night.

As for the third group, I see quite a number of children who vomit deliberately when they cannot get their own way. For this I have developed a very firm routine, which works in most cases. Take as an example one of my cases, a friendly, cheerful five-year-old boy who is moderately mentally retarded and has a condition that causes a voracious appetite. The family used to sit down to meals together, but his plate was empty before you could say "pass the sauce." He then took food from everyone else's plates and, when prevented, deliberately vomited on the table.

The technique we used was to make as little fuss as possible, swallow hard, and carry him off to the bathroom, leaving him inside with the door closed. The soiled area was then cleaned without him being allowed to watch. When the time was right, he was changed and sponged clean in a matter of fact way. His clean clothes were given to him to put on without much help and the whole affair was treated as clinically as possible. The habit was successfully extinguished within about three months, to the great delight of the parents.

More commonly, I see young children who get so angry when the Time Out technique is used that they vomit over their beds. The above method can also be used with a great degree of success. The important thing is not to allow the child to think that his actions have in any way upset you, and not to give him the satisfaction of seeing the trouble to which you have been put when you have to clean up the mess.

SMEARERS

This unpleasant habit is mostly seen in young handicapped patients, although occasionally normal toddlers aged about 18 months will indulge in it. It is usually restricted to the early morning—the damage is done to the accompaniment of the dawn chorus. The toddler wakes before the rest of the household, is bored and has a dirty diaper, so to while away the hours he engages in some "finger painting" on the walls.

This ghastly behavior pattern sickens and depresses parents, so we use two methods to cope with the problem. First, the parents must get up and change the toddler's diaper the moment he wakes in the morning. Second, the child must be prevented from getting his hands near the diaper area, which is achieved by dressing him in high dungarees or similar "high rise" garments, fastened firmly in place with safety pins. If the right style of garment is used only a Houdini would be able to get his hand into mischief! Luckily, smearing in normal toddlers tend to be a very short-lived problem.

PLAYING WITH THOSE FORBIDDEN "PRIVATE" PARTS

Most toddlers play with their genitalia at some time or other. They may touch, rub, rock or move their legs, all for the pleasurable effects these motions afford. It is normal toddler behavior, and it has no true sexual overtones.

Historically, so much fuss has been made over children masturbating that even the most broad-minded parents still have a twinge of concern when they see their own children doing it. Tales of how it would make you mad, or deaf, or both still ring in their ears. In earlier times, it was thought so vital to control this deviant habit in its earliest stages that young children were immobilized on their beds with straps or subjected to other horrifying regimes.

These days, parents are encouraged to relax, ignore it, and not let their own hang-ups get in the way. Playing with the genitalia occurs in both boys and girls. It starts in the second year when the diaper region is unveiled and a new area of discovery is made available. The treatment is to completely ignore what is, after all, a perfectly innocent habit. If this does not work, the child may be gently diverted or the offending hand otherwise occupied. These techniques are particularly useful in public, when parental embarrassment is more likely. The child is much more prone to indulge in it when he is tired, tense, or bored.

Some time later, in the pre-school years, children discover that little boys and little girls are not identical. This leads to a certain amount of innocent interest, which once again is a natural stage of development. This needs to be viewed with a broad mind and a blind eye.

Some years ago I was asked to see a four-year-old boy, referred to me from his pre-school as being a "sexual deviant." His particular weakness was to jump on top of little girls, knocking them over. I was asked to "investigate his hormones." The boy in fact needed no investigation. His real problem was a lack of sense in not realizing that little boys were not allowed to jump on little girls in pre-school. The pre-school teacher probably had a bigger problem than the patient!

HEAD BANGING

Head banging is undertaken for one of two reasons. Either the child is in a temper, or he does it as a form of innocent entertainment. Parents fear that the child will damage his brain in the process, but when you look at football players and boxers, you realize that toddler's efforts are pretty trivial by comparison. Some parents believe that it is a sure sign of retardation or mental disturbance, but if the child is normal in every other way, head banging is not a sign of significance.

Children who are in a temper may hit their head against the wall or the floor, but it is rare that they hurt themselves, and, if this happens, it is not intentional. Generally they carefully seek out the surface with the greatest noise producing capacity that will also afford the least harm to them. They never choose a tiled or concrete floor—a nice, hollow partition wall is ideal.

Some people get very upset by tantrum head bangers, thinking that they must be protected at all costs. I do not fuss, because I believe that it is a quickly self-limiting situation, as the child soon realizes the futility of the exercise. It's like the robber who enters the bank holding an iron bar and says, "Hand over the money or I'll bash myself over the head!" There is not much future in it.

Other children head bang when bored or tired. This is usually done in the crib and, if accompanied by rocking, generates quite a bit of movement. The crib may move across the floor or become so rattled that it collapses. This form of head banging is an entertainment that gives as much pleasure as thumb sucking or nail biting.

For treatment, it is best to prevent long periods of boredom, to ignore most head banging completely, and if this is not possible, to gently dissuade the child or place suitable padding around him. Unless head banging is very long-lasting or severe, it is a harmless pastime.

TOOTH GRINDING

The noise of grinding teeth sends a shiver down any parent's spine and conjures up all sorts of thoughts of madness. Grinding the teeth during sleep is a common, normal occurrence. It doesn't indicate that the child has worms or is suffering from any form of lunacy. There is little to be done to help the situation, although in very extreme cases dentists have been known to intervene.

Normal toddlers occasionally grind their teeth noisily by day, but in my experience, it is almost exclusively the behavior of a child with a major handicap. Some people report success with these children, but it has not been my experience that any therapy has lessened the amount of nerve-shattering noise.

9

SLEEP PROBLEMS—
AT LAST, THE CURE

Toddlers who don't sleep well can be the cause of great unhappiness to their parents. Sleep deprivation, as any well-practiced torturer will avow, is a sure method of breaking your spirit, determination, and ability to think clearly. The mother who says, "He's not getting enough sleep," is in fact talking in code. What she really means is, "Forget the kid, I'm a walking zombie!"

The night-time antics are really only half the story. It is the after-shock the next day that causes the real harm. Then a tired, irritable mom with a befuddled brain has to struggle valiantly to manage a tired, irritable, and unreasonable toddler. The result is often complete disaster.

In their first year of life, some babies will wake repeatedly every night. Unfortunate though this may be, you may have to accept that this is their normal sleep pattern and adopt the philosophical attitude that it's all part of the joys of being a parent. Although this may be permissible for some young babies, in toddlers this disturbance is quite unacceptable, certainly no joy, and what is more, it doesn't have to be tolerated.

For those readers who have toddlers with major sleep problems, may I say that your state of exhaustion is now to be relieved. In the following pages, there unfolds a 90 per cent guaranteed cure for most sleep problems within seven days.

THE SCIENCE OF SLEEP

Babies spend their time in the womb with their "wake-sleep" time clock in a poor state of adjustment, as far as we are concerned. Daytime is their main sleeping time, and as soon as night falls, they turn into a combination of Dracula and a front-line forward, when parents are trying to sleep. By the third week after birth, the clock becomes better regulated, distributing the sleep pattern equally throughout the entire twenty-four hours. By the sixth week, sleep has become much more of a night-time occupation, and by three months a definite adult pattern has appeared, with most sleeping taking place between seven p.m. and seven a.m. and most wakefulness being in the afternoon and early evening.

Brainwave studies (encephalograms) show different patterns of sleep throughout the night. Most sleep is of the "deep" type, which shows up as a special tracing on the encephalograph. Interspersed with this are short periods of a more active stage of sleep, often referred to as "dream sleep." This cycle of deep, followed by active, sleep continues throughout the night in about ninety minute rotations. Adults have a similar sleep pattern, sometimes being aware of passing cars or rain on the window pane, and on other occasions being "dead to the world."

A recent study made video recordings of children as they slept in the quiet of their own homes.[5] The parents of most of the children studied believed that their children slept soundly right through the night, but the recordings showed otherwise. It appeared that even apparently good sleepers may wake up a number of times, often sitting up, looking around and perhaps muttering quietly before slipping back to sleep.

In the light patches of "active" sleep, both adults and children come near the surface, often being aware of where they are and what they want. Most children have learned to turn over, keep quiet, and go back to sleep. It is my belief that many of the night-time wakeners I see are those who have not learned to turn over and go back to sleep. Instead, they bring themselves to full wakefulness and insist on immediate gratification for hunger, sucking, or comfort. I also believe that these children can easily be taught a more peaceful and charitable code of night-time behavior.

THE STATISTICS OF SLEEP

No two studies have ever shown exactly the same instance of sleep problems in a population, but a few figures are shown in Tables 1 and 2 that give some insight into how other people's children behave at night.

Table 1. Average Number of Hours Sleep Taken Each Day

Age	Hours of Sleep
Birth	14–18
4 months	14–15
14 months	13–14

Table 2. A Profile of Some Sleeping Habits[6]

Problems	Percentage of Age Group				
	1 year	2 years	3 years	4 years	5 years
Wakes once or more every night	29	28	33	29	19
Wakes at least one night each week	57	57	66	65	61
Requires more than 30 minutes to fall asleep	26	43	61	69	66
One or more "curtain calls" before settling	14	26	42	49	50
Requests comforting object to take to bed	18	46	50	42	20
Goes to sleep with lights on	7	13	20	30	23
Nightmares at least once every two weeks	5	9	28	39	38

The Chamberlain study in New York found that 70 per cent of two-year-olds, 46 per cent of three-year-olds and 56 per cent of four-year-olds regularly resist going to bed; 52 per cent of two-year-olds and three-year-olds and 56 per cent of four-year-olds regularly wake up during the night; 17 per cent of two-year-olds, 18 per cent of three-year-olds and 36 per cent of four-year-olds regularly have nightmares.[4]

By comparison, studies in the United Kingdom gave lower figures for waking up at nights with only 27 per cent of one to two-year-olds[5] and 14 per cent of three-year-olds doing so.[2] Another survey in the United Kingdom found that 37 per cent of two-year-olds living with their parents were waking up at nights. These were compared with children of the same age who lived in a residential nursery and found that only 3.3 per cent awoke at night.[7]

This lends weight to my own belief that the more readily available the comfort at night, the worse the sleep pattern of the child. Certainly when the child enters a period of semi-wakefulness, he is more likely to roll over and go back to sleep if he realizes, from past experience, that crying does not bring rapid Grade A attention.

WHAT IS A SLEEP PROBLEM?

What appears to one family to be a massive sleep problem may not concern the next. A problem is, therefore, only really a problem if parental well-being and happiness are compromised. A child who wakes up ten or more times a night may not necessarily have the worst sleep problems. He may merely wake, cry briefly, and go straight back to sleep after a reassuring pat on the back, and the parents may return to sleep within seconds with no real problem occurring. Another child may only wake once or twice in the night, but each awakening may be followed by considerable difficulties before sleep returns. By the time the parents have paced the floor, bounced the child up and down, sung every nursery rhyme in the book, and done the complete repertoire of Chuckles The Clown, the child may be fast asleep again, but the parents are wide awake, wound up, and incapable of further sleep.

It's not the number of times a child wakes up at night that constitutes a problem, but the effect this disturbance has on the parents.

JUST WHO SUFFERS?

When a child has a major sleep problem, a great many people feel its effects. The mother, father, other children in the house, the neighbors and not least of all, the child himself.

Mothers

Parents who have not had enough sleep tend to be irritable and less patient, and they give poor service to their children by day. Many get so tired that life with a toddler is viewed as a penance to be endured, rather than a time of excitement and fun. I have seen wonderful mothers in tears, because they are genuinely scared they will hurt their children unless they get some sleep. Others have slipped past coping and sunk into a pathological depression. It seems strange that the toddler is often the instrument of his own destruction. He has the power to greatly damage his mother or father, who, unintentionally and unavoidably, then transfers the wound.

The marriage

A tired mother makes a tired wife, who needs the help and support of an understanding husband. Where this is not forthcoming a great strain is placed on the marriage. I see many husbands who deliberately spend as little time as possible in the disturbed atmosphere of home, while others have to put up with being ousted from the marital bed to make way for a sleepless, kicking child. Husbands and wives need to have some time alone together if they are to communicate effectively and remain a strong team. If a child stays up half the night, destroying all meaningful conversation, this is almost impossible.

Brothers and sisters

Most brothers and sisters of sleepless toddlers develop an amazing ability to sleep through most of the night-time antics. A few are, however, sufficiently sensitive to noise to become sleep-deprived, just like their parents. They suffer the consequences twice, which is most unfair: once from having their sleep disturbed, and again next day when they inevitably suffer unjustly from the wrath of tired parents.

Neighbors

If you live in a house with thick walls set in the middle of no-where, you can afford to ignore the neighbors. Unfortunately most of us don't live in these ideal circumstances, and complaints from irate neighbors always add to parental harassment. Even worse, I have known excellent parents who have been reported to local

child welfare agencies as child abusers, such has been the racket
the sleepless child has put up.

The child

I used to reassure parents that, when the toddler would not sleep,
they were the only ones who suffered, the child always getting all
the rest he needed. Recently, I have altered my opinion. I now
believe that the child who sleeps all night becomes more settled,
happier, and easier to control by day than the child who has sleep
problems. An even stranger phenomenon has come to light with
some of the younger children I see. Once the night-time sleep pattern improves, there seems to be a lengthening (or reintroduction)
of the daytime nap. This is a paradox, but it appears that more
night-time sleep encourages more daytime sleep as well. It must be
due to the combined effect of both child and parent being more
relaxed and calmer, thus producing a sleep-inducing environment.

THE BIG THREE

The three main problems are:
  1) the middle-of-the-night screamer;
  2) the child who will not go to bed, and
  3) the child who comes to the parents' bed each night
Whether your toddler has one, two or a full-house of these anti-
social habits, I can offer a quick and relatively painless cure. It
must, however, be said that, if the child is sick or the household is
undergoing some sort of an upheaval, either physical or emotional,
he must be allowed to wake up and, if he wants, come into his
parents' bed. If the child is under the age of 14 months, he may
well have the right to exercise a baby's prerogative of disturbing
the parents!

For the healthy toddler in an otherwise calm atmosphere, there
is a cure, and I guarantee that nine out of ten will be sleeping
properly within seven days after following this technique. This is
no "flash in the pan," easy-come, easy-go cure, but one that will
last forever, once the parents see their new-found strength and
have felt the benefits of a good night's sleep.

The middle-of-the-night screamer

Being woken up in the middle of the night by a screaming toddler
is one of the really low points of being a parent. You can spot the
mothers of these nocturnal screamers as they walk down the

street. They have a characteristic stooped walk, a look of utter defeat on the face, and prominent dark circles under their eyes. What riches they would offer for a solution to their predicament! There are few greater wonders to behold than the reincarnation of these destroyed parents after several days of simple treatment. The backbone straightens, the face takes on an air of mastery, and the eyes sparkle once again. This miracle also produces happier and more relaxed children.

It is, however, an extraordinary fact of life that some parents seem to derive a strange pleasure from boasting about their child's difficult behavior, and when help is offered, they make innumerable excuses to maintain the status quo. Other parents are interested in a cure, but only if it involves no effort on their part. I must stress here that, as a prerequisite to any attempt at treating sleep problems, parents must be certain that they want a cure and that they are determined to see it through at all costs. I have rarely seen anyone fail who has followed this path with determination.

The child who wakes crying in the night emits such a noise that parents are generally sure that he's frightened and immediately rush to comfort him. I do not believe, however, that fear is responsible for the chronic, repeated night-time wakenings of the toddler, and if it were, a dim light in the room would be all that was needed to ease the problem.

THE TECHNIQUE

1. Let cry for three to ten minutes, then give comfort. The length of the time you should leave the child to cry before giving comfort depends on the strength of the individual parents and the sensitivity of the child. Many health workers tell parents that when their child cries at night they should not go near him, but leave him to cry himself to sleep. This can often take three to four hours; I think it is not only a cruel, but also an ineffective method of treatment. After ten minutes, most children become hysterical and have no idea why they are crying. They get themselves into a lather, sweat profusely, their heart pounds, and they become very frightened. Fear is not a good way of teaching any child good behavior.

My controlled-crying method employs short, individually tailored periods of crying, calculated to give the maximum message, while at the same time making the child aware of what is going on. With the average determined parent, I suggest ten minutes is an appropriate length of time: delicate, ground-down moms can take only about three minutes. Although the longer period of crying may be more effective, it is the parents' determination to be firm and their ability to give only Grade B comfort when they go to their child that decide the eventual outcome.

2. Grade B comfort. Pick up, cuddle and put the child down as soon as the crying is under control. The individually tailored length of crying time is important, but what the parents actually do when they come to the child's room is even more important. Some experts suggest that the child shouldn't be lifted, but just turned over and patted. Many parents, however, offer bottles, breasts, pacifiers or endless walks across the floor until the child goes back to sleep with his head on their shoulder.

I believe it is best to lift and cuddle so the child is in no doubt of your love, concern, and wish to comfort him. It is not at all a good idea to offer comforters, such as bottles or pacifiers, or to let him go to sleep with his head on your shoulder because, charitable as these may be, they encourage habits that are hard to break. Don't put the child down while he is crying; wait until he stops and knows exactly what is happening.

The psychological moment to put the child down is when the crying turns to "sniffing." He then knows that his parents have come, that they love him, and that they have given him Grade B comfort. He should then be put down firmly and promptly left alone.

3. Increase periods of crying by five minutes each time. Never give better than Grade B comfort. Once you have put the child back in bed, he will probably start crying again. This time, he should be left for five minutes longer than the previous occasion. He should then be attended to the same way as before, getting adequate, but inferior, comfort. The next time he cries, an additional five minutes is added, and so the technique continues.

The aim of the controlled crying method is to gradually build up the periods between attention, without letting the child become frightened and always keeping him aware of why he is crying. This technique is a little like an auto insurance policy. Motorists are discouraged from making minor claims by the inclusion of an excess clause in their policy, which says that they will have to pay the first so many dollars of each claim themselves before the company steps in and takes care of the remainder. This gives great security for major problems but makes one think twice before bothering the insurers unnecessarily over trivia. After one claim, the excess is often raised to act as a further deterrent, while still affording full security.

With the controlled crying technique, the initial excess is ten minutes of crying before help becomes available. After the first claim has been made, the excess increases to fifteen minutes, and then to twenty minutes and so on. Eventually the claimant says to himself, "I know that they will always pay up in the end, but it isn't worth the effort." At this point the sleep problem has been cured.

4. Sedation: the safety valve. When I first started using this controlled crying method, I insisted that parents engage in a fight to the death, never giving in until the child finally fell asleep. Most parents seemed to rally immense strength to see this through, but others dropped by the wayside, finding the cure harder to cope with than the disease. Consequently, over the past two years, I have inserted a "safety valve" into the system. This is in the form of a sedative, which must only be given once one full hour of treatment has elapsed. This ensures that the parents can give of their best, safe in the knowledge that, if the worst comes to the worst, help is at hand. Although most parents actually buy the sedative to keep as a form of insurance, only about one-fifth of them ever need to uncork the bottle. Most youngsters seem to get the message long before the prescribed hour has elapsed.

I suggest one hour as the average time a parent should stick it out before administering the knock-out drops, but for those parents who may be delicate, depressed, and exhausted, a shorter waiting time is allowable. It is, after all, the powerful message given before the child falls asleep that is decisive, rather than the time itself. A child who has been awake and crying for this length of time in the middle of the night is particularly susceptible to sedation, and it usually takes just a sniff of the cork to send them reeling into the Land of Nod.

5. The follow-up operation. If the child wakes again, either the same night or the next night, start resolutely at the beginning again. The child who has settled quite quickly after controlled crying will often wake many more times that night. On each wakening, the parents must be 100 per cent firm, starting again with the ten minute crying period and following the regime without faltering. If a sedative has been used, the child will usually sleep through the rest of the night, although there are exceptions to this rule. No matter what happens on the first night, the technique must be re-introduced with absolute firmness the following evening.

6. The result is a guaranteed 90 per cent cure in seven nights. The speed and pattern of the cure depend on the age of the child; those treated between nine months and 14 months have an odd response to it. Although they come under control quickly, the gains are often short-lived and will come and go for two to three weeks before some sort of stability appears. Not only do these

younger children take longer to cure, but no more than about 70
per cent of them are completely cured. After 14 months, however,
the response is more predictable. On the first night, there is a
major showdown, but in most the fuss is over by the third night;
90 per cent of parents are overjoyed by sunrise on the seventh day.

Children aged three and over are a joy to work with. Although
they have the same success rate as the younger ones, almost half of
them can be given an instant cure without ever "a shot being
fired." Once I have told the parents exactly what I expect them to
do, I then explain it all over again, this time in the child's hearing,
using words of one syllable. Children at this age are compulsive
eavesdroppers, so they take it all in and in many cases realize that
the game is up. Half of them will confound their parents by suddenly sleeping through the night without disturbance. These miracle cures are a source of great entertainment to my colleagues, who
jokingly claim that I appear to have given up the practice of real
medicine and that cures now come by simply touching "the hem of
my garment!"

The child who will not go to bed at night

Over half of all toddlers act up at bedtime if they know they can
get away with it. Some obstinately refuse to go to bed; others infuriate their parents by popping in and out of their rooms like jack-
in-the-boxes. Other, more subtle, toddlers create a smokescreen
with requests for drinks, the toilet, and various comforters, which
succeed in keeping the parents on the hop and giving them great
attention.

"Bed refusal" problems are much less damaging to parents than
the antics of the middle-of-the-night screamers. All this in-and-out
drama is a pest and the parents are irritated, but at least they are
not losing any sleep. Parents deserve the chance to have some time
alone together, so their children should be expected to go to bed at
a reasonable hour. Clever doctors have so far not yet discovered a
way of putting a child into bed and making him go to sleep if that
child doesn't want to. Whether he sleeps or not, I do have a way of
keeping a child in bed and out of mischief.

THE TECHNIQUE

I. Have a later bedtime (temporarily). If parents want to
have their child asleep by seven p.m., but he never settles before
10 p.m., it is pointless to put him down at that early hour. He
should be put to bed between nine p.m. and nine-thirty p.m.,
which should be late enough to give you a sporting chance of getting him off to sleep. Once a proper sleep pattern has been estab-

lished, then bedtime is brought forward five minutes each night. Since the child cannot tell the time at this age, he will be totally unaware of the trick being played. Gradually, a normal bedtime is achieved and you can breath a sigh of relief—at least until daylight saving is introduced for the summer!

2. Soothe him—don't stir him. When children have difficulty settling down at night, they must not be allowed to get wound up and excited just before bedtime. Rough games, wild play, and verbal stirring should be avoided at all costs. Instead, a quiet story should be read while the child is sitting up comfortably in bed. This should be accompanied by gentle, Grade A comfort, and, if necessary, security blankets, teddy bears, and a dim night-light.

3. Put him down firmly and decisively. Do not argue, debate or become diverted by his manipulations. When the child is put to bed, there must be no conflicting messages, and no sign of weakening on the parents' part. When the usual smokescreen of requests is thrown up—for a drink, the toilet, mom to lie down with him, or for him to sleep in another bed—it must be ignored. Once the child is in bed the parents must beat a hasty retreat.

4. Jack-in-the-box behavior. If the child comes out of his room once he has been put to bed, return him firmly and at once.

5. If he comes out again, get his father to put him back. If dad is available, get him to put the child back the second time. The return by the father is very effective, as it gives a strong message that both parents are united in their determination to keep him in bed.

6. If he returns, change tack and ignore him. Some parents tell me that my method doesn't work. "We put him back twenty times last night," they say. This is not a failure of my method but a failure to recognize when a discipline has turned into a game. After the child has escaped twice, an equally firm, but different, response must be used. I now suggest that when the child re-enters, he is completely ignored. The television set should be turned off and the parents should depart for the kitchen, talking together as they clear the dishes. The todder will initially be puzzled, wondering why he is being ignored, when ten minutes before he was the star of the show. He is now receiving the clear message that he is an unwanted visitor. In order to get noticed, he will stage one of his finer attention-seeking ploys. At this point, the parents notice him and put him straight back in his room.

7. If he re-enters a fourth time, sit, spank or tie. By now, even the most inventive parent is running short of both patience and ideas. In practice, other than hoisting the white flag, we have but three options left:

1) sit with him in his room;

2) give him a sharp smack, or

3) use the patent rope trick.

The first option is a gentle one and may not work. The other two are rather more potent, and when used, they generally herald the end of the reign of the jack-in-the-box child.

Sitting with the child is probably the kindest way of handling the situation. The parent sits silently in the room reading a book, thus providing a presence, but not an object to be manipulated or man-handled. This can work, as long as the child does not try to manipulate the situation by asking for drinks, the toilet, and so on.

At a certain point, when the child has emerged multiple times, and all the gentle techniques have failed, one is either obliged to give up the struggle or change the rules of the game. Let me say here, that if you give up at this stage and let the child win, he will immediately sense who is boss and give you hell from there on. Many parents, who are determined they will not be thwarted in their quest for a cure, at this stage give the child *a short, sharp smack*. The child realizes that the game is up and thereafter re-mains firmly in his room. Unfortunately, he also changes the rules of the game and starts to cry vigorously in another attempt to break the resolve of his parents. This, of course, will not work as the parents have already been instructed in the controlled crying tech-nique and the battle is all but won for them. On first reading, this may seem a hard way to treat a child, but bearing in mind that a complete cure can be guaranteed in under a week, it is a small price to pay to bring peace to the family.

For those who cannot bring themselves to spank their child, but are rapidly getting nowhere, I strongly recommend the *patent rope trick*. This is one of my better inventions, which came from the drawing-board when I was trying to curb the escape-artist antics of my own children. All that is required is a short length of strong rope.

Before you get worried, I'm not going to suggest that you now tie your child to the bed—tempting though this might on occasion be! No. What you do is loop one end of the rope around the inner handle of the bedroom door and attach the other end to the handle of another, nearby door. Carefully adjust the rope so that when the bedroom door is forced open, the aperture is just one inch less than the diameter of the offending child's head. This will effectively keep your child in his room, and although he may now resort to crying to break your resolve, the ploy will again fail because you are now in full command with the controlled crying technique. A light should be left on in the passage outside the bedroom, so that the child can see and hear what's going on around the house. This means the child will not become frightened, but at the same time he is made aware that bed is the place he is meant to be.

Before you all rush out to the nearest hardware shop ordering up miles of rope, let me just relate one cautionary, and somewhat embarrassing, tale. One late evening it had become quite apparent that there was no way our two active "super-boys" would stay in their room, so a loop of rope was attached in the approved manner. Following this there was some crying, which suddenly reached such fever pitch that we ran to investigate. The boys were still in their room, but unfortunately I had made the rope a fraction too long and our older son had skillfully pushed his brother's head through the crack in the door where it was by now firmly jammed. Extrication was as delicate as defusing the trembler device on a ticking bomb, and the realization that even the simplest things in life require great care was a salutary lesson. Don't let this put you off, however. The patent rope trick works.

8. The results: a 90 per cent cure in seven days. As with the night screamers, this technique is extremely successful for children over the age of 14 months. Nine out of ten cures can be guaranteed with confidence within a week. But let me emphasize that this is not a way of making children go to sleep. It is only a means of making sure that when you put them to bed they stay there.

The child who comes to his parents' bed each night

Many philosophers extol the virtues and joys of a family sleeping together in one giant, bed-bound commune. Although this may be a terrifically enjoyable state of affairs for those who are deep sleepers or are lucky enough not to have children who behave all night like soccer stars at a goal, the vast majority of parents I see wish their bed to be a private, peaceful place. They greatly resent those little intruders making an appearance in the small hours of the morning.

My experience is that nocturnal wanderers tend to be the more active members of the child population, and they are incapable of lying quietly in the parental bed if they are put there. They are skilled in the art of using both arms and legs to simultaneously kick one parent and punch the other. Many mothers can often tolerate this intrusion, but fathers, I find, are far less long-suffering. The prospect of a busy day after a disturbed night's sleep will force them to flee to the peace and comfort of a neighboring settee, or even the child's vacated bed.

Many lonely mothers, whether alone because their husband is away on business or because of a marriage break-up, subtly encourage their children to come into bed with them each night as company. It is then difficult, when life returns to normal, to persuade the child to discontinue the practice.

A sick child, on the other hand, has a rightful place in his parents' bed, although it is sometimes hard to evict him once his health has returned to normal. And all children are entitled to that enjoyable, early morning romp in their parents' bed—just as long as the cock has crowed and the coffee has been made!

Apart from these rare situations, I believe that children should be excluded from their parents' bed at all other times. Peace and privacy are important to people, and that includes parents. Of course, it's up to you, but if you want a good method of evicting even the most determined toddler from your place of rest, read on.

THE TECHNIQUE

1. The moment the child appears he must be put back immediately. On a cold night, a tired parent must be very strong to resist slipping the little intruder into bed, but such an action only reinforces anti-social night-time behavior and must be discouraged. Some unwelcome little nocturnal prowlers can slip into their parents' bed with all the stealth of a cat burglar and lie there unnoticed for quite some time. If you are determined to stop this habit, I suggest putting a wedge under your bedroom door, which allows it to be opened a short distance but causes an obstruction that alerts you to the child's approach.

2. If the child returns, give a stern warning and, if possible, have the other parent return him to bed. More democratic parents give the child a stern warning, leaving him in no doubt as to what lies ahead if he is seen again, and then put him back to bed (preferable the other parent than the one who dealt with him the first time). I must admit, however, that most parents feel that this degree of civility is quite unwarranted at that time of night, and they move straight to the next stage.

3. If he returns a third time. In this case, either a light, symbolic smack should be used before returning him to his bed, or various doors should be immobilized with the patent rope trick or a therapeutic little wedge. Following this, the controlled crying technique is used.

4. The results: ten out of ten if that is what you really want. Coming to the parents' bed in the middle of the night constitutes the least damaging of the three major sleep problems of toddlerhood. It is up to the individual parent to decide whether to tolerate this behavior or have a showdown. The methods outlined may seem rather harsh, but the middle of the night is no time for playing games, and it is worth being firm, because the chances of a quick and permanent cure are good.

OTHER SLEEP-RELATED PROBLEMS

The light sleeper

Most young children, once asleep, are dead to the world and would not wake even if set down in the middle of the New York Philharmonic Orchestra playing the last movement of Tchaikovsky's 1812 Overture, cannons and all! Some, however, are uncommonly sensitive to sound, which leaves the parents tip-toeing round the house at night, frightened to run a tap or flush a toilet. This is easily overcome by placing an ordinary household transistor radio beside the child's bed. On the first night, turn the radio on with such a low volume that the sound is barely audible to all but a passing bat. As the nights pass, gradually increase the volume until, after two weeks, most children are well and truly desensitized. From there on, most children should sleep through garbage collections, car horns, the football final on television, and the odd cannon.

What station should your child listen to, I hear you ask. Assess his interests. Budding merchant bankers should be tuned to the station that gives the best stock market reports, punk rockers in the making will be happy with a rock-'n'-roll station, and a possible candidate for the clergy is probably happiest listening to hymns. Of course, I am joking. It really doesn't matter which program the radio is tuned to; the child isn't listening to it anyway, just to the noise it makes.

The afternoon sleep

Children in their first two years of life enjoy their daytime nap—and not only the child I may say. Mother looks forward to this time with equal glee. Unfortunately, this peaceful event disappears somewhere between the ages of two and four, and every parent mourns its passing. But in the final days before the changeover, parents are in a dilemma. If the child does not get an afternoon nap he is unbearably irritable in the late afternoon, but he goes to bed early and sleeps soundly. If he does sleep in the afternoon, the peace is enjoyed, but it is paid for when the revitalized child romps round the house until all hours of the night.

There is, I'm sorry to say, no answer to this problem. Parents simply have to make a choice. I favor the sacrifice of the already waning afternoon nap, believing the good night-sleeping pattern to be more important.

The right bedtime

There is no universal "right" bedtime for all children. In my experience, seven-thirty p.m. appears to be the accepted time that most toddlers should assume the horizontal. This may be the case for the sleeping majority, but a significant minority won't settle to sleep at this time in a month of Sundays. The offenders are usually those difficult children who have been poor sleepers from birth. They are mostly active boys, which is surprising, because one would expect them to need more sleep considering the massive amounts of energy they use up during the day.

All we can do is accept that children, like adults, have different sleeping needs. As for the late settlers, they need a later bedtime, and although they cannot be forced to sleep, there are at least ways of keeping them in their rooms, which must surely increase the chances of them inadvertently falling asleep.

The procrastinator

Little children who do not wish to be parted for the night from their loving parents have an immense repertoire of procrastinating techniques. "I want a drink," "I feel hungry," "I want you to lie beside me," "I want a different pillow," "I don't want a pillow at all," "I want two pillows . . ." and so on, and so on. This is a genuine wish to hang on to the parents' attention for as long as possible and put off having to go to sleep. This is all part of the charm of these tender years, but it must not be allowed to get out of hand. A little procrastination is fun, but if handled badly it can turn into a major case of manipulation. Know your child and know when to say enough is enough.

The early riser

Some children love to sleep late, while others are up and on the go from the first peep of the dawn chorus. Once again, this tends to be the prerogative of those over-active members of the toddler population. I have to admit that I have never been of any help to parents with this problem. In theory, a later bedtime should cure the habit, but I find that its only effect is usually to turn a happy

early riser into a tired, irritable early riser. Cutting out the
daytime sleep seems to have equally little effect.

One approach that occasionally works is to ensure that the television can be easily turned on and quiet toys are left strategically
placed for the child to play with in the early morning. Sometimes
this enables the rest of the household to remain asleep, but more
often than not the toddler wants to be fed and wishes to share the
beauty of the sunrise with his parents. All I can offer is sympathy
but not a cure!

The night prowler

Some children wake up in the middle of the night wanting something to eat, or to play or explore the house. Recently I was
brought a three-year-old who had discovered that getting up at two
a.m. and turning on the vacuum cleaner had an amazing effect on
his befuddled parents. Another three-year-old of my acquaintance
loved to play with his toy cars in the middle of the night. As he
could not reach the light switches, he had to find an alternative
source of illumination, which he achieved by setting up his auto-
mobile collection in front of the refrigerator, then pulling open the
door and playing by its cold, bright light. This would have been a
quite innocent pastime, except that he was often overcome by sleep
in mid-activity and would be found in the morning surrounded by
piles of defrosted vegetables.

If children are determined to play in the middle of the night,
that's fine, just as long as they are quiet and do not damage themselves or other people's property. It is usually safest to deal with
night prowlers by resorting to the patent rope trick, as well as
making sure there are deadlocks on all the exterior doors and
wedges on others to limit the child's access to danger.

The shared bedroom

Often, with the midnight screamer, parents are defeated before
they ever start. They are quick to point out that my techniques
will never work as they are too disturbing for the other children. I
can assure you, however, that if you are really keen on finding a
cure, then a shared room, although inconvenient, is not an impossible hurdle.

All I ask for is one week of absolute firmness, during which
most families should be capable of rearranging themselves for a
short while. Older children who share the crying toddler's bedroom usually have a much higher tolerance for nocturnal noise

than their parents anyway. The controlled crying technique can usually be used without causing any great disturbance to the other room occupants. If this is not possible, a temporary sleeping arrangement must be organized and the other children moved from the bedroom to the comparative quiet of the living room. This will leave the toddler pretty well soundproofed for the duration of the treatment, and once a good sleep pattern has been established, the children can be reunited.

It's only when the entire family live in one bedroom that my techniques fall sadly apart. In these difficult situations parents simply have to give in to the child in the interests of the family's peace.

The crib in the parents' bedroom

Many newborn babies sleep in a crib close to their parents' bed, taking some of the effort out of the night-time feed. Some parents with older children prefer, for a variety of reasons, to keep them close to their bed at night. This may be fine if the parents are sound sleepers and the child remains quiet at night. But it may not be such a good idea for light-sleeping parents who are stirred to consciousness every time the child coughs, turns over, or passes wind. Even children with epilepsy or other medical problems should be encouraged to sleep in a separate room, as unbroken sleep has great curative powers for the entire family.

The lost pacifier

Some young toddlers can only survive those wakeful periods at night with their mouth firmly plugged by a pacifier. If it becomes disconnected, help is summoned by loud wailing and gnashing of teeth, and the cries will only subside once the missing piece of junk is replaced. Many parents get sick and tired of this constant midnight drama, but they don't know how to rid themselves of this offending object. Some disposal suggestions are mentioned later in this book, but one way of keeping track of the thing is to tie a tape onto the pacifier and pin it to the child's night clothes. Children of an advanced age, who shouldn't have a pacifier in the first place, are thus able to locate the lost object. Unfortunately young children seem to be unable to make contact with the tape and, even if they can, find it well nigh impossible to reel in and plug their mouths.

The only reliable cure for repeated wakening as the result of a lost pacifier is to get rid of the object completely. Certainly this may lead to several difficult nights, but in the long term, it is well worth the momentary inconvience.

Night feeds

There is a major relationship between night wakening and night feeding. If night-time breast feeding continues after the first birthday, there is a strong likelihood that this will be accompanied by multiple nocturnal wakenings. So great is the comfort from breast feeding, that the child will demand the breast as an adjunct to sleep—comfort rather than sustenance is the object of the exercise.

If late breast feeding is being considered, it should be given by day, on going to bed, and on wakening in the morning. A strict curfew must be imposed during the hours of darkness. Bottles give less comfort. When compared with a warm breast, there is minimal joy to be gained from sucking a cold rubber nipple. But these should also be suspended during the hours of sleep if night wakening is to be cured. When given, they establish a bad pattern, which once again encourages the half-asleep child to cry out for sustenance rather than turn over and go back to sleep.

A basic law also decrees that "What goes in must come out." The more fluid the child drinks, the greater the number of wet diapers, wet beds, discomfort, and excursions to the toilet.

Don't be fooled by advertisers' attempts to encourage you to combat "night starvation." Children don't starve at night. For the sake of peace and quiet and an undisturbed sleep, all midnight snacks, be they from breast or bottle, should be discouraged.

The crib escapee

Long before they reach their first birthday, some children have developed strong mountaineering skills. They lie quietly in their cribs for months, planning their escape route down to the final detail. The time of the first successful escape attempt varies greatly from child to child, and from crib to crib. These miniature mountaineers are rarely less than 10 months old, however, and more often closer to 18 months.

No matter how energetic and ambitious the young child may be, he is unlikely to scale a high side that has no horizontal stepping bar from which to take off. The first effort usually ends in a hard fall, as he finds the climb up considerably easier to control than the journey down the other side. Some children never consider climbing out of their cribs at all and would probably remain there happily until school age.

Parents often ask at what age the child should be moved from a crib to a proper bed. This often happens precipitously when a new baby arrives, but on other occasions it is a well-planned move. If the child has a good sleeping pattern, little harm will come from the change. The trouble comes with the child who sleeps poorly in his crib, and parents misguidedly think that the move to a bed will help. All it does is transfer the bad sleeper from one mattress to another with no attendant benefit. I am all in favor of toddlers remaining in their cribs at least until well into their second year. There seem to be very few advantages in an early release program.

When the toddler starts climbing out of his crib, parents are usually terrified that he will fall and hurt himself. At this point, they have to decide whether to leave the side of the crib down or put him in a bed, both of which allow easy escape and will possibly lead to night-time problems. If they leave him in the crib, it should be situated against two walls with a soft floor covering the exposed side. It may seem a rather callous thing to say, but in my experience most young children who have a nasty fall from their cribs usually have the sense to postpone further attempts until they have become sufficiently mature to guarantee a soft landing.

The nocturnally deaf husband

This is a fascinating phenomenon, which I have studied assiduously for years. My observations show that when the child cries at night, most husbands appear to become suddenly stone deaf, and thus their wives are forced out of bed to cope with the problem. I don't believe this is, in any sense, true deafness, but rather a conveniently learned response to an unpleasant situation. My wife claims that, when our children cried at night, she found that my hearing could be toned up with the aid of a sharp kick! Certainly in these enlightened days, I believe there should be more sharing of the less pleasant parts of parenthood, and if kicking is what it takes, then that is as good a method as any.

Fears

When a child starts to cry at night, many parents worry that he may be frightened and thus will not allow my firm methods of control to be used. Certainly younger children do have fears and some of these are discussed in Chapter 13. Separating from parents at night can cause anxiety in some toddlers, but it must be coped with if both parents and child are to get any sleep and the anxiety overcome. To help with this separation, it is quite a good idea to use comfort items, such as a favorite teddy bear or a security blanket.

Fear of the dark is common among children, and indeed to quite a large number of adults. A dull, low-wattage light is a small investment that will relieve a great deal of stress. Some academics dispute the value of night lights, believing that the shadows they throw make the child even more frightened. This is a typical academic response, and it certainly doesn't seem to be the case with any of the children I have ever seen.

Nightmares

Nightmares are much more common at an older age, but they can occur in toddlers. As the child wakes from active dream sleep, he may still be in the midst of some alarming escapade. He has an unmistakable frightened cry and is easily soothed by the rapid appearance of a parent. He quickly becomes aware that it was a dream, not a real event, and in some cases he can even remember all the details. Nightmares may occur quite regularly, and although there is some association with stress and anxiety, it is usually the sort of normal stress of life that we cannot change. The most loving, attentive, angelic parents, who have the best possible relationship with their child, will find that the child still has nightmares. He's probably dreaming in this case that he has become separated from them!

The treatment for nightmares is simple. Go quickly to the child, hold him, talk soothingly, and stay as the child slips quietly back to sleep.

Night terrors

These occur in a slightly younger age group. The child wakes from a deep, sound sleep in a state of utter terror. He sits up in bed, looking through glazed, staring eyes and cries profusely. His parents run to his aid and are confronted with a difficult situation, as the child seems almost paralyzed and stuck in a different world that they cannot reach. The thing to do is cuddle the child, talk quietly to him, and after a while the child will gently relax and go back to sleep. This can take anything up to ten minutes. In the morning, the child will have no memory of the night's events, although the parents will find it much harder to forget.

Once again, there may be repeated episodes, but it is extremely rare that any treatment is required other than letting time do the healing. As with nightmares, it is unlikely that there is any treatable anxiety-provoking event that causes night terrors.

Sedation

Sedative drugs are abused and over-used by many parents. In some
families, they are almost a nightly routine, being used for sleep
problems that could be more effectively and safely treated by simple behavioral methods. I disapprove of sedatives being used unnecessarily, but there are three situations in which I think their
use is justified:

1) as a safety valve to be used after one hour of my controlled
   crying regime;
2) as a safety valve for delicate families to use in times of crisis,
   when sleep is imperative to maintain sanity and stability; and
3) to sedate the severely handicapped child, who is extremely
   irritable by day and is awake, crying, all night.

The secret with sedation is to give the right dose at the right time.
Most doctors quite gratuitously write the instructions "to be taken
at bedtime" on the bottle. It is, however, unrealistic to expect that
a sedative given at six p.m. will miraculously ensure sleep right
through until next morning. When I want a child to sleep, I give
the drug, in its correct dose for the child's body weight, on the first
occasion that he wakes in the night. This is more effective than
administering it before the child goes to bed, because he will probably sleep perfectly well for the first few hours anyway. This way
those golden early morning hours are protected.

Occasionally I see families who are so exhausted and fragile that
they need immediate relief before they can see through one of my
behavior programs. In these cases, I may prescribe a week's sedation for the child to allow everyone to get back on an even keel
before embarking on a more permanent cure by more effective
methods. There is no harm in having a sedative in the house, as
long as it is used with sense and as a last resort, or when an
unbroken night's sleep is vital for survival.

As much of my work is with handicapped children and their
parents, I am only too aware of the terrible sleep problems that
may occur with these children. Some severely handicapped babies
may be immensely irritable by day, requiring almost constant attention, and they go on throughout the night with negligible sleep
and almost continuous crying. It takes a strong parent to cope with
the difficulties of the day, let alone being asked to cope all night as
well. No one can cope this way twenty-four hours a day and it
should not be attempted.

In an effort to preserve the parents' health and strength in these
cases, I use individually designed regimes, which may use several
drugs before achieving reliable sleep. But giving drugs to children

can have an alarming paradoxical effect. Sedated children can become irritable, overactive, unreasonable, and poorly co-ordinated. They can adopt all the worst characteristics of the obnoxious drunk, staggering around the house, slurring their speech, walking into doors, and generally being quite uncontrollable. They are danger to both themselves and others. So remember this before administering drugs to your child, particularly before car, train, or plane trips. Drugs can sometimes do more harm than good.

Sensitive neighbors

Parents with children who sleep poorly are often sabotaged in their attempts to implement controlled crying by complaining neighbors. I recommend the direct confrontation approach in these instances. On returning home from my office, the parents go straight in to see the neighbors and tell them that the child is now in the hands of a marvellous doctor from the Children's Hospital, who has designed a new treatment for sleepless kids. They explain that this is quite revolutionary and the doctor has insisted that they let the child cry a number of times at night, but that the cure will come inside a week. On most occasions this super-scientific approach, blaming everything on the doctor, has worked. So far I have no reports of parents being set on by the neighbor's dog, and very often the thought that they too are participating in a new, scientific experiment can work wonders.

10

TOILET TRAINING

Despite anxious parents, mothers-in-law, the interfering lady next door, and a host of other people who think they know better, children become toilet trained when they, and only they, are ready. No child can be trained until the appropriate nerve pathways have sufficiently matured, a process that is completely outside the influence of even the most brilliant parent or doctor. Once sufficiently mature, the process is controlled by the child's will to comply or his determination to defy, which, in turn, is dependent on the child's temperament, as well as the skill and cunning of the trainer.

It seems that at the beginning of this century children were trained much earlier than today, with the process starting at about three months, and there are many reports of children being completely trained by their first birthday. There was a lot to be said for early training in those days of cold water, poor detergents, and washing by hand. It was also a time when people had a great obsession with bodily functions and the clockwork regularity of bowel movements. It was vigorously drummed into new mothers that if the baby was started off on the right path in his earliest months, he would be saved in later life from the scourge of constipation. Most of what was labelled as toilet training was in fact an unrecognized, involuntary bodily reflex that bore absolutely no relationship to super-parents, advanced development, or even toilet training. Although we are now eighty years on, the myth of early toilet training still confuses and worries parents.

Most toilet training difficulties today are really non-problems caused by unrealistic expectations and misleading advice. Parents often start training too early, motivated by ideals more akin to the 1890s than to the 1980s. Turn a deaf ear to all those well-meaning, but interfering, friends and family. Do not start too early; it invariably leads to unnecessary problems. Remember that the child alone has the ultimate power to go where and when he wishes. Don't hurry; don't fight. Just relax.

TOILET TIMING, TOILET TRAINING

Babies, from their earliest days, tend to empty their bowels or bladders when their stomachs are full after a feed. This is a completely reflex action, being no more clever or voluntary than a knee-jerk reaction. If put on the potty after a meal there is a sporting chance that something will "pop out." This is most interesting, but it is nothing to get excited about. This is toilet timing.

Toilet training is something completely different. Here an older toddler uses his brain to decide whether he wishes to go to the toilet and then makes a deliberate attempt to oblige. This is a voluntary action, and the child is in full control.

Most of the crazy ideas concerning early training are put about by those interfering know-alls who mistake toilet timing for toilet training. No child is toilet trained at the age of one year, and children who give this appearance are just demonstrating a particularly strong toilet timing reflex. The effect may be to reduce the load on an overworked washing machine, but this is a temporary lull, usually relapsing as soon as the child starts to exert voluntary control.

TOILET TRAINING: NORMAL DEVELOPMENT

During the first one-and-a-half years of life, there is no proper bowel or bladder control, just the toilet timing reflex. As the child approaches 18 months, this reflex appears to weaken, and voluntary control begins to take over.

It is quite pointless to consider toilet training until the child knows at least when he is wet. The realization rarely dawns much before 18 months of age. In the months that follow this discovery, the child becomes aware of his toileting needs before the event rather than after. This great breakthrough occurs somewhere between 18 months and two years of age, but it has one unfortunate flaw. Although warning is given, the child's early warning system is only adjusted to tell of the impending puddle five seconds before it arrives! By the age of two, the amount of warning has increased and you can start to notch up a few successes. At about this time bowel control will also become established, in some children before urine control and in others after it. By the age of two-and-a-half years, about two-thirds of children will be dry most of the time; the majority can take themselves to the toilet and handle their pants without too many mistakes. At this age night-time wetting also starts to come under control, the child initially needing to be lifted onto the toilet in the middle of the night, and later holding on unaided. Although most children are dry and bowel trained by the age of two-and-a-half, there still remains a great sense of urgency about the whole procedure. The child needing to go "now" rather than when convenient.

In toilet training development, there is great variation from child to child. There is a strong relationship with family history, and parents with late bladder training, especially at night, frequently find that their children are endowed with similar characteristics. Girls tend to become trained slightly earlier than boys, possibly because of their slightly more advanced development, different anatomy, or perhaps a more compliant personality at this age. Early training is no more a sign of intelligence than early development of teeth. As far as I am aware intelligence comes from the brain, an organ somewhat distant from the bladder!

Our teaching today is clear. Eighteen months is the earliest age to start toilet training: two years is probably a much more realistic starting age. Night-time training is unlikely to succeed while the night diapers are consistently wet. Some parents believe that no training should commence before two-and-a-half or three years, and if their washing machines can stand the strain, the child will in no way be disadvantaged, I can assure you.

BLADDER TRAINING: THE PLAN

1) Does the child know when he is wet?
2) Consider training pants.
3) Sit regularly—don't force him.
4) When he uses the pot—reward him.

The futility of starting training before the child realizes that he is wet has been mentioned. One trick, however, may hasten this realization. The child who wets a large, well-insulated diaper may squelch around in warm humidity, quite unperturbed. Exchange this for a pair of trainer pants and life ceases to be quite so comfortable. These pants are made of thin towelling, with little insulation and, when wet, they have a great potential for evaporation. As the winds whistle around the child, the chill factor increases, giving icy feelings in sensitive places. These are quite effective in speeding up the child's awareness. Trainer pants have the further advantage of quick release, most useful in the average toddler's usual delicate state of urgency. Unfortunately, they also have one major disadvantage. There is no barrier to the moisture, allowing the child to make puddles on the carpet almost unhindered. For older girls who lack this awareness, some mothers use tights, finding the added wet acreage against the legs effective.

Once the child is aware of that damp feeling, the time has come to sit him regularly on the pot throughout the day. This should probably be done before going out to play, when coming in from play, and before and after a major meal. Some children will be enthusiastic and wish to oblige; others with a negative temperament will view it as a convenient excuse to exert some of their new-found power. Forcing these toddlers is totally unrewarding. If a child refuses to sit on the pot, the parent should show no irritation, but when he obliges, he should be accorded the usual praise and rewards.

If taken gently, bladder training causes no real problems. It is with bowel training that the struggle really begins.

BOWEL TRAINING

There are many different ways of bowel training a toddler. Most are effective as long as they are not started too early and not pushed too hard. There are three methods that you might consider:

1) the "grunt and catch" method;
2) the "broody hen" method; or
3) the "sit and wait" method.

The *grunt and catch method* is self explanatory. The parents do nothing until they hear a grunt, and see that strange look which appears at times like these on the toddler's face. This is accompanied by an ominous silence, an odd posture and finally a characteristic smell. At the first sign, the child should be rushed to the pot in anticipation of the big event. This may be easy in theory, but it often fails in practice. First, the parent needs all the speed of an Olympic sprinter to reach the toilet on time and the dexterity of Houdini to untangle the obstructing diaper. Then, if all goes smoothly and the child reaches the pot on time, there is a sporting chance that he will then announce he has changed his mind! It is not a bad method to try, but I suggest it be used only as a back-up to the more reliable sit and wait method.

The *broody hen method* is my term to describe one of the common, but perhaps slightly bizarre, training methods. When the child dirties his pants, he is immediately taken to the potty instead of being changed. Here, his offering is placed in the sacred chamber, and the child is made to sit above it like a hen incubating a new-laid egg. This is a form of conditioning, getting the child to associate bowel movements with the toilet. I know many parents who swear by this method, but I cannot really share their enthusiasm.

I favor the *sit and wait method*. It works well on toddlers, as well as those older children who have the unfortunate habit of continuing to dirty their pants. It is both simple and effective. The method is easy:

1) Start after 18 months at a time when both you and your child feel ready;
2) Sit the child three times a day, after meals;
3) Do not force him to sit there—use cunning;
4) While he is sitting, give him gentle reminders;
5) When eventually "it happens"—reward! reward!

Though 18 months is the earliest time you should start with this method, two years old is probably more realistic. When choosing the time, not only should the child be ready, but the parent should also feel strong enough to see it through. Like everything else, it is not going to work unless the parents are fully committed to its success and are prepared to persevere with the technique. It is foolish, for example, to start in the last few days before the arrival of a new baby, or at times when the household is in a state of tension or disorganization.

Sitting the child on the potty three times a day is ideal, but twice may be enough. It is best to sit him there after each meal, when the stomach is full. In young children, as already noted, toilet timing means that a full stomach stimulates the bowels to empty, this being the basis of toilet timing. At the age of two, the toilet-timing reaction is weakened, but it still has a little power and it is best to harness whatever help does exist.

Forcing a toddler to sit on the pot against his will is a sure recipe for failure. If he refuses, there must not be a fight; if he does sit properly, this action must be built up and encouraged with a positive reward. As for the length of sitting, that will depend on the child himself. Some active toddlers find it almost impossible to sit for two minutes; others are content to remain static for most of the day. The law of diminishing returns operates here, however, and if there has been no sign of action after four minutes, then it is unlikely that there is going to be any point in prolonging the agony.

If the child is sitting quietly, this is the time to engage in a little amateur psychology. Gentle hints should be dropped, such as "You're a big girl now, almost two. You will soon do big poos in the pot," or "Gosh, grandma is going to be pleased when you do a poo in the pot." Nothing must be said which suggests anxiety, impatience, or frustration on your part. The best way to ensure that a stubborn child will not go is trying to force him. The child has the upper hand and is very aware of his power. Even if two minutes after leaving the pot empty he dirties his pants, this must be dealt with coolly, saying nothing more than "Next time perhaps you will be able to do your poo in the potty. Daddy would be pleased."

If the child sits regularly, is relaxed and encouraged, not forced, eventually something has got to drop into the pot. That is the time for genuine praise. At this age the "soft rewards" of fuss and attention are best, grandma is contacted, and dad dragged to the phone at work to hear the earth-shattering news. This might seem a trifle excessive, but it works. I draw the line, however, at placing an advertisement in the personal column of the *Times* to announce the event to the world!

Once training is established, there shouldn't be a relapse except in times of diarrhea, sickness or major stress. By two-and-a-half years, most toddlers proudly take themselves to the toilet, pulling their pants up and down without help. At three-and-a-half, the first attempts will be made to wipe the bottom, although it will take a further year before the operation is at all reliable. At this point, toilet training can be declared complete.

TODDLER BED WETTING

Most doctors say that bed wetting (nocturnal enuresis) is so common in the toddler that it is a "non-problem." This may be scientifically quite sound, but it offers little comfort to parents who know that their child is still wetting the bed, whereas their friends' children were all dry by the time they were three.

The average age of attaining night-time dryness is about 33 months, but 10 per cent of five-year-olds still wet their bed regularly. After this age, about 15 per cent of them are cured of the habit each year, until it becomes relatively rare in the teenager. The parents of the five-year-old who wets his bed must be reassured that, although other parents are not openly declaring the fact, two other children in their child's class will also be regular bed-wetters.

Delay in bladder training at night seems to have an extremely strong genetic relationship. Some studies have shown almost 70 per cent of wetters to have a parent, brother, or sister with a similar problem. Bed wetting is also more common in boys; while I find that day-time wetting in the older child is almost completely confined to girls.

Some doctors get very worked up when they hear of a dry child who regresses to becoming a wetter again. They believe that this secondary enuresis is caused by infections or emotional trauma. Certainly infections can cause a relapse, but other unmistakable symptoms such as urgency or pain are usually very much in evidence. As for emotional trauma, it may well be a triggering factor, but in most of the children I see, I doubt whether even Sherlock Holmes could find the real trigger.

Treatment for bed wetting

The best time to start night training is when a few diapers have made it unannointed through the hours of darkness. Attempts can be made before this, but it tends to be a long, uphill battle.

It is unwise to remove the diaper and start training in the middle of cold weather. When a warm child lies in a warm bed, he sweats and loses fluid. When a cold child lies in a cold bed, there is little reason to sweat and the fluid chooses another route to escape. This leads to a full bladder, probably a wet bed, and cold parents, who have to tramp around the house in the middle of the night changing bedclothes. Once the diaper is removed, all that is needed is a good, waterproof undersheet, a sturdy washing machine, good clothes-drying weather, and lots of patience.

As pediatricians, we are taught that cutting down on fluids before bedtime does nothing to help bed-wetting. Many parents are, however, sure that over-drinking encourages wet beds and, unscientific as this may be, I must admit to secretly supporting this theory. Many parents find that if they get the toddler up and put him on the toilet late at night, just before they go to bed, this ensures a dry night. This is a good practice, as long as the child is not too distressed, and as long as it works.

When the toddler has a dry bed, that is the time for encouragement and praise. When the bed is wet, notice is made of it but no fuss, punishment, or implied blame. I remember asking one silly mother if she punished her child when he wet the bed. Her answer was, "No, I don't punish him. I just rub his nose in it."

At a certain age the child should come out of night diapers, whether wet or dry. I usually encourage removal at three-and-a-half, and suggest total abandonment before the fourth birthday. This, of course, depends on the child and the parents' ability to cope with the volume of wet sheets generated. There is now little more for the toddler to do than just wait for nature to take its course. Some doctors will prescribe special medication, which may have some benefits in the older toddler, but unfortunately its effect is often only temporary. If the child is still wetting after the age of five, a urine alarm system is worth considering. This electronic gadget rapidly helps over two-thirds of children.

POTTY OR TOILET?

One of the decisions that parents have to make is whether to use the toilet or a potty. There is no right answer to this; the method of using them is more important than the equipment itself.

Most parents start their child sitting on the potty, and most toddlers prefer this to the toilet. It has the great advantage of being portable, so it can be taken from room to room and even out in the car. There are, however, a number of independent little toddlers who are bored with being children and who wish to use the toilet like grown-ups. If this is the case, I offer the following suggestions.

Sitting perched high on the toilet with legs waving in mid-air is not the physiologically ideal posture for moving one's bowels. If the child is using a toilet, I recommend that a step is built at the front of the pedestal, which makes it easier for the child to climb up, while at the same time giving support for his legs when pushing down. A small child's toilet seat should be put inside the adult one. This will give the child more stability and dispel any fears of falling into the bowl.

In chain flush toilets, an extension rope should be attached to the dangling chain, allowing the child the reward of flushing the toilet after use and obviating the necessity of him having to climb up to reach it. One old hospital I used to work in had these vintage toilets in the children's wards, giving one adventurous toddler a most terrifying experience. After using one of the toilets, he climbed on to the seat, just managing to reach the dangling chain before losing his balance. The toilet started to flush, and still holding on tight, he hung terrified over the raging whirlpool below. Eventually, as his strength ebbed, he fell, becoming wet to the knees and having his toilet training delayed by at least six months! Toilets should never be flushed while the child is still sitting on them; it often causes fear and delays the training process.

THE RIGHT THING IN THE WRONG PLACE

Some children have good control of their bowels, but they insist on displaying the fact in various places around the house and garden. This can cause anxiety and anger in parents, many of whom believe that it is an early sign of deviant behavior. All that needs to be done is to quietly mention to the child that this is not welcome, and give great rewards when the right thing is done in the right place.

BOYS: SHOULD THEY SIT OR STAND?

Some little boys learn to wee while standing, before any other training has occurred. They enjoy this new-found skill, especially being able to control this jet of running water. This is a harmless enough occupation, just as long as there are no carpets in the bathroom. Occasionally, however, a child who has become firmly established in this pattern will resist sitting on the potty and bowel training will be delayed. This is only a temporary problem, which can be rectified by using one or other of the methods outlined in the next section.

THE CHILD WHO REFUSES TO SIT

I have seen children from two to twelve years old who refuse to sit on the toilet. This bad habit may be due to pure stubbornness, to being too busy to spare the time, to fear of toilets, or the pain of trying to move constipated bowels.

No child of any age should be forced, rather encouraged. With the very young, I get the parents to read to the child as he sits on the potty, initially with his diaper on. Once the sitting has become an established pattern, then the diaper can be removed. If he leaves his seat prematurely, there should be no fights, but the reading and the attention simply stop. Most young children respond very well to this simple technique.

For those who are frightened of being left on the toilet, it is best if the mother initially stays near by, gradually moving away until eventually the child learns to "fly solo."

Other children will establish a good sitting pattern if rewarded with praise and attention when they comply. In the older child (over four years), I use a star reward system which is very effective, or I negotiate a simple, no-fuss agreement such as, "You go and sit and I will have a milkshake waiting for you when you come out." Strong-arm tactics do not work on toddlers. There are much easier ways of getting things done. If the child has been constipated and possibly also has a small tear in the anal area, there may be great fear of using the toilet. Laxatives and fecal softening agents are useful, as well as a little lubricant cream for the tail end.

TODDLER URGENCY

When you are out shopping with a toddler, you learn very quickly that when he says "Wee wee, now," he means now—and not in five minutes. At this age, parents are forced to throw modesty to the wind, aiming the child towards the gutter or helping him water the flower arrangement outside the Town Hall. Car travel is also difficult, with frequent stops often being required, usually in places where it is impossible to pull over.

Urgency is normal in toddlers. Small patches of dampness appear, particularly when the child is excited or engrossed in play. Major accidents also happen for at least a year.

THE OBSESSION WITH REGULARITY

Parents' concern over what goes in the feeding end of their child is rivalled only by their obsession as to what comes out at the other. It is best to interfere as little as possible with toddlers' bowel patterns; there is a wide range of "normal," which nature usually takes care of quite adequately. A doctor once claimed that the normal toddler's bowel habit was between five times a day and once every five days. This may be rather an extreme view, but it is probably more sensible than many parents' over-concern.

The two common conditions that upset parents most are constipation and diarrhea. Some children are born with a "sluggish" bowel and always tend to be constipated. Others become constipated as a result of bad toilet habits, and others have problems that started following a feverish illness. Whatever the cause, parents need reassurance that the bowels do not need to open every day and that a bowel pattern as irregular as, say, once every three

days, does not cause headaches, bad breath, or lack of energy.
Constipation does, however, lead to a vicious circle in which the
more constipated the child becomes, the more difficult it is to have
a movement, and the more reluctant the child is. If this is associated with a small tear in the anal margin, the resultant pain may
cause a major problem of withholding.

Diarrhea can occur as a result of the slightest variation of diet
or even minor illness. There is also a strong relationship between
the extremely active child and an extremely active bowel. This
often results in the condition known as "toddler diarrhea." The
child has many movements a day, which are often very watery and
usually contain undigested peas, carrots, and other bits of fiber.
When the parents view this vegetation, they fear the child has
some major malabsorbtion syndrome and rush off to their doctor.
This is far from the truth. Toddler diarrhea in these active children is benign and temporary. Treatment for it is covered in Chapter 11.

CONCLUSION

You can't go far wrong, just as long as you don't start too early,
don't force the child, don't panic, and just take your time.

MYTHS ABOUT DIET

When you see animals feeding their young, it all seems such an uncomplicated affair, but, for some reason, humans find it extraordinarily difficult. Paradoxically, the more good food and the more expert advice that are available, the greater parents' anxiety over diet seems to become. All this is compounded by those who write books giving long lists of daily nutritional requirements and ideal foods. Academics and authors may thrive on this sort of "junk jotting," but most toddlers to not view the consumption of food with quite such a scientific eye.

Our society seems to have become obsessed with food intake and weight gain. Pediatricians listen patiently as worried mothers say, "He doesn't eat a thing, doctor," while there for all to see is a child displaying the physique of a miniature King Kong. In my practice, about 50 per cent of mothers complain that their children eat too little. Surprisingly, if they are asked "Is he energetic?" 100 per cent answer "Yes, he never stops!" In my view, health bears little relationship to food intake or fat deposit. Energy combined with that mischievous zest for life are the real signs of well-being. In a world in which 75 per cent of the population is short of food, we lucky parents should pull ourselves together and stop fussing.

WHAT SHOULD TODDLERS EAT?

Adults revel in variety and enjoy being presented with an extensive menu from which to choose. Toddlers are different. Often their tastes are quite monotonous, and they are totally unimpressed by having their food varied. Nutritionists impressively trumpet the benefits to the toddler of raw carrot, liver, spinach, and brains. I am well aware of the scientific rectitude of their utterances, but have you ever tried to get a toddler to eat brains?

Both adults and children require six different types of nutrients to survive: proteins, carbohydrates, fats, vitamins, minerals, and water. These may be given in the form of the ideal balanced diet, or equally well in the hit or miss hodge-podge of food and drink consumed by the average toddler. Look at monkeys in the wild, for example. If there is plenty of food about they will fill themselves full and then not eat for the rest of the day. If food is scarce, they will eat snacks all through the day, picking up whatever they can. They survive splendidly in this way, and so too will your own little monkeys!

Protein

Many parents complain to me that their children never eat a bite of meat. "What do they eat then?" I innocently ask. "Only things like chicken, hot dogs and hamburgers," comes the reply. Although chicken is white and comes from a bird, it is still meat, and although hot dogs are often filled with breadcrumbs and other additives, they still contain meat and make an excellent snack for the toddler. We really must dispel the myth that the only good source of protein is a thick, juicy slice of red, fibrous meat. In reality, most red meat contains more fat than body-building protein.

Protein also occurs in eggs, dairy products and other, less publicized sources, such as potatoes, bread, and many vegetables. If your children eat a minute amount of meat, eggs, or milk, and then fill up on bread and other protein sources, they will thrive, I can promise you.

Milk

How many of you can remember being told as a child to drink your milk because it was needed to produce "growing bones and strong teeth?" Certainly cow's milk is good for little cows. It is questionable, however, whether it is a necessity for little humans. If you want to be pedantic about it, the nearest thing to mother's milk is probably otter's milk, but it's in pretty short supply, mostly because it's no picnic trying to milk an otter! Seriously though, many parents worry too much that their child will not drink udders full of milk. To overcome this, they add highly sweetened flavorings, which only succeeds in nurturing a sweet tooth and probably leads to excessive dental bills and the loss of various molars. Milk does contain some worthwhile calcium and vitamins, but it is not necessary to obtain these benefits of nature from a bottle. Milk also comes in a hard yellow block known as cheese, in a plastic carton called yogurt, in puddles of yellow custard, in great cones of ice cream, or a vast array of different shaped loaves of bread. There is no need to force this liquid down children's throats! So important is this substance in the minds of many parents, that if their children are allergic to cow's milk, they go to great lengths to get a substitute liquid made from squashed and whitened soy beans. Silly, isn't it?

Vegetables

One of the great out-cries of parents is "eat your greens." Many parents are greatly upset when their children won't eat their vegetables. They generally fail to realize that their youngsters are usually eating plenty of them, even if the parents don't recognize them. There is a myth that vegetables must be of the green, leafy variety, as favored by Popeye, or orange-colored roots, as devoured by Bugs Bunny. Peas, beans, and potatoes are also vegetables, and most toddlers enjoy them more. What child doesn't like French fried potatoes, I ask you?

The principal benefit of vegetables is as a source of fibre, vitamins, and most other nutrients. And as long as you keep away from asparagus tips and truffles, they are a relatively cheap form of food. Although vegetables are rich in vitamins, much of this advantage is destroyed by over-cooking. One good alternative is to encourage children into the rabbit habit of nibbling raw vegetables. Unfortunately, most toddlers find this sort of food better for throwing than for eating!

Don't despair if your child refuses to eat his greens. Even if he eats no vegetables at all, not even peas, baked beans, or potatoes, this is not a great disaster. He can get all the fibre he needs out of cereals and all the vitamins out of fruit.

Fruits

Most children will eat fruit when it is available and, as I have already said, it is a useful source of fibre and vitamins, particularly when the child won't eat vegetables. Oranges, apples, and bananas make good, nourishing snacks that do much less harm to the teeth than many other foods. I tend to suspect parents who tell me that their children won't eat fruit. Usually what they mean is that their child dislikes stringy oranges and unripe apples. In my experience nearly all children enjoy attractively presented fruit, particularly bananas, pears, and soft fruits.

Breads, cereals, and sugars

Bread is not a bad food source, for as well as having ample carbohydrates, it is also full of protein and fibre. Nowadays some breads even have added milk, vitamins, protein, and fibre.

Breakfast cereals are also a good, but not an essential, food source. To read the side of the package one would believe that they contain absolutely every vitamin and trace element known to man, and this may indeed be true in some cases. but their nutrient value increases dramatically when the protein of milk is added.

Refined sugars, such as are found in cakes and sweets, are a good source of energy, but they have the disadvantage of easily leading to obesity, promoting tooth decay, and encouraging the child to develop a sweet tooth. They also contain little roughage and if overused will result in the child living on a low-fibre diet which, although it may provide ample calories, is not overly desirable.

Vitamins

Many books instruct parents on the exact dose of vitamins a child requires each day. This makes feeding extremely complicated if followed to the letter, and most sensible nutritionists agree that, as long as the child follows a half-way sensible diet, he will get all the vitamins he requires. The only vitamin-deficient children I have seen in the past three years have been those subjected by their parents to some extremely restrictive "fad" diet.

Lack of vitamin C will not occur in children who eat a little fruit or vegetables, or drink fruit juices or fortified fruit drinks. Vitamin D usually comes from eggs or butter, or is manufactured in the body with the aid of sunlight. The vitamin B group is found mostly in bread and vegetables, and vitamin A occurs in butter and green vegetables.

Minerals

All children, adults, and animals need many minerals and trace elements, although most of them are required in such small amounts that any half-reasonable diet will provide adequate supplies. Iron and calcium are the two minerals we think of most. Iron is found in meat, bread, and cereals, and calcium comes from dairy products, although there are many less well-publicized sources, such as the humble baked bean and some tasty green vegetables.

WHAT MAKES A FAT KID FAT?

Children, like adults, become fat when they have a genetic tendency to lay down fat and then take in quantities of food greater than their body's needs. For years, the experts have debated whether it is the over-eating or the heredity factor that predominates. Despite years of discussion, no one is any clearer about the answer.

Over-eating

Certainly the amount you eat has a significant bearing on weight gain. Overweight toddlers often have overweight parents as well, but whether this is hereditary or simply the parent inflicting the same over-eating habit on the child is unclear. A great many parents set a very bad example to their children with the type and quantity of food they consume. Others spoil their children with food, sometimes giving it as a poor substitute for proper love and attention. Some parents seem to take a delight in fattening up their offspring, like a cattle farmer preparing beasts for market. It is almost as if these parents are saying "look how affluent we are, my child is obviously well fed." To parents, fat may be beautiful, but when the competitive teenage years arrive, few children give thanks for obesity, and by that time it is often difficult to do anything about it.

Heredity

No one can become fat without eating, but there is no doubt that all children and adults react differently to identical food intakes. Some can eat unlimited quantities of Black Forest cake without gaining an inch, while others only have to sniff a container of cream to instantly put on pounds.

The statistics relating overweight children to overweight parents are interesting. If neither parent is overweight, there is only a 10 per cent chance that the child will have a weight problem. If one parent is overweight, this increases the child's risk to 40 per cent. If both parents are overweight, the child's risk increases to 70 per cent. This would appear to give all the evidence we need to show that the child's weight is predestined by heredity. One humorous piece of research, however, has rather shattered this view. One group of researchers successfully showed that fat parents had fatter children. Meanwhile, another group came up with the added discovery that they also tended to have fat pets![8] This threw a monkey wrench into the works of the heredity lobby, and once again we are left in some confusion. In reality, both diet and heredity are important factors and still no one is quite sure which plays the stronger role.

Do glands cause obesity?

Many children are referred to endocrine clinics of big hospitals by parents who are convinced that their child is overweight because of a glandular problem. There is a widely held view that obesity is caused by a glandular problem. This is true, but only to the extent that obesity is related to the salivary gland, with the child's mouth watering whenever he sees food! Other than this, a connection between glands and overweight in children is extremely rare.

Puppy fat

At the end of their first year, babies have a very different shape from that at the end of their second year. Before children start walking, they usually have rolls of fat on their thighs, arms, and abdomen, with few muscles visible. Once they start to exercise, the puppy fat generally disappears and the more grown-up muscular body proportions appear.

Many parents become concerned at about this time, being unaware of the different weight gain rates of different ages. The baby in his first year of life gains weight at a remarkably rapid rate, but this reduces markedly after the first birthday, often becoming stationary or even dropping down for a period. At the same time as this fat starts "burning off," many children become fussy, negative eaters, which causes even more weight to be lost.

Over the past decade, numerous articles have been written expressing concern that fat babies become fat toddlers, who in turn become fat children and finally fat adults. The most recent work, however, shows that there is minimal connection between fat babies and fat adults. After the age of one year, there is an ever stronger relationship between the aging child's weight and his adult build. For the fat teenager, it is far easier to put weight on than to take it off, which can be the start of a weight problem that will dog them all of their adult lives.

QUESTIONS COMMONLY ASKED ABOUT FEEDING

How many meals a day?

Did you ever stop to wonder why we, as adult humans, insist on three main meals a day, while some large snakes eat only once every two months, lions may eat only twice a week, and cows and sheep just "snack" most of their waking hours? In our case much of it seems to be habit. We have been so brain-washed since birth that we insist on three meals a day whether we are hungry or not. For example, did you have breakfast this morning because you were actually hungry or because it seemed to be the right thing to do?

And why do we feed babies five times a day, when many of them would be happier if allowed to snack much of the time? I am told that this is the result mainly of research done by a scientist at the beginning of the century, who did some laboratory experiments and worked out the amount of food the average baby took in a day. He then measured the volume of a dead baby's stomach and by simple arithmetic he came up with the magic number "five." Right or wrong, we are still stuck with this idea more than eighty years later. Nature shows us, however, that this scientific rigidity is nonsense. A happy, healthy baby may wish to feed anywhere from three to ten times each day and should be allowed to do so.

Toddlers do not have adult hangups about feeding. As they are impulsive, they will demand food whenever they feel hungry, and as they are also stubborn, they will sometimes exhibit more sense than their parents by refusing food when they are not hungry. Rigidly fixed meal times are more appropriate for restaurateurs than the parents of toddlers.

But I suppose we have to accept that in the end toddlers will grow up and be subjected to the illogical three-meals-a-day habit, so it is probably best to condition them along this course as early as they will accept. I must emphasize that there is no nutritional basis for this habit; it is purely social custom. Three meals a day, multiple healthy snacks, or one good meal a day—they are probably all of equal good to a child.

What is enough food intake?

Children have different food requirements. They eat like birds: some like sparrows, others like vultures. There is no correct amount of food for all children to consume in a day. Food intake and weight gain are not the only indicators of good health; far more important in the thriving toddler are a good supply of boundless energy, happiness, and a devilish zest for life. If my car used only half the manufacturer's recommended amount of gasoline to cover a given number of miles, I would not complain. I would be grateful that I had an efficient machine that was obviously tuned to perfection. Forcing toddlers to feed is futile. We need more sense and less food.

THE VARIED TODDLER DIET—A DREAM

Books tell us that it is important to give toddlers a good varied diet, so that they get a taste for all food and eat well in later life. This theory is not unlike the fable of the mice and the cat. The clever mice decided to put a bell around the cat's neck so that they would be warned of his approach. The idea was indeed a sound one, but the implementation was far from easy. So it is with giving toddlers a varied diet.

Some years ago I was working at a hospital when a new dietitian was appointed to the staff. She was full of missionary zeal and believed that the children were being mistreated by not having enough variety in their diet. True it was that for years every meal had consisted of either hotdogs or hamburger, or hamburger and hotdogs. Except for Christmas day, when they had hotdogs and turkey! Anyway, she designed a revolutionary new menu, which she thought was varied, interesting and balanced. And so it was, as the garbage men discovered when they came to empty the trash cans. The children were unimpressed.

We should aim for variety in order to accustom the child to the future. But if this does not work, it is pointless fighting about it. It is better to introduce small amounts of new foods from time to time until a varied interest is achieved.

Another common area of confusion is toddler taste as opposed to adult taste. When spooning baby food into a baby, many adults complain about the lack of taste, and some even add salt or sugar. Both are unnecessary and undesirable. Likewise, parents who themselves dislike liver, brains or other offal will never give these to their child. In fact the toddler may be quite happy with these foods, but parental tastes prevent them from being tried. Let's face it, adults have some pretty odd tastes of our own, such as oysters, anchovies, and chili sauce; toddlers have a right to their own tastes.

JUNK FOOD IS NOT ALL JUNK

By junk food we usually mean foods that contain too much fat, sugar, salt, and unnecessary calories. Soft drinks, sweets, chocolate cookies, potato chips, and all those seductively crinkly bags of commercial "nibblies" are the main culprits, although you could also add to these so-called "fast foods."

The problem with sweet foods and soft drinks is that they produce soft teeth and fat, soft tummies. With products like potato chips, there is some concern over the excess fat and high salt content in them, which is definitely frowned upon these days, as many doctors believe that too much salt in the diet can lead to high blood pressure in later life.

"Fast foods" are probably not quite as bad as most people make out, however. Although "long-time-no-sea" fish in batter may not improve your brain power in the way that P. G. Wodehouse's estimable butler, Jeeves, would have us believe, it is still a fairly good source of protein. A hamburger and chips washed down with a glass of milk constitute a reasonable meal. It can be devalued, however, by adding 10 per cent sugar solution cola drinks or heavily sweetened milkshakes, which tend to throw the balance toward the side of excess refined carbohydrates.

There is no doubt that, if they are introduced as a regular part of a child's diet, potato chips, chocolates, and very sweet foods are undesirable. On the other hand, the long-term intake of fast foods is probably no great evil, if the child can cope with the monotonous lack of taste.

HEALTH FOODS MAY NOT BE ALL THAT HEALTHY

The present craze for health foods is fascinating. Much of what is now called healthy food is the same old basic material mixed with undesirable substances of the natural variety rather than undesirable substances of the refined variety. For some reason, you are meant to believe that the addition of glucose, raw sugar, or honey instead of refined sugar immediately endows the food with some magical, health-giving property. Glucose is just another type of sugar in a slightly more digestible form than those sugars we deem unhealthy. The so-called "health drinks" with glucose, often recommended for invalid children for example, give an immense sugar load to the body. Dentists loathe these substances, which have few benefits in reality but have a great capacity for causing weight gain and cavities. They are much worse than that much-scorned product, lemonade.

Aesthetically, honey may be a preferable form of sweetener, as it is natural and tastes pleasant. But honey is only a blend of sugars that have been refined by their passage through the intricate insides of a bee. This apparently is more acceptable than sweetness that has passed through the intricate insides of a sugar refinery. Honey, like glucose, may be marginally preferable to refined cane sugar, but it is still a cause of children developing a sweet tooth, obesity, and cavities.

Some health-promoting syrups are also advertised as being high in vitamin C and they usually come in a blackcurrant or rosehip form. Although undoubtedly a pleasant way of taking vitamin C, the syrups are many times more expensive than the mass-produced tablet available at little cost from your friendly neighborhood pharmacy. My main dislike of these syrups is their immensely high sugar content when given in large quantities, which can greatly upset the balance of the diet and is a disaster to teeth. Even the varieties that boast no added sugar are not without some effect; one of the more commonly used artificial sweeteners produces a most colorful pink diarrhea in some children.

Powdered bran is good for health enthusiasts and horses to eat. Toddlers, however, dislike its sawdust quality and will only take bran in the form of fibre-enriched breads and breakfast cereals. If children will eat these products, then they should be greatly encouraged to do so.

Apples, bananas, oranges, and raw carrots are just a few of the good health snacks available, and they are much kinder to developing teeth than most other foodstuffs. But beware! Parents who send their children to school with a lunch box full of raisins, nuts, dates, and carrot slices may not be as clever as they think. Nibbling raw carrots is certainly to be highly commended and nuts are a good health food, but peanuts and toddlers are generally a bad combination. Hospitals spend many hours each year removing inhaled nuts from little children who have sent them down the wrong tube! Raisins and dates are most enjoyable, but they are sweet and stick to the teeth and may cause the same tooth problems as chocolates and other candies.

An enormous industry exists out there producing health drinks, health bars, and healthy breakfast cereals. These products, however, bear some investigation. Certainly, added roughage is to be encouraged, but if the product is then smothered in honey, glucose, or some other high-carbohydrate food, then much of the original benefit is lost. Some cereals are advertised as containing no added sugar. These are only of some benefit if the child is going to continue on a low sugar diet right through the day. For example, it is pointless to have a bowl of cereal with no sugar on it and then immediately follow it with a highly sweetened milkshake. Health drinks that contain all natural ingredients may, in fact, contain many of the substances I've just mentioned. Milk is a true natural food and it should not be loaded up with additives, but taken in its natural form for best effect.

Perhaps I am a trifle cynical, and I may have overstated my case in regard to health foods, but I truly believe that the myth has to be exploded once and for all that all natural substances must be healthy. You can rot your teeth, become fat, and poison your system just as well with natural substances as with factory-produced ones. Tobacco and opium are also natural substances . . . I rest my case.

DIET AND GROWTH

Growth in terms of height depends on genes, health, happiness, and diet. Of these, genes are probably the major height-determining factor, although an exceptionally good diet versus an adequate one may have some minor effect on height. Chronic severe illness can stunt growth and so can emotional deprivation.

When I was a child my mother insisted that I eat up my meat, go to bed early, take lots of exercise, and then I would grow up to be "big and strong." Recent research has surprised us all by almost proving these folk tales correct.

The main substance that controls the body's growth is a hormone produced in the pituitary gland, not surprisingly called the "growth hormone." When very short children are brought to the hospital they are investigated for lack of this substance. Although we can take blood samples and find the level of the hormone, the amount present throughout the day varies greatly in normal children, making it hard to get an accurate reading. For years pediatricians have tried to find ways of stimulating the pituitary gland to release this hormone, so that blood samples can be taken that would enable one to gauge the gland's ability to release this valuable substance. This may all seem rather scientific, until you look at the various things that we now know encourage the release of the hormone. It is now known for example that most of the hormone is released during the night when the child is asleep. It is also released in large quantities during strenuous exercise, a reason why you may see small children rushing up and down hospital staircases prior to having blood samples taken! Even more curious was the discovery that certain beef extracts caused a surge of the growth hormone to be released. So it appears our grannies were right. Unfortunately, although the stored hormone is released on demand, the amount produced in a day remains the same, as does the growth rate.

SPECIAL DIETS

Over the last 2000 years doctors have tried to relate health and behavior to foods in the diet. Although you might think this is sufficient time to have gathered the evidence, I have to report that conclusive data are still not yet available. Certainly there are some specific conditions in which food causes ill health, for example the allergy to wheat found in celiac disease, but there is also a great deal of confusion between fact and theory in this matter.

Some children and adults have true allergies to certain foods. A child may eat eggs, seafood, or oranges and then have an attack of itching and swollen eyes or diarrhea. There is little doubt as to the offending substance, as the symptoms appear each time it is introduced.

There are, however, claims that milk, wheat, corn, malt, and yeast are responsible for many conditions, ranging from asthma through runny noses to dyslexia, sleep problems, and clumsiness. It is also claimed that artificial colorings, preservatives, and some natural foodstuffs have a major effect on concentration and behavior. Judging from figures released each year from the asthma clinic in my hospital, it is extremely rare for milk allergy to precipitate or worsen asthma; for most, therefore, this must be regarded as a myth. Our experts also dispute the claim that milk causes runny noses. Folklore has it that milk causes the human body to produce mucus, but scientific evidence to support this is scant.

Much of my work is with handicapped children, an area in which constant claims are made that diet improves intelligence and behavior. I recently saw a mildly retarded boy whose parents had been assured that if he ate one kelp (seaweed) tablet a day his

intelligence would rise to normal within six weeks. This would
have been harmless enough, except that each tablet was about the
size of a pigeon's egg and tasted like something found in a sewage
farm. Not surprisingly, the child remained mildly retarded.

Other parents have been told that a vitamin B preparation
would cure dyslexia, but while this preparation is of enormous
benefit in the cure of pellagra, beri beri and premenstrual tension,
it has no beneficial effect whatsoever on reading difficulties. I have
been told that zinc cures autism, and that the removal from the
diet of wheat, corn, malt, and yeast cures everything from clumsiness to hyperactivity. These are all myths.

Parents are bombarded by the claims of special diets, but it is
wise to remember that real medical breakthroughs don't take 2000
years to gain acceptance. From the first dose of penicillin administered, there was never any doubt of its amazing effect. Kelp tablets, artificial colorings, and milk, despite all manner of
extravagant claims, are simply not in the same league. (See diet
and hyperactivity in Chapter 14.)

DIET AND BOWELS

There is as much variation in the bowel habits of toddlers as there
is in the bowel habits of his parents. Some children seem to be
born with normal bowel regularity; others have lazy bowels, and
some are definitely over-active. We are stuck with the equipment
we have been allocated, and it can only be regulated by introducing
certain dietary changes.

Fibre is definitely an "in" substance these days. It is said to
exert a "normalizing" effect on the bowels, speeding up the sluggish and calming the hyperactive. When a child tends towards constipation, more dietary fibre is encouraged. This roughage can be
increased with selected palatable breakfast cereals, vegetables, and
more fibrous breads and biscuits. Even the baked bean is an excellent form of fibre, having exerted a regularizing effect on an entire
generation of cowboys who won the west!

The term toddler diarrhea has already been mentioned. In this
condition, a healthy child tends to have a very active bowel. Parents worry over the apparent diarrhea, and as the children are also
generally very physically active they put on little weight, which
further concerns the parents. Gastroenterologists treat this problem by restricting the fluid intake to mealtimes and increasing the
fibre and roughage the child eats. Sugars in the diet are reduced,
fewer snacks are given, and the child is steered towards the adult
pattern of three meals a day. Toddler diarrhea is a temporary con-

dition; these suggestions just keep it under some form of control until it is cured by time.

TONICS TO STIMULATE APPETITE

In Ireland, I trained in a hospital that was particularly solicitous of the happiness and well-being of its elderly patients. Each night a well-known black, alcoholic Dublin beverage was handed out to help wash down the hospital food. Some believed this helped to stimulate the old peoples' appetites; others were more realistic in thinking that it merely stimulated their feeling of well-being! I am often asked for a tonic to stimulate a child's appetite. It would create quite a stir if I were to prescribe the black Dublin "medicine," but it would be just as ineffective as any other proprietary brand tonic. There is no such thing as an appetite-stimulating tonic for children.

VITAMINS AND IRON

Children who are on any sort of a halfway decent diet don't require any extra vitamins or iron. Though many parents swear by the beneficial effects of their favorite multi-vitamin preparations, there is really no scientific evidence to back up their claims. I recently read a review article in which the author said he had gathered together all the papers ever published on the beneficial effects of vitamin C in preventing the common cold. For every paper that claimed it was effective, there was another that presented proof to the contrary.

Occasionally I prescribe a vitamin preparation when I am confronted by an overworried mother who is sure her child is malnourished, sickly, and in need of such things. As I write the prescription I am aware that the preparation will do the child absolutely no good whatsoever, but will have a remarkable sedating effect on the over-anxious mother.

DIET AND TEETH

Our advanced, well-nourished society now boasts 50 per cent of all four-year-olds who have some tooth decay. Flouride added to the drinking water has certainly helped the situation, but modern diet continues to cause great problems. We have already discussed the tooth-decaying properties of junk foods, sweet foods, and sugary drinks. The child who is a late bottle feeder is at particular risk, as his mouth is being constantly irrigated by a sweet, sugary solution.

Many of these children, who lie in bed taking sips of sugary cordials, lose their front upper teeth with decay before their third birthday. In the interests of strong teeth, this practice must be discouraged, and more savory snacks should be introduced, such as cheese, raw vegetables and fruit.

It may seem pointless to try to preserve baby teeth, which are going to be claimed by the tooth fairy before long anyway, but there are two definite benefits. First, the baby teeth mark the spaces for the second teeth to occupy, making the final tooth positions more reliable. Second, if good dental care is not instituted before the permanent teeth arrive, it is unlikely to happen overnight, and the permanent teeth will suffer the same fate as their predecessors.

CONCLUSION

We are told that we must aim for regular, disciplined mealtimes and good feeding habits in our children. We must also aim for a good, healthy, natural, mixed diet. All this is far easier to aim for than to accomplish. Many myths surround the feeding of children, right from a sometimes evangelistic obsession with breast-feeding, through the man-made intricacies of weaning, to health foods and the school child's diet.

If you are feeling overwhelmed by all this—relax! Sensible parents do not malnourish their children, and although toddlers may be willful, no child has ever starved to death through stubbornness. There are many ways of getting good nourishment into a toddler, some more related to the laws of nature than the theories of the dietary experts. We all overeat. We can all afford to eat a little less. A toddler will eat when he's hungry and will let you know it soon enough. Next time he shuns his third meal of the day, remember that it is only tradition that demands he should eat it, not necessity.

12

FEEDING WITHOUT FIGHTS

Parents use up an enormous amount of energy forcing stubborn, but otherwise well-nourished, toddlers to eat against their will. All these parental antics are a great source of mirth to the child but, when the final score is taken at the end of the meal, not an extra pea has been eaten. Playing airplanes, dive bombers, singing, dancing, crawling round the floor barking, and threatening that they won't grow up "big and strong like daddy" are a complete waste of time. Just as adults don't eat bigger meals while being entertained at a dinner-theater, toddlers' consumption won't be improved by all this entertainment, either. What they really need is gentle encouragement.

Some children take their food extremely seriously, never lifting
their eyes from the plate until they have almost scraped the pattern
from it. Others dawdle, play, and escape at the first opportunity,
finding food a complete bore. Some children are thin; some are fat.
Some are fussy and some are walking garbage bins. Whatever the
personality of the child, trying to force food down is a monumental
waste of time and energy.

NORMAL FEEDING PATTERNS

Most babies in their first year are in no doubt what to do with
food. They don't mess about, generally getting the food to where it
belongs with a minimum of fuss. Babies start on milk, either by
breast or bottle, and at a certain age they progress to more solid
foods. This is called "weaning." As the decades go by, the "right"
age for weaning babies onto solids changes with monotonous regularity. At the time of writing, four months old appears to be the
"approved" age.

The words "wean" and "solids" perhaps need some clarification.
Weaning means to accustom the child to a different diet by the
gentle and gradual introduction of new foods. It does not mean an
authoritarian and rigid regime to be adhered to at all costs. What
we should try to do is accustom the child to small amounts of
various foods and let him guide us thereafter.

The word "solids" is also incorrect. What we really mean is the
slush we serve up to young children. At four months of age the
child has not fully sorted out the difference between sucking and
chewing, which results in the reappearance of one out of every two
spoonfuls of food put in the mouth. By six months, the food goes
down with relative ease, and the chewing pattern becomes well
established. At this stage, the first teeth usually appear, tiny, orna-
mental pearls that do little damage to the food as it hurries past.

By one year, the teeth are used more for chewing, and the child
eats a diet similar to that of the rest of the family. Many children
at this age undergo a dramatic change of attitude to food, halving
their intake and becoming extremely fussy. At this time, too, the
child's weight gain may slow up, stop, or even go down, while
activity burns up the puppy fat and stubbornness restricts food
intake. From this age onwards the negative streak is always just
around the corner, so in most children forcing them to eat becomes
unproductive.

At 15 months, independent children are keen on holding a
spoon, although few can keep it level between plate and mouth—
the contents usually fly in all directions as the arm tries to negotiate the bends. Children will also hold a feeding cup and, after 18

months, most children will suck rather than chew the end of a straw.

At three years old a knife can be used to cut soft foods and attempts to butter their own bread will follow soon after. By four-and-a-half the child should be able to use a knife and fork in a sort of way, and it is at this age that Chinese children generally learn to use chopsticks.

FEED—DON'T FIGHT

Sensible mealtimes

Toddlers have minds and tastes of their own. The dining table must never become a battleground. To ensure this, I present my 8-Point Master Plan for problem-free meals;

1) Avoid disorganized, disturbed, noisy meals. The toddler should sit and eat with the rest of the family, but if this is impractical, then a parent should sit next to the child and feed him before the main family meal;

2) Although the toddler should ideally be given a variety of well-balanced foods, if he dislikes variety, as many toddlers do, then a repetitive but nutritious diet is perfectly acceptable. After all he's the one who has to eat it, not you;

3) Adult eating habits should be encouraged, but it is no disaster if a child decides to return to the main course after having polished off his pudding;

4) *Cordon bleu* cooking and toddlers don't mix. Use labor-saving cooking ideas, because it is hard to stay calm when the willful toddler refuses a dish that has taken hours to prepare;

5) Gently encourage the child to eat, but don't use bribes or force;

6) Once it is obvious that the child is not going to eat any more, wipe his hands and face clean and allow him to get down from the table. Whether this be after five minutes or half an hour, don't worry about it. If the child is dawdling over his food, leave him to dawdle without an audience after a reasonable time has elapsed;

7) Display no anger if food is not eaten, but put the untouched plate in the fridge and bring it out later.

8) It is the child's right to eat or not eat his food as he pleases. Parents have a perfect right to fight with their child if that is what they want, but they should have the sense to avoid battles over food. If a child refuses the meal, he must not be allowed to immediately fill up on milk, cookies, and the like.

Make food fun

When serving fine food to adults, a chef prides himself not only on the taste, but also on the presentation. The same should apply when feeding toddlers. For a start, portions should not be massive. Various garnishings should be used, such as a square of cheese, some raisins, and a few fingers of fruit. Vary texture and color wherever possible and make food look appealing. For example, bread can be cut into fun triangles, home-made cookies can be baked in animal shapes, and even hotdogs and potatoes can be shaped on the plate to look like cannons from the Napoleonic wars! There is no end to the way food can be made interesting, and you should allow your imagination free rein when preparing it.

If feeding problems continue once you have made the food itself more interesting, then try varying the venue. Wonders can be achieved by transporting stubborn feeders to the balcony or the garden, where they can drink milk through a straw and eat little sandwiches out of a lunch box. Some foods popular with young children have been greatly wronged in parents' eyes, although they are in fact quite nutritious. For example, toast or bread with baked beans and a glass of milk provide just about all the ingredients any child needs.

I think we have to rid ourselves of some of our rigid, old-fashioned ideas about feeding toddlers. Within reason, try to give them what they want, where they want it, and when they are hungry. They are going to have to learn adult meal times sooner or later, but to begin with, it is more important to get them enjoying the process of eating.

Nibbling can be nutritious

All toddlers nibble between meals. For some children, this can supplement a full, normal diet, whereas it is often the main source of nourishment for others. Snacks seem to be good for many toddlers, sometimes miraculously transforming tired, badly-behaved children into much more likable little characters. Rather than worrying about children eating between meals, we should be ensuring that what they eat is less refined and more nourishing.

Sandwiches that contain sensible fillings can be at the same time nourishing and kind to the teeth. On the other hand, very sweet drinks and flavored milk need to be restricted. Finger foods make ideal snacks as they can be eaten on the run by the busy toddler. Cubes of cheese, slices of fruit, wedges of salami-like meat, slices of precooked vegetable and crackers all make good eating.

We might as well face the fact that between-meal snacks are here to stay, so they should be treated as seriously as the main meals they often replace. Properly orchestrated, this "alternative" diet can enhance children's health and prevent them from stuffing their faces full of junk food.

Labor-saving food preparation

I'm sure that at some time or other in your life you've slaved over a hot stove for hours preparing a delicacy for your dream child, only to find he takes one look at it and turns his nose up in disgust. Times like these tempt you to child abuse! Rather than taking this drastic course of action, may I recommend a bit of labor-saving cooking instead.

A blender or food processor and a freezing tray are all that the parents of babies need for food preparation. In one morning you can cook carrots, cauliflower, pumpkin, steak, chicken, fish and apples, pop them in the blender (one at a time I hasten to add!), and then put them into individual ice-cube trays for freezing. When mealtime comes, all you have to do is look in the freezer and decide on the menu, defrost it, and there you have a small portion of an instant, but fresh-made meal. This idea can be carried through to toddlerhood as well, using slightly larger containers and of course non-liquidized food. Food can be prepared as quickly as it takes an ice-cube to melt and, when refused, can be returned to the refrigerator as quick as you can say "See if I care!"

Feeding the militantly independent child

From their first birthday, some children are hell-bent on feeding themselves without any outside assistance. Unfortunately the most independent children are usually the most impatient, which is a sure recipe for trouble. These children should be given a spoon large enough to allow them to load the food with some accuracy. To cope with the spillage on the long journey from plate to mouth, a 'pelican' bib, one of those strong plastic bibs with a large catchall area at the bottom, is recommended. As the drop-out food is caught in the bib, it can be quickly recycled, cutting down on mess and waste.

To further help the impatient and hungry child determined to have a go at feeding himself, it is best to give him one spoon while feeding him with another. Finger foods are another good means of keeping little hands occupied.

The toddler who's hooked on bottles and baby food

If after eight months of age the child's diet is still milk and bland, untextured baby foods, it may be extremely difficult to change him over to a proper mixed diet. Prevention is obviously better than cure, so parents must be encouraged to provide a variety of textured solids after six months, avoiding milk as the sole source of nourishment.

For those who are hooked on milk and refuse solids, it is hard to give effective help without cutting down dramatically on the milk intake. Some people are extremely tough on these toddlers and exclude all milk immediately, substituting less calorific fluids until the child gives in and starts taking a reasonable diet. I prefer a gentler approach, which in the end achieves exactly the same results. The milk intake should be reduced by about half, and other fluids and a variety of interesting nibbly things introduced. This is usually all that is required, but if it does not work immediately then the milk can be further reduced. Like all such procedures, the parent must not weaken mid-way.

Firmness is also needed with toddlers who have remained on

slushy baby-foods for too long. These children often refuse to chew and the slightest lump causes them to gag. Amazingly, however, they seem to exert some hidden strength when a piece of chocolate is popped into their mouths! Once again, prevention is better than cure, as these children will often put up quite a fight before you can get them onto a normal diet. To cure these children, I start by halving the milk intake so that it cannot be used as a substitute food. Then I gradually start "polluting" baby food with home-made blended products, and as the days go by, I make the food more and more home-made. Gradually a normal diet is achieved in a matter of weeks.

CONCLUSION

Most toddlers whose parents claim that they never eat are in fact getting a very adequate food intake. Before jumping to conclusions, parents should try writing down every food that enters the child's mouth during the course of a day and analyzing it. There will be the bottle of milk, the bag of potato chips, the half hamburger, the handful of raisins, the chocolate cookie, the cheese stick and all the other bizarre bits and pieces the toddler can lay his hands on. When the list is complete you will usually find that the child has in fact received the correct number of "goodies," although possibly not in their ideal form.

If children wish to eat three good meals a day, that is highly commendable—and very convenient for everyone else. But for those who don't, it is usually better to channel your energies into providing nourishing snacks throughout the day rather than fighting. Time and peer-group pressures will sooner or later force the toddler into more traditional mealtime habits; in the meantime be flexible and use your imagination. Remember, food can be fun!

13

FEARS, COMFORTERS
AND SECURITY

All small animals know fear and small children are no exception.
Some of these fears may seem quite "off the beam" to parents, and
some children's comfort habits may seem distinctly strange. Parents are never quite sure what is acceptable for well-adjusted offspring. In fact, it would appear that just about anything seems
possible at an early developmental stage. In this chapter we look at
some of these fears, as well as security and various methods of
comfort.

DIFFERENT FEARS FOR
DIFFERENT YEARS

All young children have one overwhelming fear in common: the fear of being separated from their parents. Other fears come and go and are either of the child's own making or instilled in him by transference of anxiety from the parent. Whether we like it or not, fear has always been a major part of life, both for adults and children, and nothing I can say is going to make it go away.

Children have very fertile imaginations that are capable of generating great uneasiness as a result of hearing stories or watching television. The result is that they conjure up visions of ghosts, long-legged beasties, and things that go bump in the night. It's all part of growing up. At birth, babies are relatively immune to the fears that beset the rest of us. This is probably a mercy, when you think what the inside of a modern neonatal nursery looks like, with all that space-age gadgetry attached to the poor little, underweight scraps. The only things that startle the newborn are sudden movement and noise. Forty babies will leap in unison when a clumsy nurse drops a tray on the nursery floor. From birth to six months there is little progress in this department, until somewhere around the eighth month the baby suddenly becomes inseparably attached to his main caretaker, usually his mother. After this, any attempts to separate him from mom will precipitate distress and floods of tears.

At one year this separation is still a major problem, and the child will also often react badly to loud noises, such as doorbells, vacuum cleaners, or food mixers. As the decibels rise, he will cuddle in tighter to his mother for protection. Strange people, strange objects, and sudden movements can also upset him. At the age of two the fear of separation still exists, but it becomes slightly less intense and more predictable than in the one-year-old. Loud bangs will cause upset, as will the unexpected screech of brakes, ambulance sirens, or the violent barking of dogs.

Between two and four years that obsessively tight attachment to mom weakens further and a whole new package of fears starts to emerge; animals and the dark featuring prominently in this array. The fear of animals hits its peak around the age of three; fear of the dark usually peaks nearer the fifth birthday.

Between four and six years the child develops a highly vivid imagination, with fear of the dark constantly worsened by regular visits from ghosts, bogeymen, monsters and travellers from outer space. After the age of six some children are said to worry about being injured, or they may even start to fear death, although they still do not have the adult picture of either of these possibilities.

By the age of 10, the child has been lumbered with most of the burden of adult fears, which he will carry for the rest of his life. These are compounded during adolescence with the major fear of not "making it" as a fully accepted member of the peer group.

Management of fears

However foolish a child's fears may seem to an adult, they are very real to the child, and they must not be put down or ridiculed. Talking openly about anxieties helps to keep in clear perspective the division between fact and fantasy. The best way to treat childhood fears is by good parental example, lots of support and comfort, and then gradual desensitization. There is usually no reason to get too worried, as most fears at this age are temporary problems that evaporate with the passage of time. Looking back one year later, it is hard to think what all the fuss was about.

Some specific fears

DOGS

It is common for the under-fours to fear animals, especially dogs. Of course, we don't want to encourage the toddler to poke

passing Alsatians or pat every surly mongrel in the street, but
those who fear dogs are usually quite unselective, being terrorized
by even the most benign ball of fluff.

Most commonly the child who fears dogs will sight the offending
beast, stiffen, then hold on tight to his mother and start to bawl.
Rest assured if your child reacts this way that it is a normal developmental stage for many children and, even if you do nothing, it
will pass in a short time. One way of helping overcome the fear,
however, is to talk quietly to the child about "nice dogs" and introduce him to some of the gentler of the species.

A very few children have such great fear of dogs that they
hardly dare go outdoors in case one appears round a corner. Once
again, you should gradually introduce the child to dogs, possibly
starting with a small, newborn puppy or a securely caged dog in a
petshop window. Some therapists I know introduce stuffed dogs
into their treatment, but I feel that once you go to those lengths
you're only a hair's breadth away from turning serious therapy into
a sketch worthy of Monty Python.

Whatever else you do, be confident, talk openly about the animals, and try to get a toe in the door with some distant dog contact, from there building to full desensitization and cure.

BATHS

Most babies like water and enjoy splashing in their baths. But
for unknown reasons, after their first year, some take a strong
dislike to this and the very word "bath" or the noise of a running
faucet will set them to arching their backs, crying, and complaining bitterly. Once again you must use the technique of gradual
desensitization and reintroduction to the bath.

A good start for the toddler who absolutely refuses to bathe is to
stand him in an empty basin in front of the fire and sponge him
with warm water. After a time of this, some water may be put in
the basin and, when he is rather braver, he can be sponged in a
bath with a maximum depth of water of one inch at the deep end.
From here he will sit down, and you can start increasing the water
level until you have a child who takes a bath in the right place, at
the right time, and with the right attitude.

To prevent bath refusal, it is important to avoid frightening the
young child with such things as spluttering taps, gurgling plugs,
and slippery baths. Place a rubber mat in the bottom of the bath if
there is any chance of the child slipping and losing his balance.
The bath can become one of the best playtimes of the day, and this
should be actively encouraged, filling the bath with boats, sub-
marines, rubber duckies, and discarded detergent bottles, which
double as excellent water squirters. A bubble bath is always fun

and is easily provided by a quick squirt of dishwashing liquid, if you don't want to go to the expense of commercial preparations. Be warned, however, that happy aquatic toddlers and carpeted bathroom floors do not go well together—a tiled floor with a big drain is definitely preferable.

Once again fears of the bath are generally shortlived and, if handled sensibly with gentle desensitization, they are quickly overcome.

Genuine fear of the bath should not be confused with the theatrical antics of a manipulating, attention-seeking toddler, who, out of principle, refuses to bathe when told. Recently I saw a three-and-a-half-year-old girl, who greatly upset her mother by refusing to do anything she was asked whenever her father was home in the evenings. She would never take a bath unless the water was turned on by her father, and she had to be carried to the bathroom and undressed by him as well. When father was out, the child would never take a bath, because her mother thought it was never worth the fight.

This situation was cured in a rapid, though slightly devious, manner. Father continued to show great love and attention, running the bath, undressing his daughter, and putting her in the water, but one minor adjustment was made to the routine. "Absent mindedly," he consistently forgot to turn on the hot tap when he was running the bath with the consequence that the water had an Arctic chill—the balance of power was immediately redressed. Mother's care of bathtime was once again in equal demand!

DOCTORS

As a pediatrician, I have learned the hard way that busy days surrounded by anxious, crying, uncooperative children are extremely stressful. It is, therefore, important for our own sanity, as well as the happiness of the children we serve, that doctors' surgeries are made as friendly and non-threatening as possible.

As mentioned, babies up to the age of six months don't mind being separated from their mom, so it is easy for a doctor to lift them up and examine them on a couch. From eight months until pre-school age, however, this separation is a problem, and I find that examinations are best done with the child sitting relaxed and secure on mom's knee.

Some parents—and doctors for that matter—are amazingly skillful at stirring up a child the moment they enter the office. The child is bundled through the door and not allowed to touch anything, move, or even talk in some cases. A nervous mother will wrench the child's clothes up and twitter in his ear in an unnatural way like a bird warning of impending danger. Utterances such as "doctor is not going to hurt you" are counterproductive, since the thought of getting hurt had probably never even crossed the child's mind.

Children should neither be restricted, nor over-stimulated, by anxious parents when taken to the doctor. They should be allowed to sit quietly on mother's knee to allow the doctor to make the initial examination. As far as the doctor is concerned, the introductory touch is best with arms and feet being wobbled in a fun way, which introduces the doctor to the child as a human being and not an ogre. Thereafter, examinations should be quick and confident, accompanied by quiet, reassuring talk. The doctor should engage the child's eyes, communicating gently with him and watching carefully for those early signs of distress that appear in the eye seconds before the first tear is shed.

Painful and uncomfortable procedures, such as throat examination, should be left until the end, followed by a cuddle and release. Neither parents nor doctors should insist on things like painful blood tests unless they are of indisputable diagnostic and therapeutic value.

Doctors are really very nice people, as long as they keep their scalpels, syringes, and tongue depressors away from the child. A visit to the doctor should not be a fearful experience for child or mother. Most of us enjoy working with children, otherwise we wouldn't be doing it!

HOSPITALS

In the not too distant past, hospitals were places of dread, run purely for the business of curing the sick and without much interest in protecting the emotional well-being of the patient. This was particularly horrifying for children who had to go into a hospital. Between the ages of eight months and three-and-a-half years the young child grieves deeply when separated from his mother and is too young to understand the reasons and temporary nature of the separation. The unhappy toddler may feel abandoned, as if his parents had walked off, leaving him on the steps of an orphanage. The difference is, however, that in the hospital his parents should be encouraged to visit him frequently, might even stay the night, and will rescue him and take him home at the first opportunity.

Initially, the child will protest, crying his little heart out as his parents leave. Usually he will settle within five minutes, only to greet his parents on their next visit with copious tears, thus giving the impression that he has been crying non-stop since they departed. Hospitilization may be upsetting for toddlers, but it is often even more upsetting for the parents.

Generally speaking, hospitals are not places to be feared by children, and it is important for parents to talk openly about them should they pass one in their daily travels to let the child realize from an early age that it isn't some dreadful institution. Each day we have pre-schoolers from some of our city schools visit our wards, and they have a ball, realizing that it is really quite a fun place run by "good guys!"

In the last ten years hospitals and their routines for the care of children have changed greatly. Now if a child needs to be admitted, there is open visiting for the parents and in most cases some form of bed for the mother if she wants to stay.

If you get some warning that your child may have to be admitted to a hospital, it is important to prepare him, discussing openly what is going to happen and encouraging medical pretend play with dolls and stuffed animals. If you can, take him to visit the ward before admission and make sure that when he does go in he has all his favorite cuddly toys and comforters with him.

"Day only" surgery is encouraged now, so that the child can go home to the care of his parents as soon as possible. When the child goes to the anesthetic room, he is always accompanied by his teddy bear and usually his mother, and he will find both waiting for him in the recovery room after the operation. Anesthesiologists who specialize in children's anesthetics have thrown out all those cruel, old ideas that children didn't really feel pain. Now, in a good children's hospital, any child from birth upward is afforded the same, or an even greater, standard of postoperative pain relief than we might expect for ourselves.

In short, hospitals are no longer places for children to fear. Talk to your children freely and openly about them, for one day they may have to visit one.

TOILETS

Some children are afraid to sit on the toilet, which obviously makes toilet training well-nigh impossible. This fear may arise from a number of causes, maybe the association with a severe pain when passing a particularly hard stool or fear of being sucked into the toilet when it is flushed and washed out to sea down a big pipe. Some children are frightened of gadgets, like the exhaust fan in some bathrooms that starts automatically when the light is switched on and which, in a confined space, may sound like a jumbo jet about to take off. Other children refuse to sit on the toilet purely out of attention-seeking, toddler stubbornness.

I recently saw an irate mother who complained that her three-year-old daughter had lost all her previously excellent toilet training skills as the result of a stupid action by the father. Browsing through a shop one day he came upon a poster of a gorilla climbing out of a toilet bowl. So impressed was he with this piece of visual art that he brought it home and stuck it up on the back of the toilet door. Well, the little girl walked in, sat on the toilet, kicked the door shut and, after seeing this horrific vision, absolutely refused, not surprisingly, to sit there ever again.

With children who will not sit on the toilet for one reason or another, we once again must introduce gentle desensitization. For the most resistant, they should start sitting on a pot with their diaper still on. There should be no forcing, but lots of rewards given. From here, progress to sitting without the diaper; sitting on the pot beside the toilet with mom close by; sitting with mom outside giving encouragement; and finally going solo while mom rustles up some interesting treat in the kitchen.

This may all seem rather cumbersome and excessive and often you will find that some of these steps can be bypassed. The important message is that children should not be forced; give them good security and gently desensitize them.

FEAR OF SEPARATION

The fear of separation is common to all toddlers from the age of about eight months until it wanes by school age. It is at its most intense in the early years, its ebb varying greatly from child to child and family to family. Initially, the child resents being handled by anyone except his mother, but this quickly eases to allow all the other members of the family and close friends in on the act. When playing, he is never far from mom, and if outside or playing in another room, he reappears every few minutes to reassure himself of her presence.

Most parents need babysitters at one time or another so that they can maintain some outside life. The ideal babysitter is a grandparent, other relative, or close friend; leaving the child with other babysitters may be difficult initially, with profuse tears being shed on departure and again at pick-up time. Between these times there is usually relative happiness. The child should be accompanied by his cuddly toys and security items, and he should never be left in a great rush, preferably being given a little time to acclimatize, after which the parents should leave decisively, not weakening to his cries when half-way out the door.

Although most toddlers do well in the care of a good babysitter, a few are immensely unhappy and never really settle. If this happens, the parents must ask themselves if separation is really necessary and if it might not be kinder to wait several more months before continuing. Of course, in our modern world many parents are forced, for a variety of good reasons, to leave their child with a babysitter whether they like it or not. But some parents seem particularly blind to what they are doing to their children. An intelligent mother recently asked me for advice on a problem that was worrying her. For the past six months, she had attended church each Sunday morning, placing her toddler in the church nursery, where he cried inconsolably throughout the entire separation. What could be done to make the child less unhappy? I explained that I was certain that an understanding God would probably much prefer to see a happy child than a pew occupied in his church.

By the age of three most toddlers are able to separate and settle quite happily at pre-school. As this is his first major separation, the child must know what is going to happen to him when he is left, and he should be gently introduced to his new surroundings before being abandoned. Parents are never sure, when they bring their child for the first time, whether it is best to sit with him for an hour or so or leave immediately. This advice is probably best left to the individual pre-school director, who has a great deal of experience with this problem, but what I do know is that once the parent has made up his mind to go, then go he must, decisively, without lurking in the bushes to spy on the child.

Occasionally the child will not settle happily, nevertheless parents will insist on his going, believing that non-attendance will cause him to miss out in the warm-up heats for the academic rat race. Once again, where the child is very unhappy, there is little point in forcing him to go on. Better to wait three to six months and then try again.

A band of philosophical child raisers believe that it is important to rush through the stages of separation, to prepare a child for schooling and later life. I believe that toddlers were designed to remain close to their families for a number of years and in a normal seventy-year life span, rushing a child out into our far-from-perfect world any earlier than is necessary seems rather unkind and pointless. When I am irritated by bureaucrats, bullied by bank managers, and forced to read continuing evidence of man's inhumanity to man, I secretly would love to regress to those blissful toddler years with a loving mother to protect me from all this stress.

NOISES IN THE DARK, MONSTERS, AND OTHER ASSORTED BEASTIES

It is perfectly normal for toddlers to be frightened of a great variety of noises, even such common ones as household appliances.

This does not mean that the child is necessarily hypersensitive or emotionally disturbed, and the phenomenon in any case is usually very short-lived. Sensitivity to some noises never goes—dentists' drills and the screeching of car tires are two that are guaranteed to make my hair stand on end, for instance. I presume that, although these noises worry me, the perpetrators have long since come to terms with them.

At an older age, somewhere between four and five years, fear of the dark usually hits its peak and then largely disappears by the child's seventh birthday. A low wattage light is much appreciated by many children at night. When the sun sets and darkness appears, this is the time when the older child's vivid imagination conjures up visions of robbers, monsters, and other assorted bogeymen. It is popular for authors to attribute this to the "junk viewing diet" that we feed our children on television, but children have been terrified at night-time for centuries. Children listen to stories told to them by their parents, grannies, or friends or read books full of varying degrees of mayhem, terror, and violence. Ali Baba's offsider was so mutilated after his murder that they needed a leatherworker to set him up for burial. Hansel and Gretel and Snow White were all taken to big, black forests and abandoned. Snow White was poisoned by a nasty old woman. In Strewelpeter,

the boy who sucked his thumbs had them cut off with a large pair
of scissors. The Pied Piper took all the town's children hostage and
never returned them to their parents. Humpty Dumpty had a most
violent accident, relived in gory detail at a thousand breakfast tables daily, and what about those three poor mice whose tails were
so cruelly severed from their bodies. Even the Bible tells us of
some exceedingly nasty people and punishments. So let's not blame
all these childhood fears on modern films, television, cartoons, and
comics. The element of fear in childhood upbringing is as old as
childhood itself.

Imaginary fears are all part of childhood development and only
too soon fears move out of the area of fiction into the realities of
the adult world, fears that unfortunately will not go away. It does
no harm however, to be a little selective with the type of reading
and viewing matter your child is exposed to, and constantly remind
them of where fact ends and fiction begins.

COMFORTERS AND SECURITY BLANKETS

Children are not the only ones to enjoy their comforters; adults
enjoy them too. Adults relieve their tensions by sucking on a cigarette, a pipe, chewing gum, or their fingernails, or holding on to a
glass of alcoholic beverage. Toddler comforters are probably a good
deal less deleterious to health, generally consisting of thumbs,
teddy bears, pacifiers, and security blankets. There's nothing in-
trinsically wrong with any of these, as long as the habit does not
last too long. Let's examine them.

Thumb Sucking

Despite Sigmund Freud's inevitable emphasis on the sexual con-
notations of sucking one's thumb, modern thinkers believe they are
sucked because it seems a natural and good thing to do at the time.
If there were not some comfort and satisfaction in sucking the
thumb, I doubt whether children would bother to do it. Thumb
sucking is a world-wide phenomenon, although some writers claim
it is less frequent in some races; apparently little Eskimos hardly
ever do it at all, but I presume this is a practical move on their
part, keeping their hands in mittens to prevent their digits falling
off through frostbite. It's very hard to suck your thumb through a
reindeer-hide glove!

Children certainly seem to suck their thumbs more when they
are either tired, bored, frustrated, or tense, and it is a good way of
getting to sleep, particularly for those children who have not yet

attained the mathematical skill to count sheep. In times of stress, and particularly when a new baby arrives, many toddlers regress to this old habit.

By the age of three-and-a-half, most children have spontaneously removed their thumbs from their mouths, although some studies suggest that up to two per cent of children still have this habit in their early teens. Most experts now believe that there is no harm in the habit, either emotionally or physically. One doctor has even pointed out that a number of children are born with marks on their wrist or fingers where they have been sucking to pass the time before birth.[9] The danger of thumb-sucking lies, he says, not in the thumb-sucking itself, but in what the parents do about it. At worst, all it can cause the child is a sore thumb. Certainly before the age of six, thumb-sucking does not damage permanent teeth and after that, there appears to be only a very slight risk of the continuing habit altering the position of children's teeth.

Kicking the habit

Thirty years ago, splints were attached to elbows, mittens put on hands, and the fingers dipped in bitter substances to prevent children from putting their thumbs in their mouths. Some dentists, fearing a misshapen bite, used dental plates, which blocked the ability to suck the thumb. For a child's emotional well-being, there is much to be said for leaving nature to cure this habit rather than engaging in these anti-social activities.

Below the age of four I believe thumb-sucking should be completely ignored. After that age, many children can be dissuaded quite easily by positive rewards and subtle reminders that it is not the habit of a grown-up child. It must never become the cause of a fight or the child will continue it just to annoy his parents.

Thumbs are sucked, hair is twiddled, ears are rubbed, private parts are played with, "because they are there." They are childhood's version of the adult cigarette or chewing gum.

PACIFIERS AND COMFORTERS

Most doctors have a built-in dislike of these plastic or rubber devices, but no one has ever found any evidence to indicate that they really do any harm. Objection to them is more on aesthetic grounds than medical ones. It is fashionable in some quarters to claim that they are unhygienic, but so for that matter are the ten dirty fingers that would be inserted in the mouth if the pacifier were not there.

Many parents who are determined never to resort to pacifiers re-
lent when confronted with an extremely irritable, difficult child. If
the pacifier helps in those situations, then good luck to them.

I dislike the way a pacifier can make an intelligent child appear
dull, dopey, and a dribbler. I also worry about them being used at
bedtime, because, although they undoubtedly precipitate sleep,
they also have an unfortunate habit of precipitating wakefulness
when they become disengaged in the early hours of the morning
(see Chapter 9).

Kicking the habit

There are no long-term side effects from sucking these comforters,
as long as they are not of the sort that has a built-in bottle which
constantly irrigates the teeth with a sweet tooth-decaying solution.
When the time comes to discard the pacifier, it is usually best to
be brave, throw it away, and then brace yourself for the repercussions. There will inevitably be some hours, or even some days, of
trouble, but the pacifier will soon be forgotten. Those who do not
have the courage to discard it so abruptly may try a gradual withdrawal by losing it, damaging it, or letting it become slightly
scorched when the sterilizing saucepan accidentally boils dry!
After three-and-a-half, the child may well be reasoned with and
the pacifier given up after some hard bargaining of the sort described in Chapter 6.

Although I do not like pacifiers, I assure parents that they do
not cause any harm. When a child is under stress for any reason
he has the same right to his pacifier as his parents have to their
cigarettes—the difference is that thumbs and pacifiers are not
proven health hazards. When the time is right, preferably before
two-and-a-half, discard the object nevertheless. It has to go some
time.

Teddies, cuddlies and security blankets

Most youngsters have some object that they seek out and cuddle up
to when tired or upset. This can be some exotic imported stuffed
animal, mom's own battered but much-loved teddy, a sheepskin
rug, or even a rapidly disintegrating bit of old fabric. Whatever the
"real world" value of the object in the eyes of the child it is
priceless. These items are often referred to as "transition objects."
They give security, continuity, and comfort to a child when the
environment and those in it are changing. At the day-care center,
at granny's, in the hospital, although the environment has altered

and mom may no longer be there, the child has a beloved familiar object to hold on to. It is his link with his home base; without it he feels a stranger in the strange world. No wonder ET wanted to go home!

As the child becomes more and more attached to his "familiar," greater is the distress when it falls apart or is mislaid. To the toddler, this is a disaster of major proportions, not unlike a death in the family. But surprisingly, despite the great attachment, a bit of high-powered salesmanship from an enthusiastic parent will steer a toddler towards another, reserve, comforter.

Security blankets of the type favored by Charlie Brown's friend Linus get progressively grubbier and grubbier, until eventually they simply must be washed. This needs to be planned with all the precision of a military operation to ensure that they are in and out of the washing machine and returned dry to the owner with the minimum of discombobulation.

When a blanket is wearing out, it may be wise to remove a part of it to keep in cold storage until the fateful day when the original is in irretrievable tatters. Even without this foresight a minute, disintegrating patch of material may be reincarnated if clever Mom sews it onto the corner of some new material. This is rather like the horticultural grafting of roses and, when properly achieved, ensures years of continuing pleasure.

Comforters and transition objects are normal, natural, healthy, and promote, rather than postpone, security. Like Christopher Robin and his trusty bear, Pooh, the young child armed with his "familiar" can accomplish many a daring feat that would never have been possible alone.

14

FIDGETS, FIDDLERS AND HYPERACTIVES

When planning this book, I deliberately left out any mention of this topic, as it is surrounded by so much professional disagreement and confusion. But it occurred to me that if my highly trained colleagues were confused, how much more so must parents be? This persuaded me to include my own views on the subject. I will also try to wade as objectively as possible through some of the jungle of literature about treatments in an attempt to separate proven fact from unsubstantiated theory.

There is great variation among children. At one extreme is the quiet, controlled, compliant child with a good attention span; at the other end is the negative, noisy, over-active, impulsive, disorganized child whose mind flits from topic to topic with all the skill of a drunk at a cocktail party. At what point normal activity merges with hyperactivity is anyone's guess. There is no clear dividing line, and it depends to a large extent on the tolerance of the observer. I do not think it matters what you call a child, be it "classic hyperactivity" or simply "difficult over-active behavior." What is important is that the child's very individual package of problems is recognized and acted on accordingly.

In this chapter I will describe the picture of the full-blown hyperactive. Many readers will have children who display only a few of these features, so they need not become alarmed. The picture I paint is considerably blacker than that of the blends, or sometimes minimal degree, of these problems that manifest themselves in real life.

THE FULL-BLOWN HYPERACTIVE

The name

The most widely known name is "hyperactivity" or the "hyperactive child syndrome." Although we know the condition we are talking about, it seems that whatever label we use will be deemed wrong by the academic nit-pickers. Although a high level of activity is usually present, other types of behaviors, such as poor concentration span, can be far more damaging to the child. If activity level is not the major problem, many people resent the word "activity" appearing in any form on the label. A "hyperkinetic" child is just a pseudo-scientific way of saying exactly the same thing as a "hyperactive" child. It is clever, but it is no better.

Many behaviors make up the condition, so a less specific title is often favored. One of the oldest of these is "minimal brain damage," but this is disliked because it indicates that something has damaged the brain and, since this damage can never be demonstrated, it seems an unnecessary diagnosis. A more popular title is "minimal brain dysfunction," which indicates that there is a minimal difference in the functioning of the brain, which gives rise to all the parts of the syndrome. I certainly favor this label to describe the kinds of behavior I am about to outline. But as always, you cannot please all of the people all of the time and this label can be criticized as an "imprecise, woolly, dustbin" term. This may indeed be fair criticism, but what else can you use in describing an "imprecise, woolly, dustbin" condition? The newest title, and the one seemingly most in favor at the moment, is "attention deficit disorder." This places the main emphasis on the lack of concentration, which is the biggest problem.

I urge the reader not to get bogged down in all the finer points of terminology. My feeling is that as long as you recognize that there is an imprecise group of behavior patterns that cause difficulties and require treatment in a certain way, then the precise label is unimportant. For the purposes of this chapter I am simply going to use the blanket term "hyperactive."

How common is it?

These problems are between four and eight times more common in boys than in girls, which is, incidentally, the same male predominance that is evident in cases of autism and certain language difficulties. Owing to the vagaries of definition, it has always been difficult to know the exact incidence of this condition. We know that it has been described much more frequently in the United States than in England. This may be explained by British doctors' reluctance to diagnose the condition unless the "human tornado" is seen in full flight before their very eyes. Americans are, apparently, more prepared to believe the word of a shattered parent or the child's edgy teacher. As hyperactive children fluctuate greatly between their good and bad days, and as they may demonstrate little classic hyperactive behavior when unstressed in the quiet of a doctor's office, the American view has to be correct.

Some teachers have described over a third of their young pupils as being restless and inattentive, but the accepted estimate of troublesome activity appears to be somewhere just below 10 per cent of all schoolchildren. One-fifth of these (a per cent of the total) have a severe problem, which will continue to greatly disrupt both school and home life despite all our best help.

The cause

The main cause of "busy-ness" in these busy little people, I believe, is not diet, or the decadence of the eighties, but heredity. Most of these children have at least one close relative, usually the father, with a similar make-up. Children of hyperactive parents adopted by average parents are often hyperactive, despite calm parenting. Children of non-hyperactive parents adopted by hyperactive parents rarely become hyperactive.

It is fascinating to look at the temperamental make-up of the hyperactive relatives—doctors, bricklayers, expert mechanics, and self-made business tycoons who have many things in common. As children, they were often like their own "difficult" child. They were often either school drop-outs or late starters. They find it hard to sit still and relax, or stop fidgeting at home, except in front of the television. They are impulsive, often socially inept, and not all that easy to live with. Even those who seem academically brilliant still have some attention problems; they are often substandard in spelling and not avid social readers, for instance. Winston Churchill, Albert Einstein, and Leonardo da Vinci are often quoted as people whose drive and other skills overcame some degree of hyperactive handicap.

Studies that blame hyperactivity on parental handling usually fail to take heredity into account. The often hard-to-live-with characteristics of a parent, which render the environment less than ideal, are also passed down by heredity.

The concentration of the hyperactive usually improves after the age of five, and minor offenders are much better by the time they are eight years old. More major problems stay with the child for life, although they are often well hidden as life is arranged around them.

The features

Although no two hyperactive children are identical, a group of common features will, to some extent, appear in most. Some have a "full house," exhibiting every possible problem; others have a smaller selection. The effects they have depend on the specific features involved, their severity, and the ability of the parents to cope with a child who is often far from easy.

AT BIRTH
Many hyperactives are easy babies, but some make their presence felt from the earliest days. The worst are extremely irritable, hard to comfort, and cause difficulties for the new mom and everyone else with whom they come in contact. Every hospital nursery for the newborn has at least one of these noisy little people, who often find themselves exiled to a far corner for the protection of the other babies and the staff. Other hyperactives at this age tend to sleep poorly and respond slowly to comfort. Another symptom to add is "infant colic," which may occur in some children in the first days or weeks of life.

THE FIRST YEAR
Though many hyperactives may initially behave well in the maternity hospital, most start to show their true colors soon after they

arrive home. Sleep patterns tend to become erratic, there is more irritability and crying, and the frequent appearance of the "evening colic."

We often talk about colic, but actually nobody is really quite sure what it is. Shortly after the child is fed, he starts crying profusely. This usually commences in the first fortnight of life, finishes by three months, and usually happens in the evening. However many babies become colicky at birth, continue for six months, and cry much of the day. The cry is one of pain and, as the baby stiffens and draws up his knees, most parents presume this pain is in the gut. It has been fashionable to blame colic on wind, over-anxious, inexperienced mothers, greedy feeders, artificially fed babies, milk allergy, or a leaky valve at the top of the stomach; none of these has been proven to be the cause, which remains a mystery. As the problem always improves with time and maturity, it is suggested that there may be some immaturity of gut function, possibly caused by a hormonal deficiency.

Colic can be devastating for a new mother. Within days of birth the happy, confident mother becomes exhausted and loses all her self-confidence when she finds she is incapable of comforting her own, crying child. It is not the anxious mother who causes colic, but there is no doubt that the inconsolable child soon generates a degree of anxiety in her. No amount of burping or modifying of the diet will help. Movement seems to be the most effective form of therapy: walking the floor, bouncing, rocking, or patting the baby on his back as he lies over your shoulder or arm. I have even heard of parents who take shifts at night driving their colicky baby round the block as this is the only way to console him. Again there are stories of mothers who have resorted to sitting the baby in his bouncer on top of the washing machine and turning it on to full spin. They claim that the vibration is helpful, though I reckon this is a little extreme.

Over the years various medicines have been used to cure colic, including gin and bourbon, which contain a lot of alcohol. Simethicone drops (trade name Mylicon) is an over-the-counter preparation that is becoming popular for colic and is very effective for some infants.

Many conditions that afflict mankind will cure themselves if given time. Colic is one of them, and although the cure is largely a matter of fate, the credit is generally given to whatever sort of quackery we are engaging in at the time.

Even as babies, hyperactive children tend to have little patience, disliking such things as long car trips or stops for a good gossip in the supermarket. They are not the sort of children who enjoy lying on their back contemplating the ceiling all day, and they inevitably become the sort of adults who are unlikely to sit on mountain-tops contemplating their navels. Being propelled down a busy street in a fast-moving stroller is their idea of fun. They can't wait to get up on their feet and their level of frustration and irritability improves greatly when this is achieved. "Baby walkers" are often condemned by physiotherapists and child safety workers, but they often give these children a degree of mobility that suits their level of impatience.

Despite newly-acquired mobility, sleep problems often continue, as well as a dislike of sitting still on anyone's knee and a reluctance to be comforted.

THE TODDLER

Hyperactives may walk, run, and climb earlier than other children, but one thing is certain: once they are mobile they all have an amazing facility for "getting into things." Cupboards are ransacked in the twinkling of an eye, and mess quickly replaces the order that existed in the days before he found his legs.

Towards the age of two, activity often increases, accompanied by an intolerable volume of high-spirited noise. The general behavior has much in common with that of the average toddler, but it tends to be considerably worse. The hyperactive child has a low threshhold of tolerance when things do not go according to plan, and restricting his environment will cause problems; his behavior will be particularly bad if the child is stuck indoors on wet days. He likes to be busy outside, which he finds infinitely preferable to sitting quietly doing puzzles, pencil work, or following some early-reading program. Attention is limited, and the child will flit butterfly-like from task to task. The sleep problems continue; the child often rises early in the morning and finds it almost impossible to settle at night if at all excited. Many of these children are also compulsive "touchers," handling everything they pass, a characteristic that frequently leads to multiple breakages and a trail of debris.

Despite all these difficulties, the hyperactive child is generally a very loving and often an immature and extremely sensitive child who needs a structured, calm environment and parents with unlimited patience.

SCHOOL AGE

The toddler behavior that causes most concern is the child's incessant flitting about. Once the child reaches school, he is confined to a classroom and made to conform and mix as an equal. It is then that the full impact of the hyperactive syndrome becomes apparent. Initially, the child will fidget and find it hard to keep quiet or sit still. He will be easily distracted, turning toward the slightest noise, and only maintaining his work performance if given great encouragement. It is the problem of concentration that caused the hyperactive condition to be renamed "attention deficit disorder." This is always present in toddlers, but it is only at school age that its full destructive power is revealed. Luckily, attention usually improves in the first three years at school, although in some it continues to be a major problem.

The attention deficit surprises many people, as it is highly selective. The child may play a favorite video game with great accuracy, but when asked to learn spelling or perform some reading, interest disappears within seconds. This attention deficit also shows in speech patterns. Some children will ramble on at length, or lose track of what they are saying in mid-sentence, owing to lack of concentration. Others will rudely interrupt your conversation because, unless they say their piece immediately, it will be lost forever.

Impulsiveness is another big problem and leads to a child who invariably "leaps before he looks." This is particularly dangerous on busy roads, but it can also land the child in all sorts of playground trouble when he impulsively punches the boy who's teasing him without first checking if a teacher is looking. Many of these children are already clumsy, and impulsiveness contributes to this as the child trips and bumps into things because of lack of planning and forethought. There is also a genuine element of poor coordination, poor "flow of movement," and a difficulty in performing two actions at the same time. Difficulty in discriminating right from left, tying shoelaces, and putting on clothes the right way round also occur.

Specific learning problems are unfortunately very frequent with many of these children, who perform much more poorly at school than their intelligence scoring would indicate. The difficulty in concentrating reliably is the major problem, but specific weaknesses in spelling, reading, comprehension, and mathematics are also common.

A degree of social handicap is also common. Like most children, hyperactives crave other children's friendship and attention. Sadly they are often unable to achieve this and will resort to hopping around outside a group of playing children "acting silly," poking and annoying them in an attempt to be noticed. Play is always much better with one good friend rather than in a group. With the concentration, learning, clumsiness, and social problems, it is little wonder that many of these children receive a severe battering to their already weak self-esteem. Low frustration tolerance and over-excitability are very common, and their moods tend to swing rapidly—some days are excellent and others a complete write-off.

The attention deficit, social problems, and specific learning problems often pass unnoticed at school and the stressed child resorts to bad behavior as a cry for help. I believe all children basically wish to succeed, to be popular, and mix well with their classmates. When a child has difficulties in academic, sport, and social areas, there may be little left to excel in but nasty, naughty behavior!

I have described a wide behavioral spectrum that may be seen in the hyperactive child, and in his lesser cousins, the fidgets, fiddlers and nonconcentrators. Whatever the label, many of the problems described are common and respond best to special methods of treatment. I have described them in detail not in an attempt to label normal children hyperactive, but rather to explain to worried parents with unhappy, under-achieving, and undiagnosed children that there may well be something more than simple bad behavior at the root of it all.

Treatment

BETTER EVERYDAY MANAGEMENT

Communication. All toddlers should be receiving clear, uncluttered messages from the mouths of their parents. This is particularly important for the hyperactive child who has not only a major concentration problem, but also one that especially affects the listening memory.

Before talking with the child it is wise to cut down as much extraneous noise as possible. Turn off the television, radio and blender, and wait for the dog to stop barking. First call the child's name clearly and enthusiastically to engage eye contact. Once looking eye to eye, give a clear message using the utmost economy of words and communicating with all modes, such as hands, eyebrows, and body. Many parents bury their children under a mass of monotonous, unenthusiastic verbiage and then wonder why they don't listen. Good communication is not only vital for hyperactives, but also highly desirable for all children and adults.

Structure and organization. Hyperactives are, by nature, extremely disorganized, and they tend to spread a trail of disorganization around them. Paradoxically, these children do not fare well without structure and organization and it is in everyone's interest to introduce routine into their lives.

The child needs to know when it is time to get up, what he will have for breakfast, the days he is to go to school, and if any major happenings are going to take place that day. Problems arise when the child is faced with the unexpected, like friends dropping by, dad going off on a trip, or a very late bedtime one night. For the good of the child, it is best to run a tight ship, with life aboard as well-controlled and organized as possible.

For the older toddler or school-age child, I would make out a list of tasks to do each day around the house. These would be his sole responsibility, such as making his bed, feeding the cat, tidying up his toys, or getting the mail. All this helps to give structure and responsibility to his life and encourages a greater awareness of what is going on in his environment. When out shopping, he should be encouraged to make purchases from friendly store-keepers while mom waits outside to check that all goes well and the verbal messages do not get confused. This has the benefit of providing therapy for listening memory, responsibility, and creating a feeling of usefulness and importance.

Behavior modification therapy. As the child hurtles noisily around the house day in and day out, parents' patience eventually wears a bit thin. In spite of the best intentions, it is all too easy to slip into a negative rut, handing out punishments left, right and center, instead of thinking up positive ways of altering the child's behavior. Hyperactives get wound up by tension and agitation, so this worsens their already difficult behavior. They are sensitive children, and they will soon get the impression that "nothing they do is right," which will eventually lead to loss of all self-esteem and much long-term sadness.

To guard against this, the child's behavioral antics should be viewed through the proverbial rose-tinted glasses. When good behavior seems almost extinct, the tired parental brain must try to focus on any behavior that is nearly good and then build on that. The danger with hyperactives is that they generate a great deal of negative tension as they storm around the house, so that when that brief moment of peace and quiet occurs, parents are tempted to give a sigh of relief and sit down and relax, thus ignoring the highly desirable behavior instead of encouraging it.

Under the age of three-and-a-half, praise and attention are good rewards when the child is constructive, helpful, or tries hard. After this age stars, stickers and stamps, sweets, and cheap, small plastic toys are all effective boosters.

Secure, childproof house. With all small children, a secure, childproof house leads to fewer anxieties and thus less attention being given for the wrong reasons. With the difficult hyperactive, this is even more important, as careful planning is needed to reduce the negative "vibes" and increase the positive messages.

The school-age hyperactive. It is a sad fact that many happy little hyperactives lose much of their "sunny disposition" once they go to school. Restrictions like having to sit still and keep quiet cause problems, which are greatly exacerbated when the children try to compete academically using their easily distracted, poorly concentrating brains.

These children fluctuate from day to day, and teachers often tell me that on bad days they might as well stay at home as they are impossible to work with. They also fluctuate from year to year and although maturation and environment have some role, I place most of the blame squarely on their teachers' shoulders. The punitive, by-the-book, rigid teacher will get nowhere with one of these children, and, even worse, he has the power to destroy any vestige of self-confidence the child may have as well as the will to learn. The enthusiastic, sensitive teacher who shows interest and gives as much one-to-one care as possible will boost the child's self-confidence and do well.

Hyperactive children often have to invest twice the amount of effort to achieve the same results as their classmates because of their concentration and specific learning problems. If this is not recognized and the teacher looks only at results rather than effort, the child will cease to try and, let's face it, who would blame him? I don't believe that schoolchildren set out to be lazy, badly behaved or nasty. I am certain that if given the chance to be at the top of their class, socially popular, and good at sports, they would grab the chance at once. Sadly, when none of these attributes seems available, the child has the option of either plodding on in the hope of getting some sort of recognition one day, or throwing in the sponge and becoming the class clown.

Both teachers and parents must recognize that these are special children who often have unrecognized problems of learning, concentration, mixing, staying still, frustration, impulse, and emotional control. One could write a whole book on this subject, but my main message here is to "get off the child's back." Stop focusing on failures; point up the child's success both in school and in outside activities.

The Feingold diet

Dr. Ben Feingold, a former professor of allergy in San Francisco, first suggested a relationship between diet and hyperactivity in 1973. He noted that our diet now contained over 2700 "intentional" food additives, and as these substances had increased over the years, so had the rates of hyperactivity and learning problems in our schools. He claimed "rapid dramatic changes in behavior, sleep and school work" in over 50 per cent of children put on his special diet. His ideas were soon headline news, and his diet spread like wildfire.

In the 1980s, it is so firmly accepted in the lay press that our preservative-filled diets cause hyperactivity, that what I am about to say seems almost indecent. Despite this acceptance, ten years of worldwide research has only shown that a small minority of hyperactives get any benefit from this diet. In making this statement, I am all too aware of the multitude of parents who swear by the diet. When I talk to them, they are adamant that their child's behavior "blows apart" soon after any dietary indiscretion. I also know of many studies that report behavioral improvements when the parents know their child is on the diet. I do not dispute reported improvement, but I question whether this is due to the diet itself, or simply to the more disciplined life-style that is needed to implement the diet. Or is it simply placebo effect? For instance, it is known that if simple distilled water is injected into a patient, instead of a pain-relieving drug, up to one-third of them miraculously lose their pain. There are many other such examples in medicine, ranging from patent cold cures and appetite stimulants to elixirs of youth and a whole panoply of tonics.

To ensure that the placebo effect does not influence the parents' assessment of their child's behavior on the diet, the only reliable trial is one that is "blind," in which the parents do not know when the diet is or is not being taken. Following Feingold's publicity in the early 1970s, concern regarding food additives was expressed by many agencies from Congress down to the Federal Drug Administration. This led to a number of well-constructed studies[10,11] to test the Feingold hypothesis. The children studied were all claimed by their parents as being greatly helped by the diet. Each child was assessed to ensure that hyperactivity was indeed the correct diagnosis. At this point, it was found that many of the claimed hyperactive responders had been misdiagnosed and were not hyperactive children. Before starting each study, the children were carefully assessed both on and off the diet, to give an accurate baseline reading of behavior from which to study possible changes once the diet was challenged.

To challenge the diet in a way that was completely blind to parents, the child, and the independent observers posed great difficulties. One group overcame this by arranging for all food to be brought to the home on a sort of "meals-on-wheels" arrangement.

This gave the organizers of the study the power to secretly tamper with the diet at will. Other groups placed the children on a strict diet, and each day gave one additional item, which could be secretly modified when they wished. One study gave a daily capsule that usually contained an inactive liquid, but about once a week it was heavily laced with the incriminated artificial coloring. Another gave odd-looking cookies, which were usually as pure as if straight from grandma's oven but occasionally were peppered with all manner of additives. One group gave a daily bottle of an odd-looking home-made soda pop. Usually, this was pure and natural, but once a week was peppered with all sorts of hidden "nasties." As all this secret modification of diet was going on, the behavior, concentration, activity, and performance of certain tasks were being assessed by teachers, parents, and various other experts. Those assessing the children had no knowledge of what diet the child was getting, until the code was broken at the end of the study.[10]

FEINGOLD DIET CONCLUSIONS, 1984

Ten years ago, Dr. Feingold claimed that about 50 per cent of hyperactive children were greatly improved when put on his diet. These figures continue to be true, but only if the parents know when the child is on the diet. Carefully controlled studies in the last ten years show that only five per cent of proven hyperactive school children whose parents claim them to be helped by diet could be shown to be improved when the parents, child, and other assessors were unaware whether the diet was or was not being given.

All this sounds very cut and dried, but there remains one area of some concern. The figures given refer to school-age children, who are much easier to assess objectively than their toddler counterparts. Although all rather subjective, anecdotal, and ill-proven, it did appear from a number of studies that the preschool child responded somewhat better to the diet than his older counterpart. This response figure is unknown but small.

THE DIET

There is more to the diet than the popular belief that the child only needs to stop consuming soft drinks, junk food, and products with colorings and artificial preservatives. Feingold claims that many naturally occurring substances, such as those found in oranges, are equally harmful. If the diet is religiously adhered to, it also bans the use of toothpaste and dishwashing detergent, and mom must stop using sprays and perfume.

Although chemicals in food are rarely shown to affect hyperactivity, I can only be impressed by the enthusiasm many parents have for this diet. If they consider it is helping, I do not advise that they discontinue the treatment but ask that they view the results with mild skepticism and with their eyes wide open. In medicine, we must not allow ourselves to become over-entrenched with science. My function as a doctor is to make people feel better—and as studies do show that a percentage of parents feel happier and more in control when they *know* that their child is on the diet, then who am I to dissuade them?

Medicines

If someone refers to a hyperactive child being treated with stimulant drugs, a howl of disapproval is heard from many quarters. It is amazing that while the Feingold diet remains scientifically unproven for all but a small minority, it is nevertheless fully accepted. Meanwhile, the use of medication that has been shown by much scientific evidence to have advantages tends to be discouraged. The problem is that the drugs used are amphetamines (methylphenidate, dextroamphetamine) and as such catch all the flak of the "speed" abuse of twenty years ago. I am assured that addiction to these drugs is not a problem of childhood, and more than twenty years of use with children in the United States has produced little evidence of major side effects.

The problem with medication is that it is over-used, often being given to children in place of simple behavioral advice or the sorting out of family problems. Below the age of five, only a minority of hyperactive children will respond to medication, while over this age probably over half may be helped. In the short term, these drugs help concentration which in turn helps behavior.

Other treatments

Such is the frustration and ill-founded feeling of guilt experienced by the parents of hyperactive children that they will grasp at anything that offers some chance of help. It is a long, difficult course they tread, often a steep, uphill one with little help from either doctors or teachers. It is therefore little wonder that they open their wallets and throw their money to all manner of people who claim that they can provide miracle cures.

It is fashionable these days to state that hypoglycemia (lack of sugar in the blood) or hyperglycemia (too much sugar in the blood) both upset the hyperactive. Once again, there is no scientific evidence to back this up, although it is a view most adamantly held by many parents. Equally, vitamin therapy, particularly with the B group vitamins, is claimed to help specific learning problems and many of the unfortunate behavior patterns. Once again, this is completely unproven.

Hyperactive children tend to be clumsy and poorly coordinated, so occupational therapy should be given to improve their motor skills. This must be viewed in the same light as giving remedial teaching, as both may improve only one specific area, leaving many others untreated and giving little general improvement in the condition as a whole. What occupational therapy may promote is improved self-esteem and better physical abilities, which help social mixing and leisure-time activities. Remedial teaching may have benefits as the child functions best in the one-to-one environment, and any gains may help his happiness at school, which has inevitable repercussions on his behavior.

Other children are hung in nets and treated with swinging, movement, and stimulation of the vestibular apparatus in the middle ear. Claims are made about the benefit of this treatment, but once again there is no conclusive evidence that it works.

Whether your child has devastating hyperactivity or is just a small-time fidget, help is needed in many areas. No single treatment by itself is enough. They need sensible behavior management, self-esteem boosting, help with social skills, and possibly some remedial work. Children with minor problems do well with a little treatment, while those with major problems cause much heartache and concern for most of their childhood years. A little of this heartache can be alleviated by using some common sense management techniques.

15

PLAYGROUPS, PRE-SCHOOLS AND ATTEMPTS TO PRODUCE THE INFANT EINSTEIN

Eighty years ago children lived out their earlier years in an extended family of mom, dad, and grandparents. They watched, listened, and learned, generally following the dictum that "little children should be seen but not heard" and usually not speaking until spoken to. In this way, they served a sort of apprenticeship for adulthood! Nowadays, in our more mobile society, there seems to be a move away from this natural approach toward formal, structured learning. Children from the earliest days attend playgroups, day-care centers, or pre-schools. Obsessive, driving parents arrange swimming lessons at a very early age, and cram in reading, number work, and music lessons on top of all that.

Is this really a great step forward, or is it a misguided stagger to the side? As a doctor who spends much of his time trying to support extremely sad parents with handicapped children, I admit I am heavily biased. I think that those of us who are privileged enough to have normal, healthy children should give thanks for what we've got, give them the maximum love and attention we can provide, and not seek to turn them from normal children into something super-normal. Happiness and success in life depend on many things other than parental tutoring. These academic efforts often do more for the givers' own egos and hang-ups than help the child to cope better with the real harsh world he will be forced to live in.

PLAYGROUPS

Here young children come along with their mothers, play, and attempt to mix with each other. While all this is going on, the moms chat, socialize, and watch. This has advantages for both children and parents. The toddler experiences a little bit of independence yet is never far from mom. Although he is too young to play with other children, he plays happily alongside them and generally enjoys their company. Often children have strange ways of showing this enjoyment, as this is the peak age for biting, kicking, pushing, and not sharing. They are also directed in some simple structured play and get their sticky hands on a multitude of new toys.

By attending playgroup, the mother avoids becoming entombed in her own home, and it is vital that she should get out and meet real people. She hears what problems other mothers are experiencing with their children and gets some advice on her own. She also sees new ideas for play and child care.

PRE-SCHOOLS

Pre-schools, nursery schools, and day-care centers take children from about three years old until school enrollment. The child stays at the center, where all care and teaching is in the hands of the pre-school staff. The directors of our pre-schools are constantly being sniped at by pushy parents who think that they provide too much play and not enough "learning." Despite this, the staff hold firmly to their beliefs that this is the time for the child to enjoy and to develop a wide spectrum of skills needed for life and school. They provide an opportunity for gentle separation in a child who has previously been close day and night to his parents. They also give a quality of child care that is in most cases as supportive as the child would receive at home, thus making the transition a bearable one. This is particularly reassuring to those families who by necessity, or through choice, have to "park" their children during the day while they work. Pre-school also provides a solid, caring daytime base for the child of a single parent who has to go to work.

Learning how to learn is probably the best way to describe the activities of pre-school. The child is taught basic skills necessary for life in school. The sort of skills that the child will learn at pre-school include listening, concentrating, and sticking to a particular task. Many children find this immensely difficult at first, but the skilled, trained teachers know how to hold a child's waning interest and encourage him to sit and finish a task, bringing some structure and gentle discipline into the child's life. The skilled teacher builds on the child's natural curiosity to develop an enthusiasm for learning and a quest for knowledge.

In pre-school, the child learns to communicate not just in speech, but in all sorts of other ways. Using imaginative play their little bodies tell stories just as skillfully as their mouths. Speech accelerates at pre-school, as all those busy little beings chatter among themselves. By speech, I do not mean that regurgitated, parrot-like repetition of clever sayings and nursery rhymes they will come up with, but the organization of thought to produce appropriate original expression. I think that pre-schools provide some of the best speech therapy available.

The child also mixes, learns to share, to take turns, and to respect other people's property and wishes. He learns much about structure and discipline, which will prove valuable when he enters school. As he separates from his mother, he starts to experience a little independence.

The child is not the only one who benefits from pre-school; invariably it is of great value to the mother as well. After being a twenty-four-hour-a-day provider of child care, at last she has some time to herself to "recharge her batteries." If there is a younger child in the family, he will now receive some valuable one-to-one care, which he deserves without competition from the older child. Not only does pre-school prepare the toddler for the separation of going to school, it also prepares the mother for her feelings of separation when she views the "empty nest" after the child has flown to school, never again to be a toddler.

PRODUCING THE INFANT EINSTEIN

The word "advanced" means different things to different people. Playing the piano at four, or being two years academically superior to one's peer group at five are all signs of being advanced. But will this necessarily continue and be a help in later life? Being a vivid communicator, resourceful, reliable, sensible, determined, proficient at sport, popular with one's peers, and a keen observer and lover of life may be much more desirable qualities to help a child struggle through his three score years and ten in a difficult world.

If the child enjoys learning, it must be encouraged but not pushed to ridiculous lengths. Parents must also be cautioned that many apparently clever tricks are in reality much less spectacular than they would appear.

Rote rituals

Rote learning (learning by memory) has some benefits, but it does not always indicate brilliance or academic success. I often see a child whose parents ask him to stand up and count to 100 or recite his two times table for me. As these are rote learned skills they cut little ice with the singularly unimpressed doctor! The child who knows twice one is two, twice two is four, may sound very impressive until asked the simple question: "If you pass a field in which there are two cows and open the gate and let in two more, how many cows would now be in the field?" Rote learning of the two times table is of no real benefit in answering real-life problems unless you have been taught to think laterally and use those skills. Other parents ask their child to recite nursery rhymes, which is promptly done with all the skill of a trained parrot. Having heard about the three blind mice, I might then ask how many tails were cut off by the farmer's wife. Again rote skills are seen to be "all show and no action," when it is obvious the child does not know what I am talking about.

One six-year-old autistic boy I work with has no speech, lives in a world of his own, and is severely and permanently handicapped. Despite this, each time I see him he takes a sheet of paper and as I talk to his parents he writes down with complete accuracy the name of every street he has passed on the way from his home to my clinic. He has an astonishing photographic memory, but sadly this is no compensation for the multitude of real-life skills he does not possess.

General knowledge is another skill, most valuable for television quiz shows or to be dragged out as a party piece to impress, but it is more often than not a rote learned information. For example, the child can be programed to learn that there are seven days in a week, 52 weeks in a year, and 365 days in a year, but will he understand why his birthday was on a Tuesday last year and is on a Wednesday this year? Has he realized that all those figures don't add up and that there is in fact one more day than 52 weeks in each year, which makes it a whole new ball game? And as for leap years, he has really started to think when he understands them!

Our aims in life must be to teach children in basic skills of learning, then encourage them to work from there. Computers may indeed store an amazing amount of information, but the human brain is infinitely superior when programed in the right way.

Flash cards, sight words, and early reading

Some parents with a certain upbringing and philosophy of child rearing can't wait to secure a place for their young children in the academic rat race. Reading is one skill they wish to promote, and although they generally receive little encouragement from pre-school directors or teachers, they undertake the task themselves.

This generally does little harm, and although there is no doubt that at the age of six some of these children read much better than their "uncrammed" contemporaries, there is little evidence that at the age of eight or ten these gains will still be apparent. There is also the very real danger that being forced to read and pushed too hard at too early an age can turn some children off the whole idea, and a definite resistance will appear, which might hinder an otherwise normal approach to the subject.

In many cases, it is just about impossible anyway to teach active young toddlers to read, as their interests lie more in the areas of running, playing, helping mom or dad, and just enjoying the fun life of being a toddler. Let them have that time; it is all too short as it is.

One may ask why giving a four-year-old the reading skills of a six-year-old may not be beneficial. Once again, it is because it is a photographic memory, rote learning exercise, which does no long-term good. These skills can usefully be left until a much later date.

Some young children may be taught to recognize "sight words" at the age of three. This is a skill that greatly excites most parents, who are convinced that their child is a reincarnated Einstein, In fact, this skill can be imparted to any child who is prepared to settle and concentrate and has a good photographic memory for differences in patterns. This is the same skill that is used in recognizing trade names or a favorite chocolate bar. To encourage this skill, flash cards are used (little cards on which the word is written), and when the appropriate response is given the child is immediately rewarded. Pigeons and chimpanzees have been taught to recognize shapes using very similar techniques. Of course the ani-

mal experiments can only reach a certain point because, although it is possible to reward a pigeon for recognizing certain shapes, it is impossible to teach him to use his knowledge to work out unfamiliar shapes not previously encountered.

To read properly, recognizing patterns is only the beginning. The real skill is in being able to look at a word, sound out its letters, apply a multitude of rules, short cuts, and exclusions, and then come up with the right pronunciation. Once this skill has been mastered, words never seen before can be read with ease. Coupled with good reading comprehension, this is the real adult reading skill. Unfortunately, the human brain is not sufficiently mature to handle all this computation before the developmental age of six, and it is then that we see who are destined to be the good or the bad readers. All this will probably have little relationship to the number of sight words the child could recognize at the age of five.

I believe that teaching a child to recognize words is not the same as teaching a child to "read." I believe that early reading is little more than a clever trick, but research could well prove me wrong—but for the wrong reasons. In a large group of toddlers, some are destined to do well academically, some will be average, and some will under-achieve. It is known that parents who care

and spend much time with their children will usually produce better academic results in their children than those who are uninterested. It is also known that the child who settles, concentrates,
and is receptive to learning at the age of four is more likely to
succeed academically than the disorganized, over-active, poor con-
centrator. Although statistics may show that the recognition of
sight words at an early age is associated with better eventual academic outcome, I believe that reading has nothing to do with it,
rather that parental motivation and the child's own basic abilities
bring this about.

Swimming

Swimming is very good for toddlers, not only for obvious safety
reasons, but also because it provides a valuable and enjoyable form
of exercise and family fun.

In 1939, the reactions of forty-two infants were studied when
put in the water. In the first four months of life, a reflex swimming pattern was observed with the child moving his arms and legs
in a rhythmic manner, with vague similarities to freestyle swimming. At four months, this reflex disappeared, and the child
started to show totally disorganized movement in the water. This is
the stage when little children splash and enjoy water, but do little
more than that with their arms and legs. It was well into the second year that the first, feeble attempts at real swimming were
noted with some voluntary, semi-purposeful movements. From
here it was only a matter of time, brain maturity, and practice
until the little children swam.[12]

Swimming from the earliest days of life is to be recommended, if
it is used as a form of fun for the whole family to enjoy together.
The little baby holds tight to his mother or father with one hand,
and the other splashes in the water. Later they paddle by themselves under close supervision before being fitted with some sort of
flotation device that gives them more independence. A form of "dog
paddle" swimming develops somewhere between the third and
sixth birthdays, depending on the child's determination and the
practice he gets. Swimming for older children provides a healthy
sport, which children of all physical and intellectual abilities can
enjoy equally.

There is a modern trend perpetrated in the name of early swimming to toss babies into the water soon after birth. This, like early
reading, has little long-term advantage; a communal family "splash
down" is many times more therapeutic.

Child wonders: whom are we trying to help?

All good parents want the best for their children and put a great deal of effort into encouraging and helping them to achieve. This should, of course, be supported, but it must never be allowed to progress to unhealthy extremes. Unfortunately, the efforts of some parents soon escalate from an admirable action into a pathological obsession, and academic goals blind them to the realities of life. For some, this is a gradual and unintentional progression, but for others, showing off a brilliant child is a crutch to prop up their own crumbling egos.

Recently I talked to a journalist who had just researched an article on teaching youngsters to read at an early age. In the process, she had come up against some amazing parents and their children. One six-year-old boy was so advanced that his parents insisted that he was bored with school and arranged for him to be promoted to a class with eight-year-olds. Dad installed a home computer for his personal use and then arranged for extra home tutoring in the hope of widening the gap even further. Music lessons were also arranged and the child was largely withdrawn from activities that involved mixing with children of inferior abilities. Certainly he had become an academic genius, but as he had little exposure to anything that might loosely be termed "fun," he was a pale, indoor child who was socially and physically backward. He was viewed by the school and his parents as an interesting showpiece and by his classmates as an uninteresting freak. To a skeptic like myself, it seemed that these parents were hiding from their own hang-ups in their obsessive crusade to produce a "super-child." Sadly, the other children in the family, who were "only normal," were to a large extent ignored in the process.

Another family had a three-year-old boy who was doing remarkably well in the second year of a reading program. As this was so time-consuming, the parents hired an interesting lady from over-seas to teach the child. Her daily task was to tutor the boy in reading, then to talk away to him in her native tongue so that the child would become at the same time academically advanced and bilingual. You might ask, where were the parents while all this was going on? Well, being busy professional people, they were out at work all day!

Just because pushy parents engage in these programs, all you normal well-adjusted parents must not let yourselves be made to feel either inferior or guilty. Reading and jabbering away in a foreign tongue at the age of four may satisfy some parents' egos, but I can assure you children much prefer to learn through love and living.

LEARNING THROUGH LIVING

The greatest educators our children will ever meet in their lives are their parents. The value of watching, listening, playing, and just being around them must never be under-estimated.

During the average day all manner of adventures take place in a toddler's life. A fire engine clattering by or a big, barking dog will spark off his imagination and he will want to verbalize his experiences to anyone who will listen. On the way to the shops he might recognize an advertisement previously seen on television, or he may want to talk about the stores, the cars, and anything else of interest that passes. In the supermarket, he counts out the oranges, gets the bigger, not the smaller, package and learns to spot subtle differences on the labels. Once home, he will start matching and sorting as he helps to put away the groceries—all accompanied by a non-stop chatter. In all this, the toddler looks to his parents for reassurance and guidance.

He listens to mom and dad, copying their sayings and asking innumerable questions. With this, his verbal abilities increase, and so does his general knowledge. He helps with the household chores, learning to run simple errands and generally being "mother's little helper." Unbreakable dishes are washed in the sink and helping with the cooking is a particular favorite. Pastry is rolled, cut, and shaped and his rather grubby effort at a pie crust is ceremoniously placed in the oven alongside the family meal. While all this goes on, he feels very important and loved, and he develops a great interest in life.

He builds up his muscles, not in a gym but on the arduous walk up to the park, sitting on swings, ascending the jungle gym and the sprint to chase some unfortunate pigeon foolish enough to land within a hundred yards of this active little bird scarer. Much of the day is spent in play, not with those expensive computerized inventions produced in Silicon Valley, but with natural raw materials, such as boxes, chairs, and paper.

Improvisation and free play produce an extremely inventive brain which is often lost in the "spoon fed" child. One minute the chairs are all lined up, and money is collected and counted by the toddler conductor; minutes later he is piloting an amazingly noisy jumbo jet down the middle of the living room. The cardboard box becomes a garage for toy cars; minutes later it is a rocket base from which the cardboard innards of a toilet roll blast off into space.

Academic education, like sex education, can be acquired in a number of ways. The child may be summoned to a room, alone with his father, and given a formal lecture on the facts of life. The relaxed parent usually abhors this approach, preferring to answer questions as they arise in the course of daily life. Similarly toddlers may either be sat down and taught formally, or allowed to be apprentices to their parents and learn through the activities of everyday life.

Good parents must not let themselves be browbeaten by their friends who have adopted the role of high powered educators. Being good, loving, caring parents, who teach their child through practical living, is to be commended above all. When viewed over a seventy-year life span it seems pretty irrelevant that a child reads at the age of four or six. Better by far to start life with a healthy, happy, balanced outlook. The trials and tribulations will come soon enough.

16

THE GOOD, WORKING MOTHER

Books about child care generally censure mothers who have young children and yet still go out to work. They fail to see that not all women were designed to be twenty-four-hour-a-day mothers and, try as they may, the role just does not suit them. Some brilliant career women, who are used to living life in the fast lane, will be slowed down by nothing until confronted with a toddler. This is often the first time in their lives that they have felt completely defeated, incompetent, not in control—and it hurts! Other busy individuals find that the pace of life and isolation of being a mother is hard to accept, and they feel that life is passing them by. They feel let down and cheated.

Mothers, like fathers, are social creatures and as such need to get out to meet other adults. If they don't they are in danger of starting to think, talk, and behave like toddlers themselves. There is absolutely no evidence to suggest that sensible working mothers in any way disadvantage their offspring, in either the short or long term. Sometimes mothers need to work for financial reasons and sometimes just to protect their sanity. Whatever the reason this is one book that is not going to criticize, although a few well-aimed observations may not go amiss.

GUILT

If mothers who either wanted to work or were obliged to work could just get on with it and stop feeling guilty, their lives would be much happier. Recently I attended a pre-school parents' meeting where a bevy of home-based moms turned on the working mothers in the group, telling them that they had no right to have children if they didn't want to stay at home and care for them. Even without this unwarranted assault, most of those moms were feeling guilty at short-changing their children. Let me reassure them by quoting from the internationally respected writings of Michael Rutter: "Although frequently blamed for their children's troubles, it is now apparent that working mothers have children with no more problems than the children of women who remain at home. This has now been shown in a wide range of studies using different measures of children's behavior."[13] So there you have it. What is important, however, is that there is good child care and extra attention given to the child when parent and child are together.

CARE

For those lucky enough to be surrounded by family, grandma or a close relative are the ideal care givers. If this is not available, day care can be arranged using either high quality approved centers or a local mother who takes in children. With a good day care center, you certainly will not go wrong, although it may be hard to get a vacancy and can prove expensive. With a private arrangement, the sitter must be chosen with great care. You must have complete confidence in her ability so that you can relax when at work and concentrate on the job in hand. When choosing a care giver, it is wise to watch how she relates to your little one. Does she show a genuine mothering gentleness and care, or is it a relationship based on an adequate injection of money? When the child is first left with her, enough time should be allowed so that this isn't done with a great rush and fuss. The child should be clearly told where you are going and when you will be back to pick him up. Despite the explanation, the young toddler will not understand and will shed copious tears on your departure, as well as probably punishing you by doing the same when you return. When the child attends school or pre-school, it is good investment to take some time off work and make an appointment to meet the teacher. This leaves her in no doubt of your interest in your child.

The teacher or sitter should be left a telephone number and told to telephone you if she has the slightest worry. This will help ensure a better standard of care for the child and some early warning for you if anything goes wrong.

A FAIR DEAL FOR THE CHILD

The mother who works must make sure she gives good attention to her child in the time that they are together. The work-tired mom feels little enthusiasm to start washing, cleaning the house, and cooking, let alone talking and playing with a toddler. But however good day care is, it is only acceptable if accompanied by good night care and weekend care. Shopping, cooking, and housework must not be allowed to consume all the parent's and child's time together, although if handled properly these can be a source of fun and education. If the marriage is sound and both parents work, running the house and child care must be shared evenly, 50-50. If money allows, shop well ahead so that only occasional stocking up from the corner store is needed. Prepared frozen foods are a good standby diet, but rather expensive and monotonous on a regular basis. Exotic, time-consuming dishes must be deleted from the menu and replaced by nutritious easy-to-prepare meals. For those with big freezers and an organized brain, there is much to be said for a weekend cooking binge, in which dishes are mass-produced and frozen in meal-sized portions. This allows good food to appear with all the speed of melting ice. A weekly visit to the local restaurant or hamburger joint will give the cook a welcome break and provide great excitement for the toddler.

Working moms and *House Beautiful* are not a compatible combination. Cleanliness, hygiene, and relative tidiness are desirable, but obsessive house pride is out. Family fun comes first. It is hard to communicate with a child over the roar of a vacuum cleaner and difficult to have a good, fun-filled romp around the house when an obsessive mother resents the slightest disturbance to even a cushion.

CONCLUSION

All mothers are working moms; it's just that some have taken on two jobs, one in the workforce and one at home. As with anyone who undertakes double employment, it is only fair that both must be performed with equal care and enthusiasm. Many mothers with young children work today, and probably an even larger group would be working if employment were available. I suspect that some of the criticism levelled at working mothers by those who stay home to care for their children is based on jealousy, and that in reality they would much rather have the chance to be out and about themselves.

The fact is that the children of good, working parents are just as happy and turn out equally well as those of parents who don't work. It is not the quantity of time you spend with your child that counts, it is the quality.

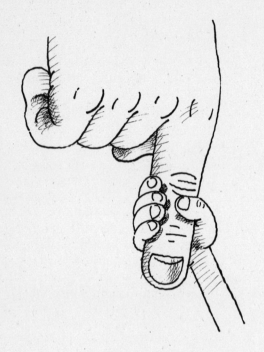

17

THE TODDLER AND THE SINGLE-PARENT FAMILY

The latest statistics show that about one in four marriages will break down irretrievably before the children of the marriage have left school. I am not an expert on this subject, but I think that any modern book on child care must give this a mention. It's no longer any use trying to pretend that single-parent families don't exist and sweeping them under the carpet.

Figures may indicate that the children of single parents have more behavioral, emotional, and educational problems than average, but these figures are somewhat misleading. They give the false impression that it is the state of being single that causes the problems, when in reality it is the events leading up to that state that have really stirred up the child.

The unfortunate, emotionally deprived girl who has never seen a proper example of mothering or experienced maternal love herself may leave home early and quickly become pregnant. She hopes that this baby will give her the love she has craved all her sad life. Unfortunately, this rarely happens and her life soon falls apart as she becomes isolated socially, has difficult behavior-management problems to cope with, and sometimes finds that in the end it is all too hard and she is forced to have the toddler adopted.

The mother whose husband is killed tragically in an accident may initially be totally immobilized by grief, which will naturally affect the child. In these difficult times those around usually close ranks, providing consistency and excellent support for mother and child. If the mother can keep on top and fight off depression, both she and the child will do remarkably well in the future.

In separation it is not the act of parting which causes the damage, but what happens before and after. In those warm-up years, if the home has been filled with anger, inconsistency and dirty, denigrating tricks, great damage can be done to the children, and the separation is the best thing that could possibly happen. That is not always the end of it. Court actions and custody battles rage on, the lawyers become increasingly rich, and the children increasingly disturbed. It is a sad reflection on human nature that the child of the eighties who has suffered the loss of a parent through death will probably fare better than one who is exposed to those extremely common, messy divorces. Unfortunately, when a parent says "All I want is what is best for my child," they often really mean what is best for themselves, and real thoughts for the child's immediate and emotional welfare are pushed to one side.

Where the parents still respect each other, but do not wish to live together, they will fight by the rules, break cleanly, come to an amicable settlement, and the child will suffer little.

Nowadays it is not only the unmarried, bereaved, and divorced who are single parents. In reality, many mothers may just as well be single, so little is the participation of the father in either home or marriage. This lack of paternal involvement, although far from ideal, may allow an equilibrium from which mom can give quite good child care, but this falls apart when the father not only refuses to help in the home or with his children, but deliberately sets out to sabotage his wife's efforts.

REBUILDING THE LIFE

In family break-ups a child copes best if supported by the safety net of grandparents, relatives, and friends who give that much-needed feeling of security and stability. Having lost one parent, the child secretly fears that the other will also abandon him, but the child will feel encouraged if all those well-known faces are still there and they still care.

After separation, the parent may often be immobilized with anger, regrets, squabbles, and grief. This is quite natural, but it is dangerous if the feelings remain for too long. A mother does not have to miraculously become "superwoman" and take on the double role of mother and father, but she must try to be an interesting person who does interesting things and gets out to see family and friends. After a marriage break-up it is never easy to get back into the social set you have known before. The separated wife may find she is more tolerated and accepted by her married friends, and many previous acquaintances stay clear as they now have divided loyalties. Having any sort of independent social life, or meeting with a new partner, is difficult. The child, having lost one parent, will guard most jealously the close relationship he now nurtures with the other. Initially, it is probably wise for the major part of any new relationship to take place outside the family home, and the new partner must realize that unless he divides his attention equally between toddler and mother, life will be far from peaceful when he is around.

The child is not a referee and as such is unaware of the rights and wrongs that split up his parents. He realizes that they both still exist, and he will still want visits from the absent partner. In our legal system, it is rare for visiting rights to be withdrawn, and they must be accepted and made to go as smoothly as possible. Some separations are so surrounded with anger that all too often these visits become a forum for the parents to further injure each other, using the child as a weapon. Often the young child will have his head filled with poisonous ideas about the absent partner, which will doubtless make the immature, irresponsible parent feel good, but will do the child immense harm. Other visiting parents over-indulge the child with expensive toys, excursions, and food which is all really only another form of "one-upmanship." Visiting should be encouraged but used strictly for the child's benefit, not that of the parents. Consistent discipline, sensible activities, and some stable home life given by both caretakers are the best way of handling this.

Money also affects the single parent, and most will experience a drastic drop in their standard of living. For many, it becomes imperative to start work, although it is often hard to find employment that will give reasonable pay for reasonable hours. Getting out to work usually helps the single mother, although the associated problems of child care—extra expense, further guilt and tiredness—all occur.

Following separation, some children develop an extremely close relationship with the remaining parent, while others feel resentful and abandoned, and behave abominably. With those who come closer, the relationship almost changes from that of parent and child to that of siblings. The child may take up a comfortable spot in the marriage bed and discipline may become difficult. In separation, behavior problems are said to occur most frequently between the ages of three and six: some children withdraw; others regress into behavior more befitting a baby; and some become angry and take this out on the unfortunate parent, who already has enough troubles without this extra burden.

CONCLUSION

Whether we like it or not, single-parent families are a major part of life today. Both parents and children are likely to have difficulties, depending on the problems that surrounded the separation in the first place, the personalities of the protagonists and their children, the availability of outside and family support, and their determination to get life going again.

Parents may find it lonely when all the family worries are carried on one frail set of shoulders. Life may be tough, but if they can quickly get over the regrets, anger, and petty squabbling as fast as possible, and try to be interesting people, then both parent and child should remain pretty firmly on the rails.

GETTING THE BEST
OUT OF GRANDMA

Grandmas and grandpas are some of our most valuable, and least utilized, natural resources. Over the last fifty years, as a result of better housing and what is called "progress," families have moved apart to live in relative isolation. This has brought with it all manner of problems. Mother-in-law jokes keep countless comedians in business, but this brand of humor is lost on the toddler, who is not interested in squabbles about his grandmother's interfering, irritating ways; he just enjoys being in her company. I write here in praise of the older generation and their great value to us and our children.

BENEFITS

Historically, in families that lived together, the younger members would call upon the experience of the older for advice. Owing to the often self-imposed isolation of modern-day living, however, parents lack easy access to that sensible advice as well as that much-needed extra pair of hands in times of stress. Other young parents view the older generation as past it, out of touch, and incapable of offering anything. This is a strange attitude, when you think that the world's most powerful countries are all ruled by people who are themselves grandfathers or grandmothers.

Life is lived at a more realistic pace as we get older, and it is viewed with that mature, "been there, done that" approach. Most older people have lived through wars, financial deprivation, and all manner of upsets, so they are in a better position to view the relative futility of the minor irritations that get blown out of all proportion in our day-to-day lives.

The older generation often has a more infectious, quiet gentleness that our fast-moving younger generation has not yet developed. Children who won't sit still are often quietened, as if by hypnotism, when in granny's care. Grandfathers may not be able to engage in high energy rough and tumbles, but they are miles ahead in other areas. The youngster will sit and listen to all manner of stories, viewing grandpa as the world's greatest wit and raconteur. They go out together on exciting safaris around the garden or the neighborhood, and although perhaps never more than 100 yards from base, there is so much of interest to see when helped by someone who can slow down for long enough to point them out.

There is no better form of temporary child care than that provided by good grandparents. This is really an extension of the parents, not least because genes and twenty years of brain-washing by grandma are bound to ensure that one parent will have much in common with her. Day care when the parents are at work, babysitting, care when sick—all these valuable services can be provided by grandparents. Some parents organize a regular afternoon or day a week when the child stays with grandma. Some take the occasional weekend mini-break, leaving their child with her, or take the grandparents on vacation to share the child-care load. There are tremendous benefits for the parents, the child, and the grandparents with this shared care.

Isolated mothers should not be backward about befriending elderly neighbors, a move good not only for the old folk, but also enriching for the young ones and one that provides much needed foster grandparents.

LAYING DOWN THE GROUND RULES

The main cause of friction with grandparents is when it is thought that they are interfering and criticizing. Their interference is perhaps understandable, because they find it hard to sit back quietly and watch their own children stumble through life making all the same mistakes that they themselves made and later regretted. A forewarning of one's errors is often greeted with either a deaf ear or much resentment. Many fights occur over trivial matters, which are irrelevant when viewed against the background of the great benefits of care-giving that grandparents can provide.

To ensure a good relationship, the rules have to be set down, and both sides have to accept that the other has rights. When the child is in the care of the parents, then the parents are in charge of the show, and although advice may be tactfully given, it does not have to be accepted. When the child is being looked after by the grandparents, then they are in charge and should not be forced to adhere to the parents' often obsessive and irrelevant ideas. A child is like a chameleon, who can blend in easily with an ever-changing environment.

Within reason, grandma should be allowed to feed the child whatever she wants, for example, and if the parents believe the sugar content will damage the child's teeth, this can be remedied with a quick brush of the teeth on returning home, rather than a family feud. Grandparents should be left to discipline the child in a way that feels best for them, and this should in no way damage the overall behavior and discipline of the child. The parents are the majority caretakers, and they cannot go through life blaming grandparents, schools, or other children for their offsprings' shortcomings. What shortcomings there are must be laid fairly and squarely at their doorstep to remedy.

CONCLUSION

It would be foolish to infer that all grandparents are of benefit to the toddler. Some have had little enough time for their own children and, having screwed them up, should not be afforded the privilege of doing the same for the next generation. But most of us under-use our greatest resource, tending to keep grandparents like Christmas decorations, to be brought out and shown only on high days and holidays. Both children and parents have much to learn from the older generation, whether it be grandma or grandpa or the old couple living next door.

For a happy partnership there are some simple rules. The younger generation must have some respect for age and maturity. They must not fight over pointless trivia, not interfere with grandma's care, and they can, therefore, expect the same non-interference when the child is in their care.

19

THE HANDICAPPED CHILD:
BEHAVIOR AND DISCIPLINE

It is very difficult to define clearly the behavioral problems of handicapped children, because there are so many different degrees of handicap affecting so many different children. There are a few generalizations that can be made, such as there being a somewhat higher proportion of restless, irritable, hard-to-comfort children among the handicapped.

The best forms of behavior and discipline techniques to use with handicapped children are exactly those you would use with normal toddlers. The good is rewarded and praised. The undesirable is ignored or pretended to be ignored. Time Out is equally useful with the handicapped, and controlled crying can be used with their sleep problems, although perhaps sedation is more often needed. One difference that we notice, however, is that, try as we may, the cure rate is less spectacular than we would like. Bearing this in mind and accepting it, we lower our sights and aim at first for a percentage improvement rather than always the full cure. This is not defeatism, merely realism. Any small improvement will be grasped by the tired parent.

As a general principle, each child should be treated with the discipline and management appropriate to his developmental (mental) age, no matter what the actual age may be. Despite this, however, you will find that outside factors can take charge and make treatment less successful. For example, children who have epilepsy that is poorly controlled are often more irritable and difficult than average. Their problems are often worse just before a fit and in the days that follow it. Some of the medications used for epilepsy can also worsen behavior, and some doctors do not seem to realize that the drugs they prescribe, although giving perfect control of the fits, can make the child virtually impossible to live with.

Children with major expressive speech problems tend to get very frustrated and often display far from easy behavior. Children born completely normal and later smitten by meningitis or head injury can develop many of the worst features of the hyperactive child. They may be of normal intelligence, but so handicapped by restlessness, poor concentration, and negligible sense that their parents are driven to distraction.

Autistic children tend to have very obsessive, repetitive behavior patterns and, hard as we may try, these can rarely be cured. We concentrate more these days on diverting these immovable problems to more socially acceptable presentations. The child who flaps his hands may be diverted to clapping, and the child who repeatedly flicks the light switch on and off can be diverted to a flashlight. Now that we have accepted the incurable aspects of our work and stopped wasting time attempting the impossible, our full energies can be channelled into improving the communication and socialization of these children which is much more important and rewarding.

DEALING WITH SPECIFIC PROBLEMS

Some severely intellectually handicapped or cerebral palsied children are extremely irritable by day. To divert them, we use movement and other techniques, although occasionally we have to resort to sedation. In the really difficult child, it is often necessary to provide care away from parents for one or two half days each week so that the exhausted parent has time to recharge her batteries.

Quite a number of handicapped children come to their parents' bed at night; others stay in their own, but cry. Parents are often much softer with these children than their normal brothers and sisters, and they are reluctant to let them cry or to throw them out of the marital bed. The controlled crying technique can be used for many of these children although in some severely retarded children I have had no success with anything other than heavy sedation. If the parents are to survive the day, they cannot afford to be up all night with a crying child. The secret with sedation is to give the drug, not at 6:00 p.m., just before bedtime, but when the child wakes up later in the night. This at least gives the parents some chance of gaining those golden hours sleep between midnight and dawn.

Some young handicapped children can take an age to feed, and mothers often spend up to two hours at mealtimes, leaving little time in the day for anything else. The best that can be done is to engage in sensible experimentation. For example, the child who takes his milk painfully slowly from a bottle may be given it from a spoon or cup, or given more solids instead. For the child who has difficulty with solids or lumpy food, different textures can be manufactured, and there are ways a skilled therapist can desensitize the mouth and encourage swallowing.

Toilet training may be difficult and sometimes toilet timing is all that can be initially achieved. Some children, particularly those with cerebral palsy, may get quite constipated. In these cases, it is a good idea to introduce a simple laxative or a "depth charge" extra fruit diet, which may ease the situation.

In the older handicapped child, all my greatest failures have been with those who have the major problem of "little sense." Day after day, year after year, the same behavior happens with these children, despite my best advice. The problem is that these children, although they may appear quite intelligent on being tested, do not learn from their experiences. Their poor parents try their best, but as nothing helps, they soon begin to feel quite impotent. Unfortunately they may be further disadvantaged when advised by some newly-qualified academic "whiz kid" whose university education never taught him that a child may have the severe handicap of lack of sense. He will misread the situation, blame all the lack of success on the poor parents, and make their lives even harder than it already is. The parents should be given all the support and encouragement possible. If things are not going well, some temporary respite care should be arranged to keep the parents on the beam and to allow the other children of the family a more equal share of their parents' time.

UNDERSTANDING AND HELPING THE PARENTS OF THE HANDICAPPED CHILD

Many parents of a special child are determined to remain completely unchanged in their attitudes and expectations, but most do treat their child differently from his brothers and sisters. Many are over-protected, never allowed to cry, and usually given their own way. Behavior techniques are often not seen through with determination, because the parents find it hard to be tough on a child who has physical or intellectual problems. And even the most robust parent has considerable inner sadness and is under much stress.

I will digress for a minute and give a brief outline of the common reactions of the parent with a handicapped child. Once these are understood, it is easier to give them help. Following the realization that one has a handicapped child, the parent may go through a form of grief reaction, not unlike the feelings experienced after the death of a loved one. Initially, when they hear the news, there may be a short stage where they feel stunned and disbelieving. This soon progresses to a long, painful stage where they try to come to terms with the situation they find themselves in. This may take months, years, or even a lifetime. At this stage, the parents need to protect themselves from the harsh reality of the situation by closing the shutters of their mind and only letting a little of the realization sink in each day. Denial, anger, and activity are all methods they use to survive these difficult times.

With denial, the parents may refuse to accept the degree of the problem and shop around from doctor to doctor in the hope of hearing better news. Some deny they have even been told anything, and others embark on ill-proven miracle cures. Anger is a strange defense that we all use when under immense stress. It seems at times like this that displacing a bit of the anger we feel onto those around us often makes us feel better. When the home football team has lost the game, you come home and kick the cat, not that the poor animal has done anything wrong, but it just makes you feel better. Activity is a defense that we all engage in when under great stress. Sitting immobile and worrying only makes problems seem even larger. The parents may take up a good cause, take on full-time employment, or work day and night for their special child. The activity will probably make them very tired, but it does help them to feel better.

It is not clever for anyone to try to break these defenses down. [14] Once the shutters are torn down and the full light of the problem hits the parents, they may be precipitated into that state of immobility, isolation and guilt called depression. I believe that with time, talk, good friends and good practical help, a better state of mind can soon be reached. The parents may still feel the hurt, but they can look past it to talk realistically and plan constructively for the future.

HOW CAN FRIENDS HELP?

The reactions I have mentioned are all normal and healthy. With good friends and good time, the presence of these defenses will become unnecessary. With denial, a friend should not force the issue, but equally must not be afraid to talk gently and openly about what has happened. Pretending that the handicap doesn't exist fools no one and only serves to upset the parents. When parents are about to risk bankruptcy and destroy their other children's well-being all for the sake of some ill-proven miracle cure, they should be firmly encouraged to visit a top local expert beforehand rather than some crank known to them only through the pen of a sensation-seeking journalist.

Anger is quite natural and may land on even the closest of friends. The anger is not really aimed at the friend; it is more a sign of the parents' tension and upset at their lot in life. Friends should be philosophical, and view it as a privilege that some of the anger that is probably leveled at the Almighty is landing on their humble shoulders!

Never criticize the mother who wishes to work or strive for some noble cause. She may well need this, and to suddenly remove it would be as ill-conceived as removing the crutch from a limping man. Activity is far preferable to immobility, isolation, guilt, and the lack of enthusiasm that it generally replaces. Those who have become isolated need great understanding. They need encouragement to get out and mix, as well as practical help with child care. Last, but most valuable, they need your listening and non-condemning ear.

The message is stick with the parents. They may not say it in so many words, but they need friends and will be grateful, if not openly, certainly in their hearts.

CONCLUSION

Such is the variety and degree of handicaps that there is no universal remedy for behavior and management problems. As a general rule, use the same behavioral techniques with the handicapped child as you would use with a normal child of similar mental age. Bear in mind that other factors will sabotage your best efforts, such as increased irritability, specific medical conditions, lack of concentration, and lack of sense. Always remember how stressed the parents of a handicapped child are, and how you can help by hanging in there with them.

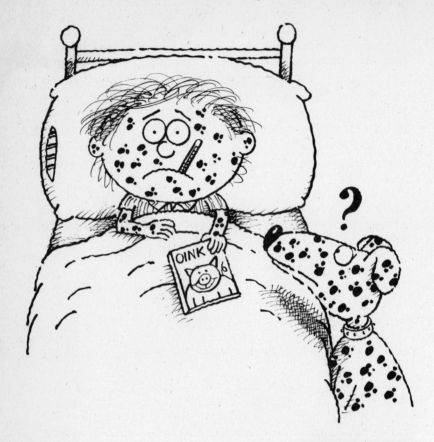

20

COMMON
TODDLER ILLNESSES

For the parents of a toddler, hardly a day seems to go by without their child suffering from something, be it tonsillitis, German measles, or the common cold. As part of growing up, the child goes through a whole series of illnesses, each one apparently more ghastly than the one before, but nevertheless all quite common and in most cases nothing to be feared. To be forewarned is, as they say, to be fore-armed. This chapter deals with the most common medical problems, and it is designed as a pointer to the parent. Naturally if you are worried by any of these symptoms, take your child to a doctor.

THROATS, TONSILS, COUGHS, COLDS AND VIRUSES

The common cold

Colds are caused, not by one, but by a number of viruses, which explains why one infection may follow straight after another, giving the impression of a non-stop nose run. As they are viruses, they do not respond to treatment with antibiotics but cure themselves, usually within four or five days of appearance. When the child first goes to pre-school, he is coughed over by a multitude of virus-splattering infants, and this is frequently his worst year for infections. Eventually some immunity is acquired, and the number of illnesses gradually decreases each year until adulthood. Most of the natural immunity which a baby inherits from his mother is lost by the age of six months, and the first winter thereafter is often a prime one for colds.

Average toddlers will get up to nine colds each year, with six being about the usual number. This works out at about one every eight weeks. Colds are spread by playmates and other people with whom the toddler comes into contact; they do not come from getting wet or playing out in the cold, whatever the myths may be. Despite years of trying to prevent colds with various vitamins and other treatments, there is still absolutely nothing one can reliably do to help.

A further area of confusion arises because the common cold often starts with a sore throat, slightly pink ear drums, and even a slight cough. When all these symptoms come together it shows that the child has indeed contracted a common cold; individually they indicate tonsillitis, ear infection, or bronchitis. There is no specific treatment for colds, although aspirin-type preparations may make the child feel more comfortable.

Tonsils

It is almost impossible to find tonsils in anyone over 25 years of age, because in years past they were whipped out at the drop of a scalpel, being regarded universally as useless appendages. Nowadays, removal of the tonsils is relatively rare, and the operation is not performed unless there are some major reasons for doing so. Tonsillitis is not the sore throat found at the beginning of a cold; it is rather the specific infection of the tonsillar tissues at the back of the throat and their associated glands at the angle of the jaw. The tonsils are not just red, but "angry" looking with flecks of pus, and as this is usually caused by bacteria, antibiotic treatment is needed and usually effective.

The severity of the tonsillitis or the need for surgical removal is not dependent on the size of the offending part. Tonsils are minute in the young toddler, reaching their peak size somewhere around the age of seven years. Large does not mean unhealthy, and large tonsils certainly do not cause feeding problems.

Croup

This is a juvenile form of laryngitis, usually caused by a virus, which creates an infection in the region of the child's voice box (larynx). Antibiotics are no help and probably the best remedy is the good, old-fashioned one of inhaling steam from a basin or kettle or sitting in a steamy bathroom. The child with croup makes a characteristic and often frightening "crowing" noise when breathing in, accompanied by a cough like the sound of a sea lion. In its mild form, it can be easily treated at home with humidity. A small minority of children can become quite seriously ill, and if their condition deteriorates rapidly or there is any other medical concern, seek help immediately.

Bronchitis

Bronchitis is another viral infection, which will probably start as a cough and go to the chest. Once again, this ailment will not respond to antibiotics. Despite making quite a lot of coughing noise, the child should be relatively happy and show little sign of illness. When the coughing is associated with wheezing and shortness of breath, it may be wise to consider asthma as a possible cause. When fever and general sickness are also present, then it may be a more major chest infection and a medical opinion should be sought. Bronchitis may be the first symptom of approaching measles in some children, even before the very first spot has appeared.

Asthma

Asthma affects about 10 per cent of all children. Its hallmark is a musical wheeze that comes from the depths of the lungs, mostly when breathing out. It is made worse by exercise and viral respiratory infections, and it is often associated with periods of dry coughing in the middle of the night.

Many parents are obviously distressed when I diagnose asthma, thinking immediately of their schooldays when friends with severe asthma spent more time at home than at school, were excluded from sports, and were regarded as moderate cripples. This is not the case today. Most children have the condition in a mild form, and they can live a completely normal, unrestricted life.

Treatment uses certain medicines to open up the air passages, and they are best administered as inhalants. These products are now extremely safe and highly effective, and they do not lose potency with continued use. Allergy testing, milk withdrawal, chest exercises, antibiotics, and restrictions of life-style are not prescribed for my patients.[15]

Summary

- Expect your toddler to get up to nine colds a year.
- Colds do not respond to antibiotics.
- Tonsillitis is an infection of the tonsils, not to be confused with the common cold. It is treated with antibiotics and only very rarely by the surgeon's knife. Big tonsils do not mean bad tonsils.
- Croup is a respiratory crow with a sea-lion like bark. In the minor form it responds to humidity; the major form requires urgent medical help.
- Most coughs are of viral origin and do not require antibiotics. When associated with wheezing, shortness of breath, or significant general sickness, medical help must be sought.

EAR PROBLEMS

Hearing

At birth the baby is startled by loud noises and changes the pattern of his crying when comforted by his mother's voice. At six months, he will turn his head towards the direction of quiet sounds from objects he cannot see. Just before one year, there is much tuneful babble in some strange, unintelligible foreign language, which is soon followed by repeating appropriate words. At this stage we know there can be no gross hearing problem. Although most children who have severe hearing loss are now diagnosed between six and nine months of age, I still see quite a few who have remained undiagnosed until 18 months. If the child does not respond to quiet, unexpected noises, if his speech development is slow, or if there is the slightest doubt in the parents' minds, a proper hearing test should be arranged.

The middle ear

The human ear is made up of an ear canal, which often contains some wax and goes from the outside to the ear drum, and inside the drum is the middle ear, which is a small chamber filled with air. In this chamber a number of delicate little bones transmit the sound waves from the ear drum to the hearing nerve and then the brain. This middle ear is connected by a thin tube (Eustachian tube), which communicates with the outside atmosphere through the back of the nose. This causes the "popping" of ears associated with the pressure increase of a vigorous nose blow or when going up in an airplane.

For the middle ear to transmit sound efficiently it needs to be filled with air, which gives it resonance, rather like some musical instruments. When full of fluid, the tone and hearing volume is diminished much in the same way as filling a drum with concrete would affect its musical quality. Fluid gathers in the middle ear when the tube from the nose gets blocked, as may happen briefly during a heavy cold. If the fluid in the middle ear is associated with infection, this may cause an acute ear infection (acute otitis media). If the fluid is present but not infected, it deadens the hearing in a chronic manner.

Ear infection (otitis media)

Following a cold, a swim, or diving into a pool, bacteria may enter the middle ear, and if the tube blocks, an infection can develop. The child becomes sick, irritable, has ear pain, partial hearing loss and, on examination, the ear drum looks angry and red. Nature will cure this condition either by re-opening the tube to the nose and releasing the infection or through a perforation in the ear drum. As the infection is usually caused by bacteria, antibiotics are given, along with a minor pain-killer such as aspirin or Tylenol. Most doctors tend to greatly over-diagnose and over-treat ear infections, such is our concern to protect the young child's hearing. Even if the ear drum does perforate, this almost always heals by itself without problems, although, of course, prevention is a better course of action. Even if you don't halt the complaint in time, it is not the end of the world.

Fluid in the ear

Sterile fluid may collect in the middle ear in association with a cold, flu or after an acute ear infection. This is most commonly seen in the early-school-age child; a teacher will note that a child's hearing has deteriorated when he starts to talk louder than usual and ignores much of what is said to him. If the teacher fails to notice the condition, the parents must let her know, so that the child may be brought to the front of the class to avoid missing anything that is said.

Pain is usually not a problem with fluid in the ear, and there is no great urgency in treatment. With time, most cases will resolve themselves, although the process can be hurried along by a simple operation in which plastic tubes (gromets) are placed in the ear drum to let the fluid escape. The tubes drop out after a number of months and usually do not need reinsertion.

The insertion of these tubes has taken over from the tonsillectomies of earlier days as the most common operation performed in childhood. Studies showing definite long-term benefits are so far inconclusive, and it is uncertain whether this will prove to be a passing fashion or an operation for the future.

With the children I see, I steer a middle road, insisting that a proper hearing test is conducted, which must show definite hearing loss before surgery is contemplated. I also prefer to leave at least six weeks before surgery, since nature has an obliging way of resolving the situation, although not always permanently.

Summary

- If a child who does not turn toward quiet, unexpected sounds at six months, has no work-like babble at one year, and is slow to develop speech, a hearing defect must be considered.
- If infected fluid is trapped in the middle ear (acute otitis media), it causes pain and fever, and antibiotic treatment is needed.
- When sterile fluid is trapped in the middle ear it thickens and is referred to as "glue ear." This is not an acute condition. It will be cured either by time and nature, or by the insertion of tubes if the condition is not considerably better within six to ten weeks.

VOMITING AND DIARRHEA

These are both extremely common in the toddler. When vomiting and diarrhea are present together this often means an infection in the gut (gastroenteritis); if vomiting occurs alone, it is more likely to be due to an infection in the body, possibly a cold, flu, or occasionally some more serious problem. If your child is very sick or you have any doubts, medical help should be sought. If the child is not too unwell, however, and vomiting and diarrhea are a problem, here are a few tips.

Children with acute gut infections need fluids, not solids. If they are going to be harmed, it is not through loss of body "fat weight," but "water weight" when too much water and salt have been lost. If vomiting and diarrhea are caused by gastroenteritis, it is almost always of viral origin, so they are not helped by antibiotics, which can often compound the problem and cause diarrhea where none previously existed.

I never cease to be amazed by the stream of odd cures I am confronted with by parents with vomiting toddlers.

"What's the problem?"

"He vomits everything up, doctor."

"What are you giving him?"

"Oh, not much. A glass of milk with a spoonful of sugar, a little salt, eggnog and a little added custard to keep his strength up!"

After all that, the parents are genuinely surprised when the child throws it all back at them.

The correct treatment for vomiting is to give *small amounts* of *clear fluids, frequently.*

Small means no more than one ounce of fluid at a time.

Clear means clear, not milk, not solids, not body-building protein, just fluid. The corner druggist will sell mixtures which, when added to water, are designed to replace all the water and chemicals a vomiting child may lose. Theoretically these should be given, but in practice there is a far simpler, cheaper, and more readily available solution: clear lemonade. Lemonade contains about 10 per cent sugar, some minerals and, if not too fizzy, is pleasant for most children to take. It seems silly to force nauseated children to drink fluids that they normally would not like, and you cannot go too far wrong with lemonade. You can even freeze it and make ice-blocks for the child to suck. Milk is best abandoned altogether, as it is less easily digested, and as every mother knows, it is very much more unpleasant to clean up than second-hand lemonade.

Frequently means each quarter or half hour during the day. Although this may seem very little fluid, you can in fact administer a quart and a half a day in this fashion quite effortlessly.

When a young child craves fluids and the parents accede to his requests on demand, this will probably result in vomiting. A simply way to overcome this excess intake is to set a cooking timer bell to ring every 15 minutes. This will let the child know when his allotted fluid time arrives and, if treated patiently and not rushed, the vomiting will soon come under control.

Acute infective diarrhea is almost always of viral origin, and antibiotics should only be used in some rare and very specific cases. If clear fluids are given, the bowel has little to discharge and the diarrhea will come quickly under control. Chalk medicines to "slow the bowel" are unnecessary in children and, as anyone who has tried to chew chalk when feeling sick will tell you, is far from pleasant. In the days that follow gastroenteritis, the child usually becomes extremely constipated. This does not need treatment and merely indicates that the bowel is quite empty and has nothing more to get rid of.

Summary

- Vomiting in toddlers is common and may accompany any childhood illness, even the most trivial.
- When the child has considerable vomiting and diarrhea, the cause is usually viral gastroenteritis, in which case the child does not need calorific foods, milk, chalk medicines, or antibiotics.
- He should be given only clear fluids, in small amounts, frequently.
- If the child looks sick, "distant," dull-eyed, weak and passes little urine, or if you are at all worried, get medical help at once.

FEVERS

When the body is upset by an infection, whether it be a common cold or something more serious, the temperature will rise in response. Some illnesses, such as measles, can cause extremely high fevers, while others, which may in fact be more serious, may have quite low fever levels. The presence of a fever is merely an indication that the child is sick; its height of temperature is not an accurate barometer of the severity of the problem.

High temperature will upset the already unhappy child and make him feel even more miserable. His parents will start to worry since they know that some children with fevers are also prone to convulsions. For both these reasons, young children with temperatures tend to be treated more vigorously than their adult counterparts.

A feverish child must be dressed sensibly, not wrapped up in extra shirts and woollens and put into a bed heaped up with blankets. He should be given one of the commercial children's preparations of either Tylenol or aspirin. Children usually find aspirin in its liquid form pleasant to take, and it has few side effects.

Note that aspirin has been exiled from use for infants and children because of the belief, by some, including the FDA and CDC, that it may precipitate Reye's syndrome.

Plunging the hot child into a bath filled with water straight from the Arctic is not only exceedingly cruel, but also counterproductive. When the sizzling body splashes down into the icy water the skin reacts by shutting off its blood supply and diverting the blood to those warmer regions "inland from the coast." As a result, little heat is lost by the child, despite the unpleasant experience. Being stripped and sat in front of a gale force fan is another nasty experience, which will only cause the child to shiver and thus, paradoxically, generate more heat.

The proper procedure is to strip the child down to his underwear and, if the temperature is still high, sponge him over gently with tepid, rather than cold, water. This gives a gentle, cooling effect and does not precipitate shivering or divert the blood away from the skin.

It seems a very unfair world for young children. When I have the flu or a fever I go to bed, turn the electric blanket on to "summer Sahara" temperature, and sweat it out. But for the poor toddler it's all stripping off and sponging down and general disturbance. Of course the difference is that with the toddler, we have a great fear of "fever fits."

FEVER FITS (FEBRILE CONVULSIONS)

In some children, the developing brain seems particularly sensitive to temperature rise, and this causes them to throw a fit. These fits are most common between the ages of six months and three years, and rarely happen after the age of five years. They are not uncommon: four per cent of children in this age group will have a fit, usually a febrile convulsion.

For most parents it is a very frightening experience, and they can be forgiven for thinking that their small child is about to die. The fit can come on amazingly quickly; many children are only slightly unwell beforehand and give no warning at all. The victims will suddenly go stiff, the eyes roll back, and breathing becomes labored. They will then start shaking or twitching, before relaxing to lie dazed and confused. After this they become sleepy, and, having slept, will appear fully recovered. Luckily most of these fits last for less than five minutes, although to the watching parent it can seem like an eternity.

If a child has a high fever, the cooling measures and medicines mentioned should prevent many febrile convulsions. If the child does convulse, he should be placed gently on his side to prevent choking. Difficult as it may be, try not to panic. Young children do not die, nor do they harm their brains with short fever fits. Stay with him rather than running off for help. Don't force spoons or other objects into his mouth, as the apparently difficult breathing is not due to a blockage in his throat but rather a tightening of his respiratory muscles. If this is a first fit, or if it does not come quickly under control, take the child straight to a doctor.

A child who has a simple febrile convulsion does not have epilepsy, and these fits will not continue through his life. After one febrile episode, however, the child is much more likely to have another before he grows out of the convulsion-prone age group.

Summary

- The short fever fit does not damage the child, only his mother's nerves.
- Febrile convulsions do not mean epilepsy.
- Lay the child on his side.
- Don't force objects into his mouth.
- Don't panic.
- Seek medical help when the child comes round or if still convulsing at the end of five minutes.

VACCINATIONS

Babies and toddlers should be given full immunization against diphtheria, tetanus, whooping cough and polio, as well as measles, mumps, German measles (rubella), and chicken pox. I will attempt here to set out the major illnesses and their risks.

Diphtheria

This is a particularly nasty illness in which bacteria produce a membrane, which blocks the major breathing tubes, and a poison, which can cause the heart to fail. Before the introduction of the diphtheria vaccine, it came in tragic epidemics and the gravestone of country churchyards list whole families of children and adults who were wiped out within weeks by it. Nowadays, thanks to modern vaccines, diphtheria is almost unheard of in the developed countries of the world. Immunization for babies is vital and harmless.

Polio

As a child, I can remember my parents barring me from public swimming pools and keeping me away from other children as the annual summer polio epidemic swept into our city. My mother was terrified that I would join the children who filled the hospital wards, some in iron lungs, some with minor paralysis, and others crippled for life.

In the United States, polio had, of course, come to prominence with the election to the presidency of Franklin D. Roosevelt, himself a sufferer of the disease, which he contracted suddenly in his late thirties. Such was the panic over the illness, that even though the initial vaccines produced were relatively hazardous, mothers were prepared to take the risk. Now all that is past history. The vaccine is absolutely safe and doesn't even need a needle these days. It's as easy as swallowing a lump of sugar. But many mothers, lulled perhaps by the rarity of the disease today, just don't bother with it. Every child should have a polio vaccination.

Tetanus (lockjaw)

Tetanus is caused by an infection that enters the body through wounds that are contaminated, usually by soil. This makes every one of us susceptible, and since tetanus is a long, painful illness with a high risk of death, it is wise to be protected against it. Modern tetanus vaccines are completely safe and very effective.

Whooping cough (pertussis)

Although it is much less serious than the other illnesses mentioned so far, whooping cough follows a long, difficult course. Death occurs about once in every 4000 cases during an epidemic. It has been referred to as "the cough of one hundred days," and although this may be a bit of an exaggeration, full recovery may well take three months. In the toddler, there are spasms of coughing, which often end in vomiting and go on day and night. There is no treatment other than to provide good mothering and nursing care.

Vaccination has nearly wiped out this once-prevalent disease.

Measles

Measles is basically a red rash with a cough. It is not a life-threatening illness in children who are well-nourished, although it causes very serious illness and death in Africa and other parts of the world where children are underfed. Measles is extremely infectious, and an unvaccinated child will most certainly get it. It is a nasty illness, which makes children feel extremely sick, but this and other unpleasant side effects can be effectively prevented by vaccination. The vaccine should be given after the child's first birthday, the illness being rare before then, because the baby still has immunity given by his mother.

Mumps

Recently a vaccine for mumps has been given along with the measles one, and it seems to provide quite good protection. This is the least severe of the childhood illnesses described, but it is possible for mumps to cause loss of hearing in one ear or even a viral brain infection, and consequently it is believed that vaccination should be encouraged.

The risks of vaccination

Nothing in life can be guaranteed 100 per cent safe, but all risks must be balanced against the benefits. There is no doubt that with diphtheria, tetanus and polio vaccination the benefits are immense and the risks negligible. With whooping cough vaccination there is a small risk, which must be balanced against the far greater risk of death or permanent handicap should the child contract the disease. Measles and mumps vaccine are not absolutely necessary, but as the risk of contracting these diseases is extremely high vaccination does stop quite a bit of needless suffering, and the occasional rare, but serious, complications the illnesses can produce. In short, the risks of these childhood vaccines are minute in comparison with those of the illnesses they prevent. I have had no hesitation in having my own children vaccinated against all these diseases, including whooping cough.

THE CHILDHOOD ILLNESSES

Having looked at vaccines and vaccination, let's look briefly at the common childhood illnesses themselves. In the days before vaccination, few of us would have escaped without having at least three of these four illnesses. Measles is so infectious that 100 per cent of all children would have got it, while 80 per cent of them would contract mumps and chicken pox. Rubella, or German measles as it is sometimes called, would have affected perhaps 70 per cent of children. So what are the main symptoms of these diseases?

Measles

Measles is a sick child with a red rash, a cough, and sore eyes.

This is the most infectious of all the illnesses, and it takes ten to fourteen days to incubate. At first, the child develops a high fever, a cough, and sore eyes, but not a spot is there to be seen. He has a runny nose, and as he coughs and splutters he spreads this highly infectious virus to all around, three days before anything is even suspected. About three days after the beginning of the illness the rash develops, which consists of many little red spots that cover the body. Many of us who have trained in children's medicine have made fools of ourselves at some time or other in our early careers by admitting a coughing child with a high fever to a busy hospital ward, having diagnosed the condition as bronchitis, only to find next morning a rash of red spots and an irate ward nurse wanting to know why a highly infectious child was sitting up in the middle of her nice, sterile ward!

Measles makes children quite sick, but one attack, once over, will give lifelong immunity.

Mumps

Mumps is swelling of one or both parotid glands plus a mild feeling of general illness.

Mumps is less infectious than measles and about 20 per cent of children will escape it altogether. It is caused by a virus, which takes two to three weeks to incubate. There is a mild fever and a swelling of one or both of the parotid glands, which are situated in front of the ear lobes at the angle of the jaw. Sometimes the child may have a headache and neck stiffness.

When the schoolchild contracts mumps and brings it home, most fathers get rather concerned as they have heard nasty rumors about what this illness can do to grown men. Orchitis (inflammation of one or both testicles) does not happen in the young child, and it is much less common in the adult than popular myth would have us believe. It is painful when it does occur, but that other much-talked of complication, "sterility," is exceptionally rare. Fathers can now relax!

Chicken pox

Chicken pox is an ugly, itchy rash with little fever or feeling of general discomfort.

This viral illness takes about two weeks to incubate. It starts with a crop of itchy, raised red spots like flea bites, usually on the trunk. There are often little spots inside the mouth, which is well outside the normal chewing ground of the common flea. The spots enlarge, fill with fluid, and form vesicles (blisters), which eventually burst and are covered by scabs. While all this is going on, the child may look awful and feel intensely itchy, but he will only have a low fever and feel relatively well. The old-fashioned pink Calamine lotion is probably as good as anything to ease the itching.

Rubella (German measles)

Rubella is a faint, generalized rash, with enlarged glands at the back of the neck in a child who does not appear to be sick.

This viral illness is completely different from measles. It takes from two to three weeks to incubate, and in the young child it is so mild it can easily go unnoticed. There is a fine pink rash, which may not be very obvious and lasts for about three days. This is associated with enlarged glands, particularly those at the back of the neck, on the lower part of the skull.

Rubella causes no harm and little sickness in young children, the rubella vaccination, however, is given routinely at 15 months old, along with the mumps and measles vaccine. The main danger is for pregnant women, as contact at an early stage of pregnancy can cause major abnormalities in the unborn baby. Any would-be mother can easily find out if she is immune or not before pregnancy by having a simple blood test.

BOW LEGS, KNOCK KNEES, FLAT FEET

Another area of the body that constantly concerns parents is the legs, including the knees and the feet. In the majority of minor leg and foot problems no treatment is needed. The days of night splints, irons, and wedges for self-righting conditions have passed.

When the child first walks, his untried feet can be seen pointing in all manner of interesting directions. They usually right themselves within months, at which point you will notice that the child's legs are extremely bowed and he is walking around in his diaper with the posture of a saddle-sore cowboy. At about two-and-a-half the legs will straighten, although this adjustment may be overdone and the child will then suffer from knock knees. By the age of five, most legs are relatively straight and the feet point in the right direction. Some children continue walking with their toes turned slightly inwards and, if mild, this is of no great concern. In fact, one specialist colleague of mine sports the theory that these children may make the best footballers, being able to change direction and weave faster than anyone else on the field! There has to be some compensation for having feet that point in two directions at the same time.

All babies and toddlers have flat feet. It often takes until the age of six for the ligaments to tighten up and produce a proper arch. This may never happen in some families, where there is a history of flat feet. There still seem to be two different schools of thought concerning flat feet. Some believe that the child should walk around without shoes and strengthen his ligaments; others believe that wedges in the shoes produce better arches. I believe that each year more and more are moving towards the "no treatment" lobby.

Once again these are general observations. If the bends or postures cause any concern, a specialist opinion should be sought.

TODDLER DEVELOPMENT WORRIES

Books on child care usually list a multitude of clever developmental milestones for the child to attain at any given age. Few of these books, however, distinguish between the important, high prediction, milestones and those that are best termed interesting but useless. Looking at a child's developmental profile, one is interested in his gross motor, fine motor, hearing, vision, communication, social, and play skills. When one has been working for some years in a developmental assessment unit it soon becomes clear which of these have the most value.

The gross motor area—walking, running and climbing—tends

to be of most interest to the parents. In fact, early walking bears little relationship to advanced intelligence and is much more likely to be an inherited family trait. Children who walk early often have a mother who was an early walker. When teaching psychologists, who have a great interest in motor milestones in young children, I cite the case of the greyhound, which is probably one of the most advances "gross motor animals" around. Any dog that spends its entire life chasing after a stuffed hare without suspecting it is being fooled is, to my mind at least, not very intelligent!

By far the most valuable skills are those in the area of communication. At six months, the child who communicates vigorously with his eyes, takes in everything in his environment, and "doesn't miss a move" has a good start to life. In the second year, the child with good appropriate, non-repetitive speech is likely to do well.

If the child has no speech, good comprehension is even more important, and the child should be able to point with accuracy to objects in pictures and books or to things in his environment. I learn much about a child's intelligence, when he is difficult to assess, by watching him play. I look for constructive qualities, where he uses the material provided in an intelligent way. I also look for imagination and pretend play. If these are present in the toddler, it is unlikely he has any major problem of intellectual development.

I worry when a child has little interest in his surroundings, walks around in a purposeless manner, and is slow to respond to sound. I worry when there is little understanding of simple messages and only parrot-like repetitive speech. I worry when there is apparently little understanding; for example, the child may flick through a book in an obsessive manner without displaying any interest or recognition of what is inside it. I worry when a toddler who does not talk to me with his voice does not communicate with his face or eyes either. I worry when the child has no pretend or constructive play and is stuck at the stage of throwing and banging toys together or running around the house aimlessly.

Many books are available on the developmental assessment of young children. My only aim here has been to point out those general patterns that will indicate whether or not a child is likely to succeed intellectually, and those which cause concern.

THE SICK CHILD: WHEN TO PANIC

When teaching junior doctors, I impress upon them that their greatest skill lies not in knowing hundreds of rare medical facts but in being able to reliably spot "the sick child." It is difficult and probably dangerous for me to try to express in written form what is essentially a "gut feeling." I believe that most of the clues are in the eyes and the child's alertness.

The child who has vomited all day may nevertheless appear alert, have bright eyes, and take a lively and keen interest when you walk into the room. If this is the case, he is probably safe. If the same child were dull-eyed, distant, and at all confused, then medical help must be summoned immediately. When a child is pale, sweaty, and looks anxious, it is a good idea to get help quickly. This is generally how a child will appear if he is "shocked" and may have some major surgical or other condition. The child who has sunken eyes, a lack of elasticity in his skin, a dry mouth, and is passing little urine is also a worry. Any child with a stiff neck, which is painful to move or bend, needs medical examination, as does a child with panting, over-breathing, or deep rattling breathing.

When mom is worried, I worry. When mom is worried and grandma is worried, I worry a lot!

MEDICINES: HOW TO GIVE THEM

Doctors have no difficulty in writing prescriptions for children; the problem comes when it is time to force the foreign substance down the toddler's firmly shut trap! If an unpleasant-tasting medicine has been prescribed once, it is wise to let the doctor know, as often there is a more palatable alternative for the subsequent occasions. For the child who is a militant drug refuser, sometimes preparations that require fewer doses a day may be prescribed. With antibiotics, this is particularly useful, as often two-dose-a-day drugs can supplant the four-dose-a-day ones.

Most drugs can be given in liquid form to toddlers, preferably slipped into the mouth on a spoon and chased down by a favorite drink. For the reluctant child, sometimes a syringe (with the needle removed!) is more effective, squirting the medicine through a small opening in the mouth. Watch out for the fine aerosol spray which can blow around the room once the medicine has hit the child's tongue! If capsules or tablets are given, the mouth should be moist before their introduction, or the capsules themselves can be moistened before they are put in the mouth. These measures help to lubricate them on that short, difficult journey from the tongue to the throat. Little tablets slip down with remarkable ease when placed in a little ice cream. Bigger ones may be crushed, placed on top of a thin layer of ice cream, with jam or chocolate topping being placed over that, thus making a spoon-sized medicine sandwich.

When a child has an illness that is making his stomach delicate because of copious vomiting, giving medicine will be a far from popular exercise. Certain medicines have to be given, but others are best omitted rather than vomited up. It seems pointless to administer a preparation designed to stop vomiting if all that is going to happen to it is that it is going to be thrown straight up again!

BED REST FOR TODDLERS

In modern hospitals children who have undergone major surgery will be seen up and about the next day. Meanwhile, not a mile down the road, a child with a red tonsil will be confined to his bed by a worried mother for what may seem to him like an eternity. Bed rest is now an outdated practice reserved for children with pre-paralytic polio and other equally rare conditions. If the child feels well enough to want to be up, good for him. If he leaves his bed to lie on a rug by the fire, that's just as good. If he feels so miserable that all he wants is the peace and comfort of bed, that is when he will get bed rest.

There are no black and white rules. Sense and flexibility are the important things, but you will usually find that, in these cases, the child knows best.

NOTES

1. Hornberger et al., *Health Supervision of Young Children in California, Berkeley,* Bureau of Maternal and Child Health, State of California Department of Public Health, 1960.

2. Richman, *Journal of Child Psychology and Psychiatry,* 1975, vol. 16, pp. 277-87.

3. Chess et al., *Behavioural Individuality in Early Childhood,* New York University Press, 1963.
   Chess, *Temperament and Development,* Brunner Mazel, New York, 1977.

4. Chamberlin, *Paediatric Clinics of North America,* vol. 21, no. 1, February 1974.

5. Anders, *Paediatrics,* vol. 63, pp. 860-4, 1979.

6. Beltramini et al, *Paediatrics,* vol. 72, no. 2, 1973.

7. Tizard, *The Origins of Human Social Relations,* Academic Press, London, 1971, pp. 147-61.

8. Mason *Veterinary Record,* vol. 86, 1970, pp. 612-16.

9. Illingworth, *The Normal Child,* Churchill Livingstone, 1983.

10. Connors, *Food additives and Hyperactive Children,* Plenum Press, 1980.

11. *Learning Disorders Pediatric Clinics of North America,* April, 1984.

12. Rutter, *Scientific Foundations of Developmental Psychiatry,* Heinemann, 1980.

13. Rutter, *Child Psychiatry—Modern Approaches,* Blackwell, 1977.

14. Green, *Medical Journal of Australia,* vol. 1, 1981, 402-4.

15. Green, *The Practitioner,* vol. 223, 1979, 690-5.

FURTHER READING

As well as the publications mentioned on the previous page in "Notes," I would like to recommend Ronald Illingworth's book, *The Normal Child* (published by Churchill Livingstone, 1983). It contains 300 pages of reassurance and wisdom!

REFERENCES

Christopher Farran, *Infant Colic,* Scribners, New York, 1983.

Connors, *Food Additives and Hyperactive Children,* Plenum Press, 1980.

Levine Carey et al., *Developmental Behavioural Paediatrics,* W. B. Saunders, Philadelphia, 1983.

Michael Rutter, *Scientific Foundations of Developmental Psychiatry,* Heinemann, 1980.

Index

absconding, 38, 79
allergies, 133, 167-70
appetite, 10, 12-13, 121-28, 135-36
arguing with parents, 51
asthma, 202-3
attention deficit disorder, *see*
  hyperactivity
attention given for the wrong reason,
  54-57, 59-62
attention "grades," 60-61
attention-seeking, 8, 59-62, 81-82
authoritarianism, 48, 57
autistic children, 175, 195

baby, new, and toddler, 46, 70-71, 77
baby walkers, 163
babyhood, 2-3
bad language, 61, 80-81
bath, fear of, 147-48
bed rest, in illness, 217
bed, toddler in parents', 99-101, 189
bed wetting, 115-17
  statistics, 116
bedroom as punishment (Time Out)
  57, 65-70
bedroom, shared, 66, 103-4
bedtime, 31, 96-99, 102
behavior modification therapy, 54-56,
  114-15, 166
birth control, 46
biting, 74-75
  at playgroup, 74-75
  neighbors' children, 75
bladder training, 113, 118-19
  see also toilet training
blue, going, (breath holding), 77-78
bonding, 2-3, 8, 18, 161
books on child care, ix, 23-24
bow legs, 214
bowel control, 112
bowel regularity, the obsession with,
  119-20
bowel training, 113-15

behavior modification and, 56,
  114-15
  methods, 113-15
  refusing to sit, 118-19
  regularity, 119-20
  right thing in wrong place, 118
boys, behavioral differences from
  girls, 3, 11, 73, 160
breakages, 34-35, 163
breath-holding attacks, 77-79
bribes, 56
bronchitis, 202

car, travelling in, 42
carbohydrates, 124
cereals, 124, 131
Chamberlin study, 12, 89-90
chicken pox, 213
children, number in family, 46
climbing, 10
clumsiness, 164-65, 171
colds, 192, 201, 203
  and vitamin C, 201
colic, 162
communication skills, 215
communication with children, 165
competition, 22-25, 77
consistent discipline, 28
constipation, 119-20, 134, 196, 207
controlled crying technique, 93-96,
  98, 104
controls, learning of, 3-4
convalescence, 217
"Coping with Toddlers" course, 13
corporal punishment, *see* spanking
coughs, 192, 201, 203
  with night asthma, 202-3
crib, escaping from, 105-6
  or bed? 106
croup, 202
crying,
  caused by colic, 162
    by fears, 106-7, 151-52

crying *(cont.)*
 by irritable babies, 11-12, 18, 161-62, 195-96
 by irritable handicapped, 195-96
 by separation, 151-52
 controlled,
  crying technique, 88, 93-96, 104
  at night, 92-96, 106-8
  tantrums, 65
  to punish parents, 50, 65, 98, 149
cuddly toys, 156-57
cyanotic attack (blue), 77-78

dark, fear of, 107, 145, 153
day care, 151-52, 183, 196, 198
deafness, selective, for
 discipline, 56-57
 nocturnally deaf husband, 106
debating and arguing, 51-52, 60
democracy, and toddlers, 51-52
development, behavior in normal
 toddler, 1-6
 and intelligence, 174-78, 214-15
 milestones in, 214-15
diarrhea, infective, 207
 toddler, 120, 134-35
diet, 122-25, 128-36
 and bowels, 131, 134-35
 and growth, 132-33
 and teeth, 124, 129-31, 135-36
 for hyperactives, 167-70
 variety in, 128-29
 what's enough? 128
 see also food
diets, special, 133-34, 167-70
diphtheria immunization, 209
discipline, 28, 47-57
diversion technique, 53, 64, 73
divorce, damage to child, 28, 187
divorced parents, 28, 187
doctors, fear of, 148-49
dogs, fear of, 146
 and fierce pets, 38
doors, securing, 36-39, 98-99, 103
 slamming, 60

ear problems, 203-5
early rising, 102-3, 163
early-school-age child, 16
eating, *see* feeding

enuresis, *see* bedwetting, bladder training
environment, influence of, 18, 20
epilepsy, 195

fainting, pallid breath-holding attack, 78-79
fat children, 125-27
 and fat families, fat pets, 125-26
 see also obesity
fathers, responsibilities of, 35, 45
 as better disciplinarians, 44
 lack of involvement of, 187
 return home from work, 35, 44-45
fear, 10, 106-7, 144-54
 of bath, 147-48
 of dark, 107, 145, 152-54
 of doctors, 148-49
 of dogs, 146
 of fairy stories, 153-54
 of hospitals, 149-50
 of noise, 152-53
 of monsters, 153-54
 of separation, 145, 151-52
 of toilets, 150-51
febrile convulsions, 208-9
feeding, 10, 39, 121-36
 between meals, 137-43
 dawdling, 139
 handicapped children, 196
 independent children, 142
 normal pattern, 138-39
 other animals' feeding patterns, 127
 see also, diet, food, meals, mealtimes
Feingold diet, 167-70
fever, 207-8
 how to bring down temperature, 208
fever fits, 208-9
fiddly fingers, 36, 163
fighting, with brother or sister, 75-77
first year, 2-3, 161-62
fits, epileptic, 195
 fever, 209
flat feet, 214
fluid in the ear, 204-5
foods, 121-36
 adequacy of, 128
 health foods, 130-31
 junk foods, 129-30
 labor-saving, cooking of, 141-42

made interesting, presentation,
      139-43
   snacks, 141
   solids, introduction of, 138
   see also diet, fruit, vegetables, etc.
fruit, 124

gastroenteritis, 205-6
genitals, playing with (masturbation),
      84-85
German measles (Rubella), 213
girls, behavioral differences from
      boys, 3, 11, 73, 160
grandparents, 29, 190-93
   discipline, 192
   for babysitting, 151, 188, 191
growth, 132-33

handicapped children, 194-99
   effect on parents, 197-98
   feeding difficulties, 196
   help from friends, 198
   irritability, 195-96
   no sense, 196
   sleep problems, 196
harnesses, 138
health foods, 130-31
hearing, 203
helping professionals, being wary of
      their advice, xiii, 25-26
heredity, influence of, 8, 18-20, 126,
      160-61
historical review of development,
      17-19
honesty, child's bluntness, 35-36
hospitals, 149-50
hyperactivity, 159-71
   and behavior modification therapy,
      55, 166
   and colic, 162
   cause of, 160-61
   clear communication in, 165
   clumsiness, 164-65
   described, 161-65
   diet for, 167-70
   drugs for, 170
   famous hyperactives, 161
   impulsiveness, 164
   incidence of, 160
   school failure and specific learning
      problems, 163-65, 167
   self-esteem, 164-65, 167, 171
   treatment of, 165-71

hyperglycemia, 170
hypoglycemia, 170

ignoring, 54, 64-65, 97
illness, 200-217
impulsiveness, 9, 80, 164
intelligence,
   and development, 112, 214-15
   attempts to produce infant
      prodigies, 174-81
interrupting adults, 33
intimidation, as a discipline, 48

jealousy, 77
   see also sibling rivalry
junk food, 129-30

knock knees, 214

laryngitis, and croup, 202
learning through living, 180-81
locking in bedroom, 66
lockjaw (tetanus), 210-11

masturbation, 84-85
meals, 127-28, 139
   see also feeding
mealtimes, 139
measles, 212
   vaccination, 211
media myths, 23
medicines, administration of, 216-17
mess, 34-35, 36, 37, 68, 163
milk, 123, 142-43
   allergy, 133, 162
minerals, 125, 134
minimal brain dysfunction, *see*
   hyperactivity
mixing, 6, 15, 164-65
mothers, working, 44-45, 182-85
mumps, 212-13
   fathers' fear of sterility, 213
   vaccination, 211

naughty corner, 66
negativity, 5, 61
negotiated settlement, 53-54
neighbors, 24, 91-92, 109
New York Longitudinal Study, 11
night feeds, 105
night terrors, 107
nightlight, 107, 153
nightmares, 107

noise, effect of, 31
    fear of, 152-53
    made by toddler, 60, 163
normal behavior, 8-16
no-win situations, 39-42

obesity, 125-27
    fat pets, fat families, 126
    glands, caused by, 126
    heredity, 125-26
    puppy fat, 126-27
off days, 16, 165, 167
otitis media (ear infection), 204
overeating, 125

pacifier, 104, 155-56
pallid, breath-holding attacks, 77,
    78-79
parents, rights of, 42-46, 63-64, 91
personality differences, 11-12, 17-21
pertussis, see whooping cough
pets, dangerous, 38
playgroups, 24-25, 173
playpens, 38
polio vaccination, 210
potty, or toilet? 117-18
pre-schools, 24-25, 152, 173-74
privileges, removal of, 53
protein, 122-23
punishment, 30, 49-51, 53
puppy fat, 126-27

questions, incessant, 51-52, 60

reading, 176-78
    difficulties, 164, 167
    normal development of, 177-78
    teaching before school, 176-78
refrigerator, closing of, 37
rewards, 55-56
road sense, 9, 38, 164
rote learning, 175-76
routine, 27-28, 165-66
Rubella (German measles), 213
rules for early-school-age child, 16

safety in the home, 37-38
screaming in the night, 92-93
security blanket, 106-7, 156-57
sedation, 108-9, 195-96
self-centeredness, 6, 51-52
senselessness, 5, 196
separation, child's fear of, 145
    no fear of, 38, 79

separation, parents' divorce, 28, 187
    access and visiting, 188
    damage of messy break-up, 28, 187
    parents' new relationships, 188
sharing, 6, 15
shopping, 40-42
shouting, 52
sibling rivalry, 70-71, 77
single-parent family, 186-89
sleep, 40, 84-6, 88-90
sleep, problems, 89-109
    and breast-feeding, 105
    and sensitive neighbors, 109
    and the controlled crying
        technique, 94-96, 98, 104
    and the handicapped child, 108,
        196
    and the hyperactive child, 163
    and "the patent rope trick," 97-99
    brainwave studies (EEG), 88
    crib or bed, 105-6
    daytime, 10, 92, 101-2
    early risers, 102-3
    effect of disturbed sleep on
        families, 90-92
    interrupted, 92-93
    light sleepers, 101
    night feeds, 105
    nightmares, 107
    night terrors, 107
    night wanderers, 103
    sedation, 108-9, 195-96
    shared bedrooms, 66, 103-4
    fear of dark, 107
    fear of separation, 106-7
    statistics, 89-90
    treatment for problems, 93-95,
        96-99, 100
    see also bed, bedtime
smearing feces, 84
snacks, 141, 143
soiling, see bowel training
solids, introduction of, 138
spanking, 14, 49-51, 52, 98, 100
speech, 179-80, 203, 215
stealing, 81
stubbornness, 5-6, 12
sugar, 124
    and behavior, 170
    and teeth, 124, 129-30, 135-36
supermarkets, hazards in, 40-42, 162
swearing, 61, 80-81
swimming, 178

tantrums, 62
  in car, 42
  diversion of, 64
  incidence of, 58
  pretending to ignore, 63-65
  in supermarket, 40-42
  Time Out for, 65-70
teeth,
  and biting, 74-75
  and chewing, 138
  and diet, 124, 129-30, 135-36
  grinding, 86
  and thumbsucking, 155
teething, and behavior, 16
television, effect of, 23, 153-54
temper tantrums, see tantrums
temperament, 11-12
temperature, high, 207-8
tension and behavior, 29-30
tetanus vaccination, 210-11
threats, 52
thumb-sucking, 154-55
Time Out, 57, 65-70
  benefits, 73-74
  choosing room, 65-66
  failure of method, 66-70
  kicking the door, 67
  wrecking the room, 68-69
  vomiting (on bed), 83
toddlerhood, 3-6
toilet, 117-18
toilet training, 56, 110-20
  bedwetting, 115-17
  boys, standing or sitting? 118
  fear of toilet, 150-51
  normal development of control, 112
  potty or toilet? 117-18
  refusal to sit, 118-19
  right motion, wrong place, 118
  star charts (praise) for older children, 56
  toddler urgency, 119
  toilet timing, 111, 196
  trainer pants, 113
see also bladder training, bowel training
tonsils, 201-2

toys, 35, 180
trainer pants, 113
transition objects, security blankets, 156-57
"triggers," 15, 32
twenty-four-hour-a-day-mothers, 44-45, 182, 198
tying doors shut, 36-39, 98-99, 100

unreasonableness, 5
untidiness, and mess, 9, 34-35, 36-37, 68-69, 163

vaccinations, 209-12, 213
  risks of, 211-12
vegetables, 123-24
  passing undigested in toilet, 120
verbal abuse, 61
vitamins, 124-25, 135, 171
  and the common cold, 201
vomiting, 205-7
  and clear fluids, 206-7
  and crying, 82-83
  on coughing, 82-83, 211
  on demand, 82-83
  medicine for, 216-17
  treatment for, 206-7

walking in the night, 87, 88-89, 103
  see also sleep
walking, as an indication of intelligence in toddlers, 215
water, fear of, 147-48
  swimming, 178
weaning, 138
wetting, see bladder training, toilet training
whining, 46, 72-74
whooping cough, 211
  vaccination, 211
willfulness, 5-6, 12
working mothers, 182-85
  babysitting, 183-84
  and cooking, 184
  fair deal for child, 184
  and guilt, 183
  and housework, 184